WEIGHT OUT

By: Hillary "Herby" Herbst

Edited by: Carol Williams

Book Cover Art: Instagram
@jenny.gets.weird

Book Cover Photos:
www.kearstenleder.com

Dedications

To Mindy: You kept throwing creative noodles
at the wall and this one stuck.

To all my "Editors": Thank you for all of
your insights, details, and feedback.

To Elad: You truly are the best therapist /
life coach there is. You saved my life.

It takes a village to raise a child.
It takes a different village to keep Hillary sane.
To My Village: Thank you from the bottom of my heart.

PROLOGUE

Procedure words or prowords are words or phrases limited to radio telephone procedure used to facilitate communication by conveying information in a condensed standard verbal format. Prowords are voice versions of the much older prosigns for Morse code first developed in the 1860s for Morse telegraphy, and their meaning is identical.

WAIT OVER
I must pause for a few seconds.
WAIT OUT
I must pause for longer than a few seconds. I will call you back.

CHILDHOOD

I was born and raised in a really small town, Somonauk, about 60 miles west of Chicago, Illinois. To be extremely accurate (and to paint the picture), it was called "The Village of Somonauk" and the population was around 1200 people. Before Google, you really couldn't find Somonauk on many maps.

I didn't have a good or bad childhood. My parents divorced when I was three or four. My dad has been in my life my entire life. We saw him every other weekend and on or around the holidays. His side of the family has a family reunion the first Sunday in August every year, and I went to all of them until I joined the Coast Guard. When we were older, he came to every single game we played. For me it was just t-ball and softball, and then, my senior year of high school, I was our school's mascot, Bobby the Bobcat. My dad came to every basketball game I was at, and I think a wrestling match or two. My younger sister was in every sport known to man, and Dad came to all her games.

My mom remarried in 1989 when I was five. I liked my stepdad when they were dating. My stepsister actually went to the same babysitter/daycare we did, so we already knew her. She was the only "older" girl at daycare that would play with the rest of us, so my younger sister and I liked her very much and were excited she was going to be our sister . . . and then our parents married.

In real life, there is homework. My stepsister is four years older than I am and five and a half years older than my younger sister. In real life, my stepsister couldn't play with us every

6

minute of every day. My younger sister and I were too young to understand so we were mean to my stepsister. We just wanted attention.

As we got older, though, my stepsister and I ended up getting along very well, but my younger sister and I did not. My younger sister is 21 months younger than I. Until recently, I really thought my younger sister and I were opposites in every single way possible. My younger sister has always been very athletic and has had muscles and looked good. I've always been clumsy and been on the chunky side. My younger sister is quiet and observant. I'm loud and unobservant. She also had a very bad temper and was sometimes violent. As a child, I didn't have a bad temper at all, and I have never been violent.

In the meantime, my younger sister got married and really started working hard to repair our relationship. I was very skeptical at first, but she was persistent, and I finally met her half-way. We get along fairly well now. And I've learned we have more in common than we ever thought we did. We're both perfectionists; we just aim that perfection at different things. We're both stubborn as hell and extremely passionate. Again, we are just passionate about different things. And both of us have a work ethic like no one else you will ever meet.

My stepdad had a liver transplant when I was in first grade. My sisters and I walked home from school one day and when we came in the house, my stepdad didn't know who we were and told us to get out of his house or he would call the cops. I was too young to really know what was going on. My stepsister called my mom at work. My mom came home, but he didn't know who she was either. She called 911, and he was rushed to the local hospital. From there he was air lifted to Chicago and had an emergency liver transplant.

My stepdad didn't drink much at all. My mom didn't either. Growing up there was never any alcohol in our house. And he was over-all healthy for a man his age. The liver transplant came out of nowhere and shocked everyone who knew him.

After that, the medications he was on made him mean. My

younger sister and I really didn't get along with him at all when we were kids. And we absolutely hated the fact that we were forced to call him "Dad." He wasn't our dad. We saw our dad every other weekend.

As I got older and he became stable health-wise and his meds were adjusted properly, I understood that the meds messed with his moods, and he was actually a nice guy. I ended up getting along with him very well. In fact, as a teenager I would say there were a lot of fights where it was my younger sister and my mom against my stepdad and me. I don't mind calling him "Dad" now. I haven't minded for a while.

Everyone knew everyone in our town. Most of our family, grandparents, aunts, uncles, cousins, etc. were no more than an hour's drive away and that was the same for everyone else. We locked our doors at our house but really didn't have to. It was a safe town. My sisters and I walked to and from school and to and from my mom's shop. When I was old enough to drive, I would go to the local store, leave my car running in the winter, get a gallon of milk, and go home. The only time anyone's car was ever "stolen" was when a friend or family member got in and drove it a block away to play a prank on them.

My mom has owned her own printing business since before I was born. My stepdad had random jobs here and there, but his health didn't really allow him to work a regular job with regular hours. He ended up working for my mom and still does to this day. My mom's main business was the print shop, but she has had several other ventures over the years, the most recent ones being Premier Jewelry and her own rubber stamp line.

From grade school all the way through my freshman year of high school I was "bullied." I put bullied in quotation marks, because I was definitely picked on a lot, but it never really got physical. No one ever beat me up, stuffed me in a locker, gave me a swirly, etc. It could have definitely been worse. But our family didn't have a lot of money, I wore my stepsister's hand-me-downs and my pants often had holes in them. I remember setting my lunch tray down on the table, and, in unison, the entire table turned their trays the opposite way. Looking back, it was incredibly stupid. But at the time, I was deeply hurt.

In junior high I started getting mouthy and sarcastic. My classmates would call me "Ugly," and I would look them in the eye and say, "Well, stop looking at me!" My show of confidence made them back off.

In my freshman year of high school, two girls would put gum in my shoe every single day when we had to change clothes/shoes for gym class. I remember laughing in my head because they always put it in the heel of my shoe, so I always saw it. I never once stepped in it. I just calmly walked over to the garbage can and threw it out. My stepsister said I should pull it out of my shoe and, "Stick it to her forehead." While that would probably have been incredibly funny, she probably would have beaten the shit out of me. The gum thing went on for too long, really. But eventually they got the hint that they weren't really bothering me and they stopped. Other than one very minor physical altercation, also during gym, with another girl, and one very obnoxious, evil guy, I don't remember being bullied after the gum stopped.

The physical altercation was silly. The girl and I didn't get along. I don't remember if she did something to me and I threw the basketball at her in retaliation . . . or I think she threw the basketball at me and I charged her . . . Either way, the other girls broke us up before either of us really got in a good hit, and the teacher never knew.

I played softball year-round, in a summer league and a traveling league until I was fifteen. I loved it and I was good at it. I played first base and in the outfield. I was a good fielder, but I excelled at batting. I wasn't a power hitter, but I almost always got on base. One year I had a perfect season: I never struck out. As I entered high school, though, I started getting bored and stopped practicing. The other girls kept improving on their skills and I didn't. I also really wanted a car. I knew my parents were not going to pay for one for me. I had been babysitting since I was 12. I also had a few other jobs, including detasseling one summer, selling ads for the local newspaper, and cutting wicks for a candle maker. My grandfather's best friend was co-owner at the local grocery store where I started working in my sophomore year. I started as a cashier and then moved to produce. At 18, I moved to the deli. I absolutely loved it. I loved most of the people I worked with. The only thing I was bummed about was the year after I quit playing softball the traveling team went to Disney World. I, of course, did not get to go with. At 16, though, I got my driver's license and was able to buy my first car, a 1992 Plymouth Sundance.

As I mentioned earlier, in my senior year of high school, I was Bobby the Bobcat. I really enjoyed being the mascot, and I was very good at it. In my junior year, my friend, a senior, served the first year we had the mascot costume. When my year came, I did a lot of the same things he did, and also made up my own material.

Everyone loved me, adults and children, except one guy in my class. He continued to "bully" me long after everyone else stopped caring. Whenever I would run through the crowd giving people high-fives, he would pull off my costume hand. In one of my first cartwheels, the costume foot flew off. This guy picked up the foot and threw it across the gym. After that, I learned how to properly tuck it in to prevent that. I didn't really care about it for my sake, but there were kids at the game that didn't know I was the mascot. The fact that he was exposing me to them bothered me a lot. There was also a look in his eyes, too. I can't describe the look other than evil. Years later, he was arrested for sodomizing and abusing his son. It was an incredibly sad situation and it shook our small town. My mom said when the local radio station aired the story, they were very graphic about what he had done. I'm not sure why they made that decision. I hope his son is recovering, and that it does not have long lasting negative effects on the child's life. Sadly, I was not surprised at all when my mom told me about it.

My father is a nonpracticing Lutheran. My mom is Baptist. We were raised Baptist. (Anytime there was a disagreement between my mom and our dads, it was done my mom's way.) My sisters and I were also "bullied" at church. Somonauk Baptist Church was also Somonauk Baptist School. Both the school and the church were a little on the extreme side.

For example, the Bible says to not get drunk. The church's thought was, if you never drink, you can never be drunk, so therefore, drinking is a sin. As with most churches, our church believed and taught that we should witness to non-believers. However, our church took it a step further by not giving church members a chance to choose what was best for themselves. For example, all the schoolgirls had to wear skirts, not pants. The boys and girls were not allowed to have designs on their shirts, either. They weren't allowed to go to the movie theater, dance, listen to secular music, etc. None of these things are sins in the Bible, but the church kids were raised to think that they were actual sins.

My sisters and I attended public school, wore shorts and t-shirts, watched non-Disney movies and therefore were, of course, told that we were going straight to hell. The other kids saw it as their job to "witness" and "preach" to us to try to save us from our evil ways. If they were not "witnessing" to us, they would just ignore us so we couldn't be a bad influence on them.

I remember my stepsister having a really hard time with one of her Sunday school teachers and what he was preaching in his classroom. My mom talked to him about it, but he stuck to his guns. Instead of letting my stepsister stay home or finding an alternative, my stepsister had to keep attending his class. My mom would just occasionally talk to him or tell her to ignore what he said. Later, I had the same teacher. I never really paid attention in any Sunday school classes; I'm very good at daydreaming, so I didn't have the same problems my stepsister did.

My sisters and I hated going to church, though. I would try

to get out of it by sleeping in or pretending not to feel well, but it never worked. I told my mom I didn't want to go, but that was unacceptable in our house. We were going to be good Christians, whether we liked it or not!

Later in life my mom became our Sunday school teacher. In her class, the other kids behaved, and we were not "bullied." My mom preached tolerance and acceptance of other life-styles. The kids went along with it, and I don't remember any parents ever disagreeing with her. My mom sees this as a huge victory and thinks that that solved all of our problems. Yeah, right. A better situation doesn't equal a good one, and I still hated church.

After high school I started going to a church in Plano with my friend, Michelle. I was skeptical, but I still lived at home, so I thought it was better than Somonauk Baptist. Luckily, my new church wasn't a school and wasn't full of a bunch of judgmental a-holes. Most of the youth group attended Plano school and all of them were really nice. I still keep in touch with some of them to this day. I wish I had kept in touch with all of them. I wonder what they are all doing. That would also be the church where I met the youth pastor who helped me make the decision to join the Coast Guard . . .

THE PERFECT STORM

I was a junior in high school. If I remember my course load correctly, I was in American Dream (the nickname for honors English combined with honors History, a class that two teachers had come up with and fought to teach together), pre-calculus, geometry, Spanish 2, PE, and study hall. I also worked part-time at the local grocery store cashiering and in the produce department. I wasn't dumb, but I was in over my head. My pre-calculus teacher, or as he liked to be known as, facilitator, did not grade our homework on a regular basis. Instead, he was infamous for his pop-quizzes. Since math had always been my strongest subject, I stopped doing that homework in order to finish the rest of my homework. I was able to keep up for a while and then slowly fell behind. The last semester I got a D on my report card. It was the first and only D I ever received on a report card. It bothers me because on paper it looks like I struggled with that class, and that I'm not good at math, but that isn't true. Math is actually my strongest subject, along with reading comprehension.

I was preparing for college but was quickly realizing that I didn't want to go. I knew my parents hadn't gone to college, but I thought that it was expected of me. We did not have any money to pay for it, so if I did go, I would need a scholarship, or I would have to work while attending, or both. I had quit playing softball my sophomore year to get a job at the local grocery store and buy a car. I was not going to get a sport's scholarship and I was starting to think I wasn't going to get an academic one, either.

I came home from work one night and sat on the couch for a few minutes just to say "Hi," to my parents and relax a little before I went to bed. They were watching *The Perfect Storm*. I sat quietly and began watching, too, although I was so tired, I was only half-watching. It was the scene in the movie where the helicopter was hovering over a fishing boat and all of a sudden, I declared, "That is what I want to do with my life."

My mom unexpectedly replied "OK."

Thinking she was brushing me off, I said, "I'm serious. That is what I'm going to do with my life."

Again, she replied, "OK."

I'm not sure why I felt the need to clarify this—as I have never enjoyed fishing and my mom knew that well—but I continued to say, "Not the fisherman, the guys in the helicopter. I want to join the Coast Guard and see the giant waves in the ocean."

My mom again replied, "OK."

Resolved, exhausted, and a bit in shock, I went to bed.

PS I'm not very superstitious, but . . . I had heard or knew that the movie had a sad ending. I did not watch the entire movie until April 11, 2018, after I was honorably discharged from the Coast Guard. Imagine my shock and disappointment to find out it was not a Coast Guard helicopter in that scene. Oh, well. I can't imagine joining a different branch.

WILL GOD TALK TO ME?

After my declaration during the movie, I talked to the school guidance counselor. Boy, I was in for a shock! The Coast Guard was branch of the military! If I joined, I would have to go to boot camp. I was under the impression that lifeguards handled everything from the beach to the buoys and the Coast Guard handled everything past the buoys. In my seventeen-year-old mind, Coast Guardsmen were just glorified lifeguards. That was a job I could do. But joining the military?? Boot camp??

I decided to keep on digging for more information. I found a recruiter and remember him coming to my house with several pamphlets and a lot of information. He suggested I go to boot camp during the summer between my junior and senior year, then enlist after graduation. I was both excited and overwhelmed. I remember thinking I would be a good Telecommunications Specialist. He left the information with my parents and me. We said we would get back to him.

I don't remember ever wanting to go to boot camp. I was always very, very social. I had a core group of about eight friends that I hung out with all the time. Also, there was Krystal in Biloxi, Ms, who I visited every summer.

I did, however, want to join the Coast Guard. I blew off the ACT my junior year of high school, scoring a 26 on it. According to Google in 2018, a score of 21 or higher puts you above average and 24 places you at the 74th percentile. Imagine what my score could have been if I had studied or cared! I probably could have gotten a scholarship. (This is a very common theme in my life. I know I don't have to work very hard to do well on tests so I rarely score as high as possible.) I had joined other high school juniors and took the ASVAB, a mandatory test for all aspiring military members to help determine if they are eligible for military service and what jobs might fit them. I scored a 78, qualifying me for all jobs in the Coast Guard but two. All I needed was eight electives my senior year of high school to graduate, so I took eight electives. I had no interest in stacking my schedule to get into college. I was joining the Coast Guard.

After I graduated high school, I quit work. It was our

last summer together. I wanted to hang out with my friends all summer and have as much fun as humanly possible. When they went off to college, I would join the Coast Guard and then go to boot camp. That was my goal. And that was one of the best summers of my life. In the end, I knew that I couldn't go through the entire military employee processing station (MEPS) experience because I did not meet the weight requirement, and I had plantar fasciitis.

I went to the podiatrist and told him I wanted to join the Coast Guard but couldn't with plantar fasciitis. I had been wearing orthotics for a year or so, and I wasn't in pain anymore. I asked if I was healed. The podiatrist explained to me that having plantar fasciitis was like breaking a bone. The orthotics worked like a cast: the bone would eventually heal, as my feet had. However, the bone, and my feet, would always be weak, and I would have to be careful not to "break" them again. He suggested I continue wearing my orthotics as much as possible. He wrote a similar statement for the recruiter and released me from his care.

After that I began doing the Atkin's Diet. I love meat and thought it would be a fairly easy diet for me. In the beginning it was. I lost ten pounds right away. I was really excited.

After getting the statement from the podiatrist and losing the ten pounds, I went to MEPS so I could join the Coast Guard. My recruiter had been transferred to a new station and my new recruiter picked me up and drove me to a hotel in Chicago. Early the next morning, I went with a bunch of other military recruits to MEPS.

Anyone who has ever been to MEPS will tell you it is pure hell. You are required to fill out a bunch of forms such as background checks and medical history. You are repeatedly told to be honest or there will be grave consequences when they find out the truth later. Most people are concerned about past drug usage. They tell you just to admit to smoking pot. They say that everyone has and it's better to be honest. They didn't believe that I never had.

Once the administrative stuff is taken care of, you begin the medical part of the day. After dividing the men and the women, they make you strip down to your underwear and do a bunch of stretches and exercises with and in front of everyone else. Most famous is the duck walk/waddle. After that you are given a pelvic and breast exam. It isn't a full pap smear, but it is just as embarrassing and awful. Since there is a long line of girls waiting, it is just a quick "drive- by" exam. In Chicago that doctor was known as the "Dragon Lady." She was older, Chinese, and mean. Several of my friends (male and female) who joined the National Guard or Marine Corps talked about how horrible she was and how uncomfortable they were. Once the exam is over, you get dressed. Then they take your blood, make you pee in a cup, and weigh in.

Problem was, I didn't need to pee! I don't have a fear of peeing in front of other people; I just didn't have to go. I had peed that morning, and I hadn't had much to drink after that. They started making me chug water. I chugged so much water, I made myself sick. In the middle of all that, after I had literally drunk a gallon of water or more, they started weighing all of us! I was so mad! Anyone with a brain would know that the water made me weigh more than normal. How was that fair? I was tired, sick, embarrassed, and emotionally and physically drained. I was also overweight. Then I finally was able to pee and finish out the day, without qualifying.

Returning home, I went through a bit of depression. The Atkin's Diet was hard as hell. After the initial ten pounds I did not lose any more. And I missed carbs. I didn't realize how many of those I ate, too. I was angry all the time. I stopped trying to lose weight altogether, and ended up gaining everything back.

I was visiting the grocery store one day and the owner asked me if I wanted to come back. I laughed at him. But we started talking. He needed help wrapping meat early in the mornings. He would give me a raise if only I would work a few days a week. I was starting to rebound from MEPS and told him I wouldn't be there long, as I was going to join the Coast Guard. He said OK. I started working at the store again.

My friend, Nate, had joined the Army National Guard after high school so when he returned from bootcamp we ran together a couple of times. He showed me the proper way to run and taught me how to breathe. When we ran, he would lead us past my house. He said in boot camp they would take you back to the barracks, thinking you were done, then they'd make you do another lap. He wanted to prepare me for that. I really enjoyed running with him and it started becoming easier for me. Nate was dealing with a lot of personal things, though, and after we ran together a couple of times, he started blowing me off. I would go over to his house early in the morning and he wouldn't answer the door. Back then cell phones were not really common and I didn't want to wake up his family. Sometimes I ran anyways and other times I just went back home and went back to bed.

Nate had a lot going on in his life. During our senior year of high school, one of his brothers was diagnosed with stage 4 cancer. His brother passed away while he was away at boot camp. I knew he was having a hard time coping with that, but I didn't realize just how hard a time he was having. I did not understand the grieving process, how long it took, what effects it had. I did not know that when Nate blew off our running plans it was because he literally couldn't get out of bed. It wasn't personal. I should have had more compassion for him, been more patient. I didn't realize that he wanted to help me out but just couldn't. Since I didn't know what he was going through, I got mad at him instead and turned away.

Because I had been in karate briefly when I was younger, I went back to my karate Sensei and told him that I wanted to join again. I explained to him that I would learn everything required, but that I was not joining to advance to a new belt, I was joining for the exercise to qualify for the Coast Guard. My Sensei had served in the Marine Corps and understood and agreed. I started doing that twice a week. I don't remember what fad diet I tried next, but I started that, too.

After about a year, I still wasn't making much progress.

I had good friends in the area. My younger sister was about to graduate high school. My stepsister had gotten married and, a few months later, got pregnant. I was trying to lose weight, but I was also very comfortable. Life wasn't good or bad. Small town living was all I had ever known, and I wasn't quite ready to leave it. Every time I tried to diet, I felt isolated and alone. I couldn't enjoy going out with friends because they inevitably wanted to eat, and I couldn't have whatever they were eating. If I wasn't dieting, I was worried about my future. I couldn't live at home forever. What was I going to do?

I prayed and prayed and prayed, but there was never an answer. God never talked to me. I started to get mad. If God wanted me to join the Coast Guard, then he should tell me. And I should lose the weight because he could make it fall off. Why wasn't God making me skinny? I really liked the church in Plano and continued to go with Michelle. The youth group went on a weekend retreat so I talked to the youth pastor about everything that was going on. He said that whenever he was trying to make a decision, he would consider five things. I remember four of them:

1) Is it Biblical?

2) Is it legal?

3) What does his godly counsel think?

4) Once the decision is made, does he have peace with God?

I thought about all of this very carefully, discussed it with the youth pastor and with my mom. There wasn't anything in the Bible that said I shouldn't join the Coast Guard. It wasn't illegal and my godly counsel was pushing me to go for it. I could feel my passion coming back. I made my decision for a second time. I was going to join the Coast Guard.

I remember asking my mom one night "You know, alcoholics have AA, drug addicts have rehab, what is out there for over-eaters?" My mom said she thought there were "fat camps." We found a weight loss camp in La Jolla, CA. I cashed in my mutual fund meant for college and attended camp for three weeks to learn how to eat healthy and lose weight the right way. I lost several inches while at the camp, but only one pound. I went back to MEPS upon returning home and, although I had a better experience, I still did not meet Coast Guard weight standards.

At some point the store owner and I had a falling out. The manager kept scheduling me for more and more hours that I didn't want. When I told him that the hours I was working now were not the ones I had agreed to when I started working there again, he reminded me that it was supposed to be a temporary situation, but I was still there. Our original agreement was no longer in effect. I quit.

I started working in the day care room at the YMCA. I'd been babysitting since I was 12 and enjoyed being around kids. This way, I could also have a free membership to the YMCA so all the classes were free. I already had a membership and loved the step and kick boxing classes. Unfortunately, my work hours were the same as the class hours, so I started running again. I was running on the treadmills now instead of outside, but I remembered everything Nate told me and it started becoming really easy for me.

I also started waitressing at a local restaurant. I worked a few nights, every Saturday morning and every other Sunday. During the week, I would work at the YMCA in the morning and then I'd run six miles, which usually took me an hour. If I had to work at the restaurant, I'd only run three to four miles, eat, shower, and go to work. I did my best to eat the way I was taught at camp; however, Saturdays were my splurge day so I ate whatever I wanted. I absolutely loved the sausage gravy at the restaurant and would either get the croissant breakfast sandwich with hash browns covered in gravy or I would get the meat lovers skillet. The rest of the day I would eat chocolate and other junk food.

For my 21st birthday, my best friend, my younger sister, and I went up to Minnesota for a week. My entire family had vacationed in Minnesota every summer for the last week in July and first week in August. We stayed at Bojou Lodge Resort on Round Lake. In junior high, my grandfather built his own cabin on the other side of the lake. We spent a Christmas up there one year, but my mom doesn't like the cold, so we only did that once. For my 21st birthday I wanted to go back to Minnesota in the winter and I invited my best friend to experience Minnesota with me. I knew he would enjoy snowmobiling and sledding.

A month later another friend took me to Colorado for a week. We went to the Royal Gorge and Seven Falls. We also had dinner at a fancy restaurant one night with white tablecloths and a piano player. I enjoyed Colorado, but my friend and I fought the entire trip. He was a Marine Reservist and he "jokingly" said over and over the Coast Guard was not a real branch and couldn't figure out why I'd want to be a part of that. He also criticized me for not being able to lose weight. I was on vacation, so I watched what I ate somewhat. He assumed I ate that way all the time and criticized me. He was giving me a lot of advice that I didn't want. I tried telling him that I knew what I was doing and would be fine, but he argued that I wasn't having much success. I would let him talk down to me and that would put me in a bad mood. Then he would get upset that I was in a bad mood and wasn't enjoying the vacation he had planned. I couldn't win. I was happy when the trip was over.

After those trips I continued to work, run, and eat like they taught me at camp. My younger sister had graduated high school and was in college on a softball scholarship. My stepsister had my nephew and I was there for the first year of his life. My best friend was in college and doing well in his fraternity. My other friends were away at college and living their lives. In the summer of 2005, I was finally ready to leave home. I also thought I had finally lost enough weight to join the Coast Guard. On June 7, 2005, I went back to MEPS and weighed in at 138! Two pounds under the limit! It was time for me to join the Coast Guard.

I had two going away parties. Well, maybe one and ½. I went to a bar and celebrated with my best friend and my Sensei. I think it was meant to be a party. I think we invited other people, but I really don't remember. Most of the night, it was just my best friend, my Sensei, and me. Later, however, Nate came. I'm not sure how he found out about it or if he was even there for me, but I was happy to see him. Since our falling out, we hadn't spoken to each other in a year or so. But all of a sudden, there he was at the bar. I walked over to him and said "Can we just both apologize to each other for everything and be OK?"

He smiled a small smile and agreed. I looked him in the eyes and said "I'm sorry, Nate." He looked me in the eyes and said he was sorry, too.

Then he gave me the most amazing hug in the entire world. Nate always gave good, tight hugs. Nate's hugs just made everything good. When he was hugging you, you knew you were safe, and everything would be OK. The hug he gave me that night told me that we had both matured, we both knew that what had happened was beyond our understanding and control, and that we both loved each other despite all the bullshit. My heart melted. He told me congratulations and I said I wouldn't be there without him teaching me how to run. We had a few more drinks and a really good time. I will always be incredibly thankful that we were able to mend our fences before I went to boot camp.

The second party or "real" party was a pool party at a friend's house. She worked at the store with me and lived right down the street. Her mom was one of the managers at the store and her older sister and my stepsister were good friends. My brother-in-law would go over to their house after work and swim often. He built houses for a living and had built them a new deck. Everyone in the entire town was at that party! Most of my family came, even my cousin who had moved to Wisconsin! Friends from all the places I had worked showed up to celebrate with me. I asked everyone to write a small note to me on an index card, and I took a picture with almost everyone who came. Later, I put all the pictures in an album with the notes under them. I still have that album.

An unexpected guest showed up, as well! A guy I had worked with and had a pretty big crush on had been serving time for selling drugs to an undercover cop. When we worked together, I would listen to his stories of all the parties he went to, but I would try not to lecture him or judge him. Some of the stories were funny, in a disturbing way. After one party, he freaked out because he thought he was throwing up blood and might be dying. It took him a minute to realize he was throwing up his favorite drink, Strawberry Crush soda.

Truthfully, I was just happy he was talking to me. As I said, I had a huge crush on him. I would also hear stories of his friends borrowing his car and not filling it up with gas or taking advantage of him in other ways. It would break my heart, but there was nothing I could do about it. He had a fierce loyalty to his friends that I never understood. They were not great people. I really enjoyed working with him. He was always nice to me and I could tell he had a good heart. His good heart was an asset, but it was also a liability. After he got arrested, I wrote him a letter telling him how sorry I was that he had been arrested, but that I hoped he could make the best of it and learn from it. I told him that he had a heart of gold and that I wished more for him and his life than what he had made of it so far. I don't remember what else I wrote, but I know I was trying to balance what I thought of him without approving of his decisions. I just wanted him to know that I cared about him.

I didn't know that his sentence was now up. His brother also worked at the store. His brother was my age and in my class in school and we got along well, too. His parents were customers at the store and also bowled on the same league as my parents. (I told you everyone knew everyone in my small town) His family was invited to the party and they told him about it as well. He showed up with his brother and my jaw dropped!! I was ecstatic to see him!

We talked for quite a while. He went to church in jail and found God. He was clean and he was ready to lead a good Christian life. He told me he really appreciated the letter I wrote him. He said it was nice to know someone outside of his family cared about him. He was so happy, he was glowing. I was really happy for him. It was another really nice circle that was closed before I went to boot camp.

We kept in touch on and off for a few years. I even saw him when I went home to visit a couple times. We went to a Cubs vs. White Sox game together with my parents. Eventually he stopped returning my calls. My mom had told me he got married and I thought maybe my crush on him wasn't good for his new marriage. Later my mom told me he had been arrested again. I knew he was struggling. It's hard to start a new life in the same town with the same friends. It's also hard battling an addiction. I was sad but not surprised to hear he had been arrested again. I hope at this point he is out and doing well.

On July 19, 2005 I officially enlisted in the United States Coast Guard. I stayed in a hotel in Chicago after I swore in at MEPS. My younger sister and a couple friends came up and had dinner with me. We had a small food fight so I went to boot camp with stains on my shirt. The next morning, I flew out to Philadelphia and waited in the airport's USO for the bus to Cape May. I had peace with God about my decision to join the Coast Guard right up until I stepped out of the bus in Cape May and found the foot prints that my feet were to fill. . . .

GIVE ME STRENGTH

Lord I'm giving my all
But it is not enough
And I'm doing my best
But it is getting tough

The battle is long
I didn't think it would be
And the air of defeat
Is getting to me

(Chorus)
So if this is what you want me to do
Then give me strength, Lord
I really need strength from you, Lord
So I can live my life for you

I've broken down
I've hit the floor
Sometimes I wonder
What I'm fighting for

They say the best things
Are worth the fight
But in this battle
I'm losing my sight

(Chorus)

I need you now, Lord
So I don't give up
I need you now, Lord

So I won't give in
Please give me strength, Lord
To see this battle to the end

Please give me strength, Lord
So I can win
If this is what you want me to do
Please give me strength, Lord
To live my life for you

Poem By: Hillary Herbst

7 YEARS

I was in boot camp July-Sept of 2005. My company was X-171 (X-Ray). Our sister company was Y-171 (Yankee). We began with 100 people in my company and 80 in Yankee, if I remember correctly. We were told we were two of the largest companies to go through since 9/11. My company commanders were an Electronics Technician Second Class (ET2) and a Food Service Specialist Chief (FSC.) Since it took me so long to join the Coast Guard, I had gone through three recruiters. The middle recruiter, a Machinery Technician Second Class (MK2), was also a company commander in Cape May while I was going through boot camp.

In some ways, boot camp was easy for me. Since I had been trying so hard for so long to lose weight and join, running on a daily basis did not bother me. In our physical fitness tests, I completed the mile and a half in 12:30, which was not only under the required time for women, but also under the required time for the guys! Being constantly yelled at didn't bother me too much, either, as I realized it was mostly for show, just part of the game. I got along with most of the people in our company. My collateral job was being part of the laundry crew. That got us out of a lot of physical training (PT) exercises and punishment, and we got along pretty well.

In other ways boot camp was extremely hard. We were told it would take a while for us to get mail, but I was one of the very last people to receive mine. I got my first letter at the end of the third week. Even though I got along with most of the people in my company, I really missed my friends and family back home. It was hard hearing mail call at night and not hearing my name.

I also struggled to stay in step while marching. This might not have been so bad if I weren't so short, which put me in the front row of our company. I was one of the first people everyone saw, and I couldn't stay in step. Also, while I was a good runner, I did not have much upper body strength. When it came time for the push-ups fitness test, I could not do the required amount and almost did not graduate on time due to this. I was on my third and final attempt before I finally completed fifteen push-ups.

One of the hardest things for me to cope with was my ruined journal. My best friend (the one who went to Minnesota with me) knew how much I loved to write. Before I left for boot camp, he had given me a journal with the following note in the cover, "You've reached for the stars and got them. Continue to reach for what you want, and you will get it. This book is for you to record everything when you can't write a letter. Hopefully when you return, I might be able to read this and get all of our phone calls in writing. Good luck. Love always."

Before we left for boot camp, we were given a list of items we could bring with us. I added Febreze spray. One night the company commanders made us throw everything from our lockers into our sea bags as fast as humanly possible, then run outside with them. The Febreze leaked all over the journal. Some of the entries I had written were smudged and some of the pages came unattached from the binding. I was devastated.

Most of the boot camp journal survived. Some of my writings include a list of all the nicknames we gave each other, or "New York" gave us all. My last name, Herbst, is apparently hard to pronounce so everyone started calling me Herby. Some people still call me Herby to this day, and I love it when they do. Others' nicknames included Eggroll, Rat, Sunshine, and as said, New York. I wrote down different quotes, and cadences and other things we had to learn.

One thing that was easy for me in boot camp was marksmanship. I've been shooting guns my whole life. In my journal, I wrote all the qualifying scores for marksman, sharpshooter and expert. Next to all the numbers is my score. I was one of two people in my company of 100 who qualified at the range. I only qualified as a marksman, but I was still proud of myself.

In boot camp, we had a board in our barracks that the company yeoman filled out every day with all the people on duty. We were supposed to memorize it and be able to tell any company commander who was on duty any time we were asked. MK2 (my former recruiter, now a company commander) discovered I had finally made it to boot camp and waited to see me.

When he found out what company I was in, he repeatedly called me out in the galley, "Seaman Recruit Herbst, who is the OOD today?"

I had to come to attention in the middle of the galley and answer him. Luckily, I have a pretty good memory, so I always knew the answer. While MK2 gave me a hard time, he later saved my butt and gave me a good reputation.

One day our company was getting our butts kicked. As said, we had a large company. It took us a long time to come together as a company and work as one. We were in trouble a lot. In the middle of push-ups and getting lectured, ET2 suddenly called out my name. "SR Herbst!"

OMG!!! Why is he calling my name? What am I doing wrong? I replied, "PO ____, SR Herbst"

"Do you know MK2?"

"Yes, PO."

"Is it true it took you three years to join the Coast Guard?!"

Where is he going with this? Am I about to be rephased? Thrown out of the Coast Guard? Is he about to tell me I still suck? "Yes, PO, it's true"

ET2 turned his attention to the rest of the company and began lecturing them about how badly I wanted to be there and how they needed to get their act together. It was a very passionate motivational speech about how the Coast Guard was voluntary and if people didn't want to be there, they were ruining it for those who did.

He ended the speech with "Herbst worked really hard to get here. It took her a long time, so she wants to be here. Don't mess this up for her!" I was relieved, proud, scared, embarrassed, and happy, all at the same time.

As time passed, our company did come together and earn our "colors." It didn't take too long for us to screw up, though, and lose them. We had to walk on them on the quarter deck as punishment. We earned them back later the same week.

Our company commanders didn't rephase or revert many people. Yankee's company commanders did it for fun, it seemed. We did get some rephasers from other companies ahead of us. One girl snored so loud! She was nice, but none of us could sleep with her in the room.

Our last week in boot camp was more relaxed. We all knew we had to really mess up at that point to be rephased or reverted. We were getting our paperwork together to go on to our next units. MK2 came up to our floor. I don't know if he had official business or why he came up, but he ended up seeing me. He told me how happy he was to see that I finally made it to graduation. I apologized for wasting his time as a recruiter. He blew that off. At the time, I thought recruiters only got paid if they recruited people. I thought that since he wasn't able to help me join, he had lost money. Luckily, I was wrong. I was thankful for this and breathed a sigh of relief. Suddenly, I heard ET2's voice, "SR Herbst stand at attention!"

"Aye, aye, PO."

"Who do you think you are? Do you think you are back in Chicago? You are just standing there having a conversation like you are still at MEPS. You are in boot camp!! Did you forget that?!?"

"No, PO."

"Herbst, it took you seven years to get here, don't ruin it now"

"It took three years, PO."

"Yeah, well, seven sounds better"

After I came home from boot camp, I continued my journal. I wrote conversations I had with my friend. That was an inside joke between us. I think I know why. I went home for my 22nd birthday and gave the journal to him to read. The last entry is from him for my birthday. I keep the journal in my fireproof safe and consider it a treasure. Hopefully, those pages that fell out will never get lost.

We kept in touch for a while, but life took us in different directions. He is an Army veteran, married, with three kids now. We are still friends on Facebook. We aren't as close as we once were, but that is the way life is. I will always treasure what we had.

STAY HOME

Hurricane Katrina hit the Gulf Coast while I was in boot camp. After boot camp I elected to take twelve days of leave, going seven in the hole, and then I was supposed to report in at Coast Guard Station Sabine Pass, Texas. It is in southeast Texas right on the border of Louisiana, about 100 miles south of Houston. There is a small fire station, high school, and a few other businesses in the middle of nowhere, and oil fields. My Boatswains Mate First Class (BM1) called me at home and told me that Hurricane Rita was headed straight for Sabine Pass, so they were evacuating the station. I should stay home and wait for him to call me again to report. Hurricane Rita hit Texas on Sept 24, 2005.

A week later, BM1 called so my mom and I drove down to Texas. Once we hit southern Texas, we began to see a lot of damage from Rita. Driving to the station, we saw that houses and businesses were destroyed. Everywhere we looked, we saw devastation. Billboards and road signs were knocked over. We even saw a boat, high and dry, in the middle of a field.

I reported into the station, with my mother, on October 3, 2005. The small boat station had also been destroyed. There were rocks outside the gate, white and blue. The white rocks were supposed to surround the blue rocks and the blue were supposed to spell out "Station Sabine" They were in disarray. The gate was wide open. The main station building was severely damaged. Small camper trailers were set up on one side near the entrance. FEMA had loaned them to the Coast Guard for the duty station personnel to stay in while on duty. There was also a long trailer with five showers and a small kitchen trailer.

The station shared a base with the Aids to Navigation Team. Their building had not been destroyed so the station set up a make-shift communications room in one of their smaller rooms. The fire station was destroyed, but the firemen kept a couple of their trucks and a trailer on the base. The harbor pilots and one of our 87-foot cutters shared a small pier with us. It was a very eye-opening experience. I had never experienced that kind of damage before in my life. It was both exciting and scary to begin my Coast Guard career immediately after a major hurricane.

A female boatswains mate second class (BM2) showed us around the station. I met a lot of people, some who worked at the station and some who were temporarily helping out. A Lieutenant (LT) from Sector Houston was there, taking a lot of pictures. He took one of my mom and me in front of a large pile of debris that used to be the station. Later he emailed my mom the picture and wrote her this:

> Ma'am,
>
> It was a pleasure meeting you today and personally welcoming you and your daughter to Coast Guard Station Sabine. Some may think the Station is a mess. That's true, to some extent. But I hope you can see past the large pile of debris and numerous makeshift utilities to see the true spirit of our Coast Guard in every person working to get the Station back online. No doubt it will take lots of work and some time.
>
> In the past week it's been a wonderful privilege to work with Station Sabine. I am confident Seaman Herbst will have a great first tour. I wish you all the best.
>
> Respectfully,
> LT

Later my mom flew home. That is when I first met Travis.

MY TEXAS FAMILY

Travis was from Texas, just outside of Houston. He took us to the airport. I'm not sorry that my mom drove down to Texas with me, but I was teased about it relentlessly. Also, getting her to the airport when I was supposed to be settling in and getting to work was awkward. Travis tried to make me feel better on the way back by telling me that his mom came with him on his first day, too. He seemed like a nice guy. I was trying to figure out what to expect in my new situation, wanting to make a new friend, so was probably too eager. At one point I asked if the people at the station hung out a lot, saying something about Travis and me hanging out. When I eventually left for A-School I made scrapbooks to give my Texas Family on the condition that they all write me a short letter for my scrapbook. The first sentence from Travis reads, "Well, when I first met you, I honestly thought you were very weird, actually I think I've just gotten used to it Ha! Ha! I also thought you were trying to ask me out on a date!"

When Hurricane Katrina hit, people from Mississippi and Louisiana came over to Texas. When Hurricane Rita hit, the Texans didn't have many places left to evacuate to. Several people at the station had damage to their homes or lost their homes and were staying in hotels in Houston. The "normal" schedule for a Coast Guard Small Boat Station is two days on, two days off, with sliding weekends. Since so many people at the station were commuting back and forth from Houston, trying to put their lives back together, the schedule when I reported into Station Sabine was straight four days on, four days off.

While I was in boot camp, my mom had looked online for apartments for me. She had found a couple for me to check out once I arrived. There was a two- bedroom apartment waiting for me in nearby Nederland, Texas, but it had to be bleached and repainted because of mold in one of the closets.

Normally as a non-rate (E2s or E3s who graduated from boot camp but had not been to school for a specific job) I would have had to work a different schedule until I qualified to stand watch in the communications room. I did not have to do this since everything was in shambles. On my four days on, I was picking up debris around the station, rearranging those white and blue rocks, and other tasks related to the hurricane. The mosquitoes in Texas are the size of small birds so my back was covered in painful bites. Muscles, that I didn't know I had, ached. I had a hard time sleeping in the FEMA trailer. It was hot, humid, uncomfortable, hard work.

I met another non-rate around my age, The Religious Nut. The R.N. was from Texas. Her father lived in Houston. On our first stretch of four days off, she invited me to stay with them. We told each other our life stories in those four days and quickly became friends. On Oct 7, 2005, Three Doors Down, Shinedown, and Alter Bridge were playing a concert at the Pavilion in Houston, so the R.N. and I went together. I had never heard of Alter Bridge or Shinedown before, but I enjoyed them both. Three Doors Down brought down the house. I loved them already and they were phenomenal live. The last song, "Love Me When I'm Gone," with the flag on the screen in the background with scenes of troops gave me goosebumps. I was so proud to be an American in the Coast Guard, cleaning up after a hurricane. All my hard work for the past "seven" years had paid off. This was definitely where God wanted me. I was thrilled to be there.

Soon after that, my apartment was ready. I moved in and my stuff arrived from Illinois. My mom let me have my childhood bed. She also brought me a folding card table and some chairs and a few other apartment essentials. The Store Keeper

(SK) at the station offered me his couch. It had gotten moldy during the hurricane. Although it had been steam cleaned and was totally fine, he had young children and didn't want to take a chance of them getting sick. I bought the couch for $50. I loved that couch and kept it for the next eight years.

My mom had purchased a treadmill for me since she knew I loved running. On November 3, 2005, a BM2, Ken, and Corey, came over and took it up to my second-story apartment to set it up for me. It was a giant pain in the neck. After it was set up, Corey asked me if I wanted to go to the club with Ken and him that night. Excited to have plans with some new friends, I enthusiastically said, "Yes!!"

When we three went out, Ken was drinking and having fun, but I could tell he was also watching over me in a big brother way. I thought it was really sweet. He wanted us to have fun and to do our own thing, but he also wanted to make sure I was safe. I don't have an older brother so was humbled and happy that Ken was acting as one.

Ken should have been watching Corey, though. Well, he kind of was. I think Ken was the one who broke up the fight Corey got into. It was too late, though. Corey was kicked out of the club, so Ken and I left with him. I still had a good time. And I was still excited to have two new friends.

Ken was a little bit older than the rest of us. He was prior Navy and now a Fireman in the Coast Guard. He hated being at the station and working on boats. His passion was working on aircraft. He was married and had a son, but they were in Arizona. Ken and Corey had been roommates, so they hung out often. Ken hung out with the rest of us on occasion. I have a note from Ken in my scrapbook about a "wild" night on Dec 4, 2005. Apparently, at that time, when I was drunk, I liked to "sing" at the top of my lungs on the way home. Ken didn't hang out with us that often, but I still consider him to be a brother to me.

Corey. The Drunk Hottie. Oh, where do I even begin?!? I love Corey more than any words in this book will ever be able to convey. Corey and I are the same age; we're both '84 babies. Corey was one of the best boat crewmen at the station. His twin brother and he had reported a couple years before me, but his twin was kicked out of the Coast Guard. Corey is from Baton Rouge and loves the outdoors: fishing and camping and hunting. He is very outgoing and also loved going out dancing and partying. Several people at the station, including my mentor, had warned me to stay away from him. They warned me he could get me in trouble. But I loved Corey from the beginning. I loved his energy. I loved the way he treated me. I loved hanging out with him. Corey made me feel so comfortable. He was so accepting of who I was and never wanted me to be anything different. Corey is like that with everyone. He literally just wants everyone to have a good time when they are around him. If you are friends with Corey or Corey considers you family, Corey is more loyal than anyone I have ever met in my entire life. Corey is my best friend. We keep in touch to this day.

When the station went from the four on, four off schedule back to the normal two on, two off, with sliding weekends, I was moved to the other duty section. I don't remember the reason. I'm sure it was a good one; it ended up being a good one. But I was devastated. I really liked the female BM2 who had been helping me out with everything. There were a couple other non-rates who I really got along with and I was working on getting qualified. I did not want to switch sections and meet new people. I don't know why, but I didn't think I would like the new people. In general, as I have learned over time, I am not really comfortable with change.

However, the switch ended up being great!! Lee, BM2 at that time, was officially assigned as my mentor. He had been in the Coast Guard for ten-ish years at that time. His uniform was always really sharp, and he took his job very seriously. He was somewhat intimidating, but I liked him. I learned a lot from him, too. We hung out every once in a while, and I met his wife, but his rank and job at the station made him more of a boss and mentor than a friend who could hang out with us. But I love Lee and respect Lee more than I will ever be able to convey in this book. Lee is the entire reason I became an Operations Specialist (OS) and had a career. Lee has given me more advice than any one man should ever have to and has supported me every time things have been rough for me. We still keep in touch to this day, as well. He retired as a chief a year or two ago.

Now working with a new crew, I met another non-rate, a year or two younger than I, Hoestie. While talking to her at the station, I found out she needed a place to stay. The roof was ripped off her apartment and the complex was estimating a month or two to repair it. I told her she could stay with me if she wanted to. I had a two-bedroom apartment, after all. She moved in.

Hoestie was from College Station, Texas, and we became really good friends. I didn't charge her rent, officially, but she paid me. She introduced me to Cheddars, and we went there to eat a lot. She was big into reading, as was I, and she recommended I read "A Million Little Pieces" by James Frey. I loved the book and she began recommending others for me to read. Hoestie was injured and couldn't do too much at the station. She was kind of "emo" in general and the command didn't like her attitude. I appreciated how straight forward and honest she was, even if she was slightly depressing sometimes. She also had a very sarcastic sense of humor which I loved.

The Religious Nut, Hoestie, Corey, and Travis became my Texas Family along with the Lovesick Outdoorsman. I don't remember when I first met the Lovesick Outdoorsman. To be completely honest, I'm not even really sure how he became part of the family. He was a little older than the rest of us and was a BM2. He did love the outdoors and would come camping with us. I think he went fishing with Corey sometimes, too. But he couldn't hang out with us too much because he outranked us and was supposed to be an example for us. One time that actually got him in trouble. Regardless, for better or worse, the six of us were family. And it wasn't too often that you would see any of us alone. There was some sort of combination of us together, whether it be just the girls, just the boys, Corey and the Lovesick Outdoorsman fishing, Hoestie and I having lunch. Our group was always together.

STATION PARADISE

A seaman at a station is required to earn the following qualifications:

Communications Watch Stander

Boat Crewman

Boarding Team Member (BTM)

When we were standing four on, four off at the station, the primary focus was to clean up the hurricane debris and make the station attractive and functional again. We were working long days in the heat and humidity. We had gloves and rakes and were moving all the debris into one place. Some of the non-rates had to "weed-eat" or mow. The boatswain mates (BMs) would get underway and try to determine the new water depths since the sands had been shifted by the hurricane. The Aids to Navigation Team and our BMs were trying to determine where all the buoys and other aids were. They needed to know what had been destroyed, what could be repaired, what was misplaced, and what was still working and in place. They were using this information not only to repair and replace what they could, but also to update the nautical charts for the area.

Once the station was as together as it could be, we went into the town of Sabine and helped elderly people, teachers, and others in need clean up the debris in their yards. It was very hard but very rewarding work. I was hot and exhausted but also excited to be part of something so meaningful. It was also really cool to see how people come together after a disaster to help each other out.

After that, it was time to get back to the mission. BM2 Lee

had me start standing watch in the temporary Communications Room and gave me all the stuff for boat crew. The hurricane had wiped out a lot of the radio towers and much of our equipment was damaged or not fully functional. While I was learning to do the job, a lot of things had to be modified or marked as "not applicable."

A Comms Watch Stander basically listens to the radios and responds to any calls for the Coast Guard or other distress calls. They also take the guard for the small boats when they get underway and assist sector (the unit above a station) with anything they may need. While a Comms Watch Stander at a station serves a purpose, especially after the hurricane, an Operations Specialist (OS) stands the same watch at the sector, 24 hours a day, seven days a week. Sector can always assist with a case and sometimes take over the entire case, if needed.

It takes 3-4 weeks to get qualified at a station to stand the watch. I don't remember having any trouble getting qualified, other than the storm damage modifications that everyone struggled with. I really enjoyed standing watch. The comms room was air conditioned. I was out of the heat, not getting eaten up by mosquitoes, waiting to potentially save someone's life. What job was better than that?

I was also working on qualifying as a boat crewman. Our station had a 47-foot motor lifeboat. Usually 47s are used when there are rough surf conditions. Station Sabine did not experience rough surf in our Area of Responsibility (AOR). There were rumors we were going to give the 47 to another station to use instead. I started getting sign offs on it and then was told to focus on the 41-foot lifeboat instead. Later I was told to keep working on the 47. Then a little while later, I was told to stop again. It was slightly annoying, but I was also working on the 41. Eventually the station did give the 47 to another station in Florida. I never was fully qualified on it.

The 41 was a work horse. I loved that boat as much as anyone could love a boat. In the mornings, it was required to do boat checks on all the boats. We would go down after breakfast and check that the lines were tied to the pier in accord with whatever the tide was doing. Then we'd get aboard the boat and check that all the equipment was on board and in the right place. To get Boat Crew qualified you had to know every piece of equipment on the boat. Boat checks assisted with this. The Mechanics (MKs) would get on and turn the boats on. They would check the engine and make sure everything was working right. Then someone would check the radios and make sure they were working right.

We also had a 25-foot and a 21-foot boat. Those were considered non-standard boats and were fairly easy to get qualified on. They could only be used in shallow water and didn't have nearly as much equipment on them.

After boat checks in the morning, we either had work to do around the station or we'd get underway for training. We did a lot of two boat training; meaning that we would get the 41 and the 25 underway and then we would practice towing the 25 either in a side tow or stern tow with the 41. We also practiced passing the P6 pump back and forth between the two boats and hooking up all the firefighting equipment. I enjoyed all of this except that I wasn't really great at any of it. The book knowledge, answering questions, telling someone how to do it all, was easy. But when actually doing it, I was clumsy.

Every other Thursday, if I remember correctly, Air Station Houston would send out a helicopter and we would practice with them. The helo would drop a basket or the Stokes litter onto our boat and then hoist it back up. Sometimes they would drop the rescue swimmer, too. The first couple times I practiced I thought it was the coolest experience ever!! This is what I had seen in *The Perfect Storm*. This is why I had joined. And who else could say that they worked with small boats and helicopters?!?

But it didn't take long for the excitement to wear off. The helo hovering over the small boat would spray water everywhere. The saltwater would turn our boots white, so it took forever to dry them out and shine them. The saltwater also messed up our uniforms. The training was almost always done at night. We would get back late and still have to clean and prepare for duty relief on Friday morning. We continuously tried to get out of doing it—to no avail.

We didn't start Boarding Team Member training until later. I hated most of that. Boarding teams go onto vessels and do law enforcement. On smaller boats BTMs make sure the boats have all required safety equipment and the operators are sober. It's similar on bigger vessels, I suppose, but there is more stuff to check. I didn't join the Coast Guard to be a cop. I joined to save lives. I grew up shooting guns, target practicing. Everyone in my family hunts, except for my stepsister and me. I have no problem with guns at all, but I didn't want to carry one. I certainly didn't ever want to be in a position where I would have to use it. I expressed these concerns to the command, but it is a Seaman's responsibility to get qualified. So, I did my best during training and figured I would deal with real boardings if or when the time came. Thankfully, it never did.

In between standing watches in the comms room and all of our duties, we all had a lot of fun, too. Oscar is the dummy used when we practice "man overboard" drills. Oscar is similar to a Red Cross CPR dummy, except Oscar is a full person, not just torso and head. Fun fact, Oscar has its name because when a vessel has a man overboard, the signal flag used to let other vessels know is the Oscar flag.

When Oscar was not being used in training, there was no telling where he'd end up or how he would be dressed up. It may sound lame in a book, but there isn't too much scarier than a strange man sitting in the female bathroom in the middle of the night.

I also remember working by the pier one day when Corey picked up a jelly fish and tossed it at my head. I remember being dead legged several times and tripped when I was walking. Travis was infamous for trying to scare people, along with another BM2 who had a Reagan mask and liked to jump out at you whenever he could.

We were a group of adults in our early 20s who were given a lot of responsibilities and weren't quite sure what to do with all of them. So we worked really hard and we played really hard. Sometimes we played too much. For example:

The command wanted the non-rates trained. That makes sense. In spite of the hurricane, the command still wanted all duties performed. That makes sense, until you see it in action. Every night we were supposed to use the golf cart to do a round of the base for security purposes. The most important risk we were trained to watch for was holes in the fence. What didn't make sense was that there was already a known hole in the fence: the hurricane had destroyed the main gate and large parts of the fence. The family and I would joke around while we were on duty, "Look for holes in the fence. Ignore the big one in front."

The first idea I ever had for a book was an idealistic book about working hard and following your dreams. I was also very religious at the time and it was going to focus heavily on my youth pastor's advice about making decisions. I was going to talk about how if you were where God wanted you to be, you would always be taken care of and life would always work out. After everything I've been through though, I don't have the same faith as I once had.

The next idea I had for writing a book was to describe a non-rate's life at the station. Not the usual station, but rather a station after a hurricane had wiped it out. The mission was the same, but the everyday work was very different. A lot of things had to be modified or changed in order to make things work with what we had. I already described staying in FEMA trailers and using a shower and kitchen trailer. I've talked about the comm's room and getting qualified as a comm's watch stander. I could write stories about Oscar, the Reagan mask, and jelly fish. I could write stories about the silly duties and jobs we had. They weren't silly on their own, but they were when you remembered the hurricane.

I remember emailing some friends from boot camp and asking them for stories they had at their units. I just wanted to put together a book of silly stuff, military humor. I must not have worded my email very well because one friend replied that he would not take part in mocking or shaming the Coast Guard. That was not at all what I wanted to do.

I guess I talked about writing a book more than I remember because when I asked Hoestie for permission to use her name in the book, she asked what it was going to be about, and had a list of topics for me to choose from. She remembered a whole list of potential titles for the book from our previous conversations. After hearing what I wanted to write about, then reading Prologue One, she asked if one of the titles could be a chapter title instead. This is that chapter. Station Sabine was great in many respects, but it was so full of nonsense and drama that we all had a love-hate relationship with it. Hoestie called it Station Paradise.

NEW YEAR'S

New Year's Eve 2005 is one of my favorite and most unforgettable New Year's Eves ever. Corey and I were and always have been strictly friends. I did have a small crush on him when I first met him because he is HOT as hell, but after I got to know him, he was the definition of a brother. He was obnoxious, always playing pranks and just an all-around general pain in the ass. He was also a ton of fun to be around, extremely loyal, and would seriously kill anyone if they even looked at me the wrong way.

Corey had his tongue pierced. I had never kissed a guy with a tongue ring before and was curious at how much "better" or more fun it really was. We joked around that at some point when we were drunk, we would just have to make out one time, just so I could see what the tongue ring was all about.

For this New Year's Eve, we went to our normal spot, Dixie's Dance Hall on Crockett Street in Beaumont. It was Corey, his best friend, his father, and me. Of course, we were at Dixies all the time and Corey knew everyone, so once we got inside, more people joined us. Our normal routine was to go in, do a couple of shots, and begin greeting people. Sometimes Corey would dance with me or teach me how to two step, if we got there early enough for the country music. I always loved that. I love dancing, though I completely suck at it. Then once the music changed to hip-hop or club mixes or whatever, Corey would start doing his own thing, usually dancing with other girls, and I would do my own thing. New Year's wasn't any different. We were both doing our own thing when everyone started counting down:

"10, 9, 8, 7, 6, 5, 4, 3, 2!! HAPPY NEW YEAR!!'

Corey was kissing all the girls and then he turned to me. Corey is 6'4 and I'm 5'3. Corey bent down and gave me a peck on the cheek. I looked up at him and said loudly, "Get down here and give me a real kiss!"

Corey smiled, picked me up, spun me in a circle, and shouted "I love you."

Then he kissed me! A real kiss! And wouldn't you know it ... 2006 New Year's night was the one night that Corey did not wear his tongue ring!

AFTER THE STORM

February 26, 2006, *Extreme Makeover: Home Edition* "After the Storm" came to Sabine Pass, Texas. We got word at the station and everyone was excitedly hoping to meet the star, Ty Pennington. Or maybe I was excited because I wanted to meet Ty! They were going to make over the fire station so the fire department guys staying on base were thrilled to have a fire department again. They also made over the high school gym and theater, and a church. Then the show sent the towns-people on a shopping spree to Sears.

February 28, I got a call from one of the guys at the station who said if I came into work early the next day, I'd be allowed to attend the concert. I was like "What concert?"

The guy told me that the Goo Goo Dolls were going to perform the next morning in front of the washed-up shrimp boat next to the Sabine station. All station personnel were going to be allowed to go to boost morale. It was really because the TV show wanted as many people there as possible.

I didn't believe him. I kept asking if this was a prank. He wasn't one of the usual station pranksters, but this just didn't seem true to me. He kept insisting that he was not joking. I'd have to get to work around 6:30 am, though.

Figuring I didn't have much to lose besides sleep and maybe a little ego, I finally decided that I would go into work early. Wouldn't you know, the Goo Goo Dolls were staged in front of that shrimp boat, right next to the station at 7:00 a.m., March 1, 2006!!!

The song the producers wanted for the show was "Better Days." I think the Goo Goo Dolls sang it three times. Each time the producers would adjust cameras or mikes or tell the crowd to cheer louder. After the show got the shots they wanted, the Goo Goo Dolls performed two or three other songs before leaving.

I was amazed! A small-town girl, from the middle of no-where Illinois, just watched the Goo Goo Dolls perform for national television in front of a washed-up shrimp boat in Texas at 7:30 in the morning. Thank God I had pictures! It was also going to air on TV. Otherwise, no one would believe me! I hardly believed it myself.

At last, the show aired in May of 2006. My parents taped it for me, and I still have that tape! Unfortunately, it is hard to watch now because it is in bad shape. Who has a VCR anymore, anyway? I watch snippets of our show on YouTube every once in a while. To this day, it gives me goosebumps.

"SWEETHEART, ARE YOU GONNA BE OK?"

Lee, my mentor, BM2 at the time, did not want me to be a non-rate for four years then leave the Coast Guard. He knew it took me a long time to join. I was proud of that, so I was now debating a career. He also saw a lot of potential in me that I had never seen in myself.

I wanted to move on, too, for my career's sake, but I was also having a blast at the station. I had a "family" that I loved. I was making decent money; living independently of Mom and Dad. What more did I need? I could stay in Texas forever. What would be wrong with that?

I was finally done with all my sign offs on the 41. I had learned all the equipment on the boat. I knew how to hook up the fire hose and put out a fire. I knew how to hook up the P6 pump to de-water a boat. I had practiced numerous tow drills and man overboard drills. I never could get exempted from the helicopter operations with Air Station Houston on Thursdays . . .

I took my board and did better than any non-rate had ever done. Seriously, the command was stunned and impressed. I knew everything about that boat. They wanted me to know the size of the engines. I knew the horsepower and the square footage of them. I answered with confidence every question they asked. That's what a Coast Guard board is: five to six people, who already have the qualification and/or are in the chain of command, sit at a table, ask you questions and weigh your answers until they are comfortable that you know how to do the job. The people on my board were beyond comfortable.

Then I had to complete my check-ride. I went out on the boat to perform all the tasks/drills we had practiced, minus the helicopter (Thank God!). I almost failed. My check-ride was awful. During the man overboard drill, I almost fell overboard. I've always been very clumsy. Memorizing stuff was easy; performing it, not so much. But somehow, by the skin of my teeth, I qualified!

During all this time, Lee/BM2 kept hounding me. "You want to be a BM, you should go BM, I'm gonna put your name on the BM School List, you'd make a good BM, you want to be a BM…" Every day on duty and the few times we hung out after work, it was just BM, BM, BM.

I kept telling him I did not want to be a BM. My check ride should be proof; I should not be a BM. So, then he would ask me what I wanted to do instead. I didn't know. I couldn't answer. He knew that I wasn't researching or looking into anything. In hindsight, I realize he also knew I shouldn't be a BM. He kept pushing me to make a decision about my career. I was happy and willing to "settle" where I was. He was determined to see me move up.

Then one night on duty, the Search and Rescue (SAR) alarm sounded. I was qualified on all the boats. I ran down to the 41. I was the first one there. I was so excited. It was my first official case. I threw on my life jacket. I was going to start the boat up, but truth be told I had forgotten how.

The rest of the crew finally got down there and we got underway. A male on a shrimping vessel thought he was having a heart attack. We went out past the jetties. I was so excited. I was going to save a life! This was what I joined for. This is what I had trained for. This was going to be the epitome of my career! And it was! … Sort of.

We arrived on scene and the male was transferred to our boat from the shrimp boat. I was ordered to take him down to the survivor's compartment, give him a life jacket, and get basic information from him.

We were dead in the water (DIW) offshore, awaiting a helicopter to hoist him from our boat to fly him to the nearest hospital. The waves were two to three feet. I tried lifting the bench to grab a life jacket just as a wave hit the side of the boat. I tripped. I was a little embarrassed, but I got up and handed him a life jacket.

All of a sudden, I wasn't feeling too well. This couldn't be happening. I was the Coast Guard. I was here to save this man's life. This is what I worked hard for. This is what I trained for. I started asking him questions. I realized I didn't have anything to write on. I asked for paper. I kept losing my balance with the waves hitting the side of the boat. I asked what his name was. I was trying to think of something else to ask him.

Then the man who was potentially having a heart attack, the shrimper I was supposed to be saving, the "victim" in this situation, looked at me with eyes full of pity and asked, "Sweetheart, are you going to be OK?"

I was mortified. Luckily, just then the helicopter arrived. The other crew members asked for him top side. He was hoisted into the helicopter like I had seen (and even done) a million times in practice, and they flew off to the hospital. Once the helicopter was out of sight, I puked over the side of the boat.

After that, whenever the SAR alarm would sound, I would take over in the communications room and let someone else get the boat underway. Most of the non-rates hated sitting in the communications room for hours doing nothing. I loved it. I hated manual labor. I would volunteer for as many watches as they would give me. I started learning what the command wanted for watch reliefs, or shift change. I would have all the information ready when the Officer of the Day came in in the morning. The OOD's loved me. It didn't take long for Lee/BM2 to ask me, "Do you want to be an OS?"

When the first recruiter came to my house, I was interested in becoming a Telecommunications Specialist (TC). Since then, TCs were combined with Radar Man (RDs) and a new rate was born, Operations Specialist (OS). BM2 told me standing watch in the communications room was basically what an OS did all day. He saw I liked it and was good at it. I finally agreed, with a lot of hesitation, to let him put my name on the OS School list. After all, I knew I would not make a good BM . . .

THE PARTY HOUSE

Generally speaking, a non-rate at a station cannot be placed on an A-School list until the non-rate has been promoted to E3, has been at the station for six months, and is fully qualified. I came into the Coast Guard as an E3 because I signed up for a six-year enlistment instead of four. In 2006, OS was still a new rate and it was a critical rate, meaning that they did not have enough people in the rate to fill the jobs. I was qualified as a comms watch stander and on the 41, 25, and 21 as a boat crewman. All of that meant I could put my name on the OS A-School list after only four months at the station. Lee/BM2 put my name on the list in January or February of 2006. The very next day OS was taken off the critical rate list. I just made it. Talk about perfect timing! I was right where I was supposed to be, again.

At the time, Corey was living with his best friend whom he had known since childhood. Unfortunately, his friend was not paying his share of the bills. Corey wanted to kick his friend out, but without a roommate, how could he pay his own bills? We knew that I was going to leave for A-School in a few months, so I agreed to move in with him.

No one at the station strictly forbade me to move in with him, but no one, including and especially Lee/BM2 was happy about it, either. I had been "lucky" up until that point that Corey had not gotten me in trouble. If I moved in with him, he would for sure get me in trouble. Now that I was on the A-School list, I had something to lose if I got in trouble

I knew why everyone was concerned, but I also knew Corey. He easily got in trouble. Yes, this was and still is true. But

Corey also knew how important my career was to me and respected that. There is no way Corey would ever get me in trouble. If something went down, I would walk away or leave altogether, like I wasn't with him; I didn't know him. That was the rule. We only had to use it one time and it was actually when I was visiting him long after the station. I moved in with him without thinking twice.

It didn't take long for people at the station to start noticing differences in Corey and me. Corey was so laid back, and always wanting to have fun. He lived in the moment. I always worried about things. Corey made me relax. As I said in the Texas Family chapter, Corey accepted me for everything that I was, so I was my true self around him. Overall, I was a lot happier.

As for Corey, we started carpooling to work so he was never late anymore. I ironed his uniforms for him. He took work slightly more seriously. One of the BMs/OODs asked me one day how living with Corey was going. I said I loved it except we always had people over and sometimes that got to be too much. Then I made a joke about how Corey probably hated living with me, though.

The BM looked at me and was like "Are you kidding? Corey loves you. And he loves living with you. He has never said one bad word about you. And . . . we all like you both more now, too. Any reservations we had are gone."

My favorite memory living with Corey was our Easter party. Corey kept saying over and over again that he wanted to dye Easter eggs and have an Easter Egg Hunt. I could not for the life of me figure out why, but I'm always down to celebrate the holidays, so I agreed. I bought the eggs and hard boiled them. I got dye kits. I bought candy and set it out in a bowl in the middle of the table. I bought hamburgers and hot dogs to grill out. I should have known better but I invited adults and kids. I thought we'd actually have a BBQ and Easter Egg Hunt and it would be family friendly. Others thought better so no one brought their kids. People did dye Easter eggs and actually enjoyed dying them. Then they used the wax crayons to draw all sorts of "fun" things on the eggs; most of which were not kid friendly. We did grill out, and we wrestled. The Religious Nut got thrown into one of the bushes and completely took the bush out!! I mean, she won that fight!!

Corey and I used to throw food at the other to catch it in our mouths. I have no idea how or why this started. We were probably goofing off in the mall food court or something one day and it stuck. We used to do it with popcorn chicken. At some point in the party, I took a jellybean out of the candy dish and tossed it across the dining room. Corey caught it. People were surprised and thought it was a lucky catch. So, I threw another one. And Corey caught that one, too. And then Corey threw one to me and I caught it. And then it became a competition, an all-out war! Everyone was throwing jellybeans to or at each other!! The next morning, I was cleaning up more jellybeans and candy off the floor than beer bottles or anything else!!

The family continued to hang out together often. We went camping at the river and swung off the rope swing into the river all the time, especially as the weather got warmer. We went to Dixies. We went to concerts. Everyone knew that Corey and I had a special bond. We all loved each other, and we were all family, so it didn't really matter to anyone, except the Religious Nut. She was upset that she and I didn't have a special bond. I think it was especially upsetting to her since she was one of the first people I hung out with. She was also upset that I had a special bond with a male and not a female. She had reservations about unmarried male--female relationships in general because of her religious beliefs. I knew Corey and I were just friends. She had a few screws loose, in general, (Religious NUT) and kinda started driving us all nuts. But we included her in as much as she would participate. And we all had a good time.

After a while, the parties were a little overwhelming. I did not realize how much Corey enjoyed being around other people. Someone was always over at our house. A lot of the stuff in the house was mine. I was getting tired of other people using it, but not taking care of it. Corey and I did start "fighting" a little bit because I needed some space. If I had had to live with Corey for any longer, I'm not sure how good our friendship would still be. Because we both knew it was temporary going in, it worked out really well.

PEPPER SPRAY

It was expected for a seaman at a station to get BTM qualified. When I was in boot camp and we trained on the pistol, we shot a 9 mm. When I first got to the station, we shot the 9 as well. I qualified marksman in boot camp and at the station.

Later the Coast Guard switched to a .40 caliber. I loved the .40, but I did not qualify with it the first time I tried. I was going to go back to the range to qualify when my orders to A-School came through. It was official. I had a start date: June 12, 2006. The command decided that since I would not get qualified as a BTM and I would never do any boardings, they should not waste any more ammo on qualifying me. I did not go back to the range.

Another part of BTM training is getting pepper sprayed. The command had set a date for all the non-rates to be sprayed if they had not already. I was given a choice whether to or not. On the one hand, I was going to A-School, so I did not have to. On the other hand, at some point in the Coast Guard I would probably have to be trained with pepper spray and I should just get it over with. My family thought I was crazy, but I chose to get it over with.

Some units film pepper spray training. I wish mine had been recorded. At the very least, I wish there was a picture of me before and after. Despite all the pranks we pulled on each other at the station, my CO was actually very strict about hazing. He made a rule that there would be no pictures or recordings of the pepper spraying.

The day came. It was hot as hell in Texas, as normal. I think Lee/BM2 was the one who sprayed us. Travis was in the red man suit and "attacked" us after we had been sprayed. After you are sprayed you are required to yell "OC! OC! OC!" This tells everyone else on your boarding team that you have been sprayed so the situation has escalated. Then you are required to "fight" with the red man for a few minutes, again, in case you are attacked in real life. Then you have to draw your gun (which was a fake gun for the exercise) on the red man and tell him to get down on the ground. At that point the exercise is over, and you can wash the spray out of your eyes.

It was my turn. I was sprayed and then told to open my eyes. There aren't strong enough words to explain the amount of pain and how much that burns. I was surprised, though, at how well I could still see. Some people have to hold their own eyes open, then fight one-handed. I don't remember having to do that, although Travis was very blurry. I didn't fight very hard. Travis still makes fun of me for my weak "Get back!" yells and my gentle pushes. I swear I thought I was tearing him apart. I drew my gun, told him to get on the ground, and then I ran over to the bucket of water.

Some people react very differently to pepper spray. I was lucky and didn't have too bad a reaction, in comparison to others. Since it was so hot and humid and there was very little breeze, the BMs brought over one of the air-conditioned government vehicles and turned it on. We sat in the truck holding our eyes open to let them dry out.

I guess my reaction to the pepper spray was that it drained my sinuses because I kept having to spit. At one point the BM1 came over to ask how we were doing. Mid-conversation I told him to move. He looked at me funny but did. I hacked a huge loogey on the ground. "OMG Herbst! For real! Is *THAT* how you think you attract guys around here? That is so not sexy!"

After spray training, you are given a letter to prove that you have been sprayed. To this day, I still carry a copy in my wallet. I also sent one to my mom, put one in my fire-proof safe, and put one in Corey's fire-proof safe. Everyone in the civilian world thinks this is funny, but also thinks this is over-kill. Anyone who has ever been sprayed understands and may keep even more copies than I did.

Thank God, I did, too! When I got to the *USCGC Mellon,* they wanted to spray me to qualify for GPOW because they couldn't find my letter in the system. There was no way in hell I was doing that again! My CO at the station was right: at some point in your Coast Guard career, you will probably be sprayed. I was relieved that I had decided to do it in Texas, with my family. I was even more relieved when I watched the a-holes on the *Mellon* make a game out of spraying entire faces with entirely too much spray. Everyone recorded it then laughed at those with bad reactions A-holes and hazing were typical on the *Mellon*, though, and I would see and deal with my fair share of it despite getting out of being pepper sprayed.

DESSERTS AND RIVER WALKS

The Religious Nut wanted the family to go out one night dressed up really fancy, like in prom dresses and tuxedos. Hoestie and I both thought it was a decent idea, but wanted to know where she wanted to go once we were dressed up. She said we should go out for a really fancy dinner. Again, Hoestie and I liked this idea, but we were non-rates and we weren't making that much money. We thought maybe we should go to a fancy restaurant and just order dessert instead of eating an entire dinner.

The guys thought the girls were crazy, of course. But when I got orders to go to A-School the guys decided maybe we should do something special. So, on May 3, 2006, the entire family did get dressed up. The girls did not go shopping together, but we all three ended up with very similar dresses. The R.N. and my dresses were black and Hoestie's was a dark green. They were all sleeveless with hems just past our knees. The guys wore nice jeans and button up shirts. We went to a restaurant called Pappadeauxs. It was on the nicer end, but not too expensive. I don't really like seafood, but I loved their alligator. We had a really nice family dinner. And we took a lot of pictures. Travis actually framed one of them to give to me as a going away gift.

Travis also decided that we should all go to San Antonio before I left. May 26-28, 2006, Travis, Hoestie, the R.N. and I all went to San Antonio. I don't remember why, but the Lovesick Outdoorsman and Corey did not go with us. We took my car.

I'm a terrible driver and it was also super windy. I was probably driving too fast, but the wind was also pushing the car around. I swerved a lot! To this day, whenever I tell Travis that I have to drive any distance at all, he replies, "I hope it's not windy!"

When we arrived in San Antonio Travis kept asking me what I wanted to do. We had decided we would spend a day floating the river and we would have dinner on the river walk. I really didn't know the area or what there was to do. Hoestie was pretty laid back about the entire trip. She might have vetoed something, but I don't remember her being too pushy about anything. She was there to say goodbye to me and have a good weekend. The R.N. kept making plans and itineraries for the trip. Anytime Travis or Hoestie would ask me anything, she'd answer. She even had a list of restaurants to recommend. I probably would have let her plan the trip if it had been just us. I really didn't know the area and wasn't that passionate about arguing. But God Bless Travis, he repeatedly told her that it was MY trip, so everyone was going to do what I wanted to do. We would look things up online or they would throw out suggestions but the final decision on all activities was mine. I didn't think it was possible to love Travis more than I did already, but after that trip, I loved him more.

We had a good time floating the river. We took several pictures with a waterproof disposable camera I purchased. We had a great time walking the River Walk. The San Antonio River Walk is breath taking!! We ate a nice dinner, at a nice restaurant on the walk. I purchased a cool Coast Guard candle. I always looked out for Coast Guard merchandise and was always excited when I found something. I still look for stuff now and Travis still makes fun of me for that, too.

I don't remember what else we did. I have some pictures at different restaurants, but they don't say where we were. The hotel was nice. We were so exhausted after the day's activities; I think we just passed out. I don't remember swimming or using any of the facilities there, but maybe we did. Regardless, it was a really nice going away trip. And in the end, I think even the R.N. had a good time, too.

My mom insisted on driving with me from Texas to California. I didn't want her to, but I didn't tell her no either. It ended up being a good and bad thing. The road trip, in general, was God awful, but we did have a good time hiking in Yosemite.

Mom came down to Texas my last week. She was there when the movers came to pack my stuff. That could be an entire chapter by itself. I'm not writing this book in order of events, so I've written most of the Mellon stuff already. I forgot to add that when my stuff arrived, most of it was broken and some was missing. I did get a house plant, though, that did not belong to me.

But I digress. Mom came down and Corey, his best friend, her and I went bowling. The family took several pictures together, including in front of the boats at the station. I was given a station plaque and a Bravo Zulu. Bravo Zulus are sort of awards. Some awards are ribbons or medals and count for points towards advancement. A Bravo Zulu is not any of that, but it is a token of appreciation and does note your hard work. I was happy with it. And I was sad that I was leaving.

I gave everyone their scrapbooks and they all wrote in mine. A couple other people wrote in mine, too. Lee/BM2 wrote such a nice message, I almost cried. Lee is also a really good artist, so he drew some cartoons in it, too. Another guy not worth really mentioning at all except for this wrote "Say all but change the names" I guess I really did talk a lot about writing a book.

I pulled one last really good prank on Corey and then my mom and I left for California.

GOODBYE

(To My Texas Family)

Even though we always seem
To get under each other's skin
We are always there for one another
Through thick and thin

We've shared good times and bad
Shown each other who we are
And the drive to have fun
Is never very far

We were thrown together
Six strangers with different pasts
But we quickly became a family
And made memories that will last

So now as I have to leave
To California I must depart
I really hope you all know
You hold special places in my heart

And I wish you all the best of luck
As you continue on with your careers
I will never forget any of you
Or the good times we've had down here

Poem By: Hillary Herbst

A-SCHOOL INDOC

The road trip from Texas to California was mostly horrible, for several reasons. As excited as I was that I was headed to A-School and about to complete the next phase in my career, I was also miserable that I had left my Texas "family." I texted them every single day on the road, including when I was driving. I had to know what was going on. I had to know they were having fun. I had to know that they missed me. They had to know that I missed them.

Ironically, when I was texting and driving and driving too fast, nothing bad happened at all. But in Fresno, CA, I was pulling out of a gas station and couldn't see around a semi-truck. The truck driver looked in his mirror and waved me out. A car came up behind him, went around him, and hit me. No one was injured. There wasn't even much visible damage to my car. I continued to drive the rest of the way to Petaluma. Later the insurance adjuster came out and found that the frame of my car had been bent so they totaled the car. The accident was declared a "no fault" accident.

On June 12, 2006 OS A-School started. Two classes start A-School at the same time, and they are known as sister classes, just like boot camp. Usually there are two individual Operations Specialist First Classes (OS1s) who are the Class Advisors for the two classes. Since summer is transfer season, they were short instructors/advisors/OS1s, so one OS1 was advisor to both our classes.

The first week of school was known as Indoc (indoctrination). Along with our normal classes, we also had night classes. They were, in my opinion, gigantic wastes of time.

These classes covered basic Coast Guard rules and the Training Center (Tracen) rules. We were all tired and didn't want to be there. I doubt anyone paid much attention to them at all. I certainly didn't. During Indoc we were not allowed to leave base at all, for any reason.

I'm fairly certain it was during that time that I met Jack. Jack was in my class and was a reservist from Boston with the stereotypical Bostonian arrogance and attitude. I loved him from the beginning. Since we were stuck on base, we played a lot of pool in the barracks. Jack was a pretty good pool player, and I was, well, not good at all. I don't know why he decided to start showing me how to play, but I'm glad he did. I enjoyed playing pool with him and hearing some of his crazy stories.

My roommates were my California Wingman (CW) and another girl we'll just call G. CW was in my sister class. I don't remember which class G was in. At first we three got along very well. CW was married to a Marine who was overseas. She purchased a phone and phone line for the room so he could call her whenever he was able. She told G and I that we could use the phone whenever we wanted so long as we immediately ended our call when her husband called. It sounded very reasonable to me. I had my cell phone and don't remember using the room phone that often, if ever. G had a TV, and I had a radio. We all agreed that the phone, TV, and radio could be used by any of us at any time.

Our class leaders were Ed and Dee. We thought they took their job a little too seriously and sometimes their "parenting" was not welcome. I got along with Dee great and she is one of my best friends in the entire world to this day. Ed hung out with Jack sometimes and was in what would become our group of friends. Ed and I had a love-hate relationship and really don't keep in touch, although I heard he switched rates and is now a Boatswains Mate Chief (BMC) and happily married.

I'm not sure exactly when or how Sean and I started hanging out. Maybe I just started talking to him in class. I really don't remember. Sean was from Idaho and was kind of hippy-ish and shy. I got along with him very well. We kept in touch for quite a while after A-School and then he got married. Now I talk to his wife all the time. His wife, J-Babe, was a few classes behind us and we became good friends whenever she got to Petaluma. They didn't date in A-School; she was actually dating someone else. They reconnected later and are now married with two kids.

As you can see, it didn't take me too long to have a new group of friends. Between the people just mentioned and some other random friends here and there, we were never alone throughout school.

The class advisor, Sabrina, was an OS1 who had been in the Coast Guard for quite some time. She was very passionate about her job and career and she was also very passionate about helping us succeed in our careers. She was just the right mix between hard ass and compassionate. For example, almost our entire class had come from the fleet. Let me back up for just a minute:

When you join the Coast Guard, you have two options. If you are familiar with the Coast Guard or you know what rate or job you would like to have, you can join with guaranteed A-School. Once you graduate from boot camp, you immediately head to school to become rated. This is what Travis had done and why he was a Seaman Boatswains Mate (SNBM.) He had gone to school after boot camp and became a BM, but because he didn't have much time in the Coast Guard, he had to wait to promote to E4/Petty Officer.

The other option you have after boot camp is to go into the fleet as a non-rate, meaning you did not have a rate or job yet. This is the option I chose because I was not familiar with the Coast Guard. Even though I had thought about being a TC, I wanted to go into the fleet to learn, firsthand, what all the rates and jobs were and what they did. As you know, I ended up on the OS list instead of becoming a BM.

Like me, most of my A-School class and sister class had

come to school from the fleet. One of the first mornings OS1/ Sabrina came down to the barracks and had all of us line up. She then gave the command "One step forward. March!" Half the class stepped out with their left foot (the correct way) and the other half with the right foot. None of us had corrected our steps so we weren't even in a straight line. We were a hot mess. Did she realize it had been, well, eight months for me, longer for some, since we had to march?!?

OS1/Sabrina was very patient with things like that. However, after the first uniform inspection and when it came to room inspections, we all knew that she had very high standards. Most of us liked and respected her right away. She started out as my Class Advisor and Instructor and "mentor" (Yes, she was my mentor, but I still consider Lee to be MY mentor). I only referred to her as OS1 during my school days. Since then we have kept in touch, and I'm proud and honored to say that just like Lee, she is also a good friend. She retired as a Chief so now I can call her Sabrina.

On June 21, 2006, our class was granted "Cinderella" liberty. We could finally leave the base and do whatever we wanted, BUT we had to be back on base before midnight. The front gate kept track of anyone who got back after midnight and they would be in big trouble. Our class decided to go, as a class, to Chili's. That was the first time that we really started to see each other's personalities outside of class.

Sometime soon after that, we were done with Indoc. Unless we had duty, we were free to come and go as we chose, so long as we were always in class on time.

SCHOOL ROUTINE

A-School was broken into different units. We would see OS1/Sabrina (class advisor) most mornings from 7:30-8:00. She had to split her time between us and our sister class. We would discuss any class business we had or have uniform inspections or whatever. After Class Advisor time, a different instructor would come in and present the lesson or sometimes OS1/Sabrina was our instructor. The first couple weeks we learned about the different security classifications and how to receive and destroy classified material. We also had to take typing tests every morning. We had to consistently type 50 (I think) words per minute in order to graduate. I don't remember anyone struggling with that too much. We then learned how to build different radio circuits. That instructor seemed insecure because he was a younger OS1. Since OS was a fairly new rate, it didn't take people long to promote to higher ranks. This OS1 had made OS1 in 3-4 years and, we found out later, was only 25 years old. I don't know if that was the only reason or if he was just kind of a jerk in general, but in class he was definitely a jerk. You could tell he was really just trying too hard to earn our respect. I didn't enjoy that class much, but I don't remember it being too hard, either.

I don't remember the exact order, but from there we either started Basic Comms or Maneuvering Boards (Moboards). A Moboard is a square piece of paper with a giant compass on it. You can plot your vessel and other vessels on it to determine when the other vessel will either pass your vessel or intersect with your vessel. From there you can decide if you want to avoid the other vessel or if you want to intersect with them.

With the Moboard, you can figure out an exact course and speed to do either. That is what we learned in A-School, but Moboards can be used for several other things, too. Our Moboard instructors were retired from either the Coast Guard or the Navy and taught at the school as civilian contractors.

I enjoyed Moboards at first and then became really, really bored with them. We had to do several Moboards per day and whatever we didn't finish in class; we'd take for homework. I never had to take any home, and often I was done way before class ended. Jack and I would get in trouble for talking to each other because he would finish early, too.

The Golden Compass Award was given for excellent Moboard work and was an actual gold compass. I wanted the Golden Compass Award so badly. The final test was five, I think, Moboards and all five had to be perfect. The Golden Compass was rarely awarded, mostly because of stupid errors caused by students rushing through. We were warned about all of this. That didn't stop me from rushing through one of them, though, and making a stupid mistake. I passed the final test with flying colors, but I did not earn the Golden Compass Award.

Basic Comms was fun. That is when we started doing the things that I came to A-School for. We learned the phonetic alphabet and prowords. We learned how to do radio checks, the proper way—Turns out BMs at stations just do them however they want. If you follow radio etiquette, though, there is a proper way to do them. That was true of almost everything, and I did have to correct some station habits.

I will admit I was kind of annoying/obnoxious during class and sometimes after. I loved my time at Station Sabine, and I missed my family. I came to A-School because I had been on the radios and I had run cases and I enjoyed it. So, I was very much like the girl in the movie *American Pie*. Instead of "one time at band camp," at least once a day I would wistfully say, "at my station..."

Jack had finally decided he had enough and one night while

we were playing pool, he told me to quit saying that. He told me how annoying I was and that no one cared about my station or how I used to do things. It sounds rude as I'm typing it. He probably was rude. But that is what I loved and still love about Jack. Jack is very straight forward. You never need to guess what he is thinking because you always know where you stand with him. After that night, I tried to not say it as much.

We had been in school for a couple of months and we all had our routines, dramas, and friendships. All of the OS classes marched down to class around 7:15 every morning. Each class would head in different directions and as said, class advisor time was 7:30-8. Actual class was 8-4, I think. My times might be off a little bit. (Hey, it's been 10+years) Mondays and Wednesdays (or Tues and Thurs?) we had to work out together as a class after regular class. Our class loved playing ultimate Frisbee and did that as often as OS1 would allow. We then had the rest of the night or weekend off unless we had duty.

We were all put into duty sections and the duty rotation was 1 and 5, meaning every 5th evening or night you had to stay on base; you were not allowed to leave. There were different watches the duty section would have to stand. Horsley Hall Quarterdeck had to answer the phone or check in new people. The movie theater watch made popcorn and sold candy during the movie and then had to clean up the theater afterward. The gym watch had to clean up the gym. The colors team had to raise and lower the flag at the proper times. None of it was too hard, although we all complained about it plenty.

I very clearly remember lunch time, specifically after lunch. We'd all go up to the galley and eat, and then we had some time left over before we had to march off to class. Not just our class, but all the OS A-School classes would sit in the Steadman Hall lounge and watch the TV show *Cheaters* until the very last minute when we had to line up.

There was drama, too, between the OS classes. Our class leaders always wanted us to line up early and march to class early so we'd have time to get seated and settled. The senior class did not feel the same way and we got tired of waiting for them.

We had a prior Army guy and a prior Marine in our class, so we would sing cadences as we marched. One time Jack made up a cadence, too. We lined up after lunch and as we stepped off, he yelled out proudly, "Bill's class is always late, I don't think they'll graduate." We all repeated it, just as loudly.

It was funny, but it didn't go over well with the other class or with any of the OS1s/instructors. We were told to apologize. And, so, we made up a cadence for that, as well. "Bill's class we are so sorry..."

There was, of course, roommate drama, too. I mean, we attended class together and lived together, and we were from all over the country, different ages and different backgrounds... there was bound to be some conflict.

CW and I got along well, and I got along with G all right. I had my car for a little while, even though it was totaled, and G loved me when I went out and got food or ran some other errand for her. She accused me of being racist any time I did not want to do something for her. She annoyed me, and I probably annoyed her on some level, too, but there wasn't much tension.

G and CW, on the other hand, did not get along at all. I'm not sure what, exactly, started the feud, but tension started growing between the two of them. Then one night, G did not end her phone call when CW's husband beeped in. CW was beyond mad and told G she could no longer use the phone which then escalated into G deleting every single answering message on the phone—all of which were from CW's husband. CW lost her mind and tried to attack G. I don't remember who or what broke them up, a punch was never actually thrown, but the look on CW's face said it all. Both of them were told to leave and cool off. From that point forward our barrack's room was a war zone. The two of them turned into little kids. If CW had the lights on, G would turn them off. If G was watching TV, CW would turn on the radio. It was incredibly annoying, to say the least.

Jack got along well enough with one of his roommates but absolutely hated the other. To be fair, I don't think anyone in our class really liked that other one, except the one girl he was sleeping with—even though he was married. None of us would have really cared about that, except he had a guaranteed billet so he could be co-located with his wife to a place a lot of us wanted to go. His cheating on his wife added salt to that wound. He was also pretty arrogant and had a bad temper. I don't know if there was anything specifically Jack didn't like about him, or if it was a general thing. I know the dislike was mutual.

Jack and my roommate drama, however, did NOT hold a candle to what Dee was going through. It started off with just her and one other girl. They were both a little bit older and mature. Both of them were morning people, so they both went to bed fairly early. They got along well until they got a couple other girls in their room who had been reverted into our class. Reverted means that they had to repeat their training because they screwed up. Both of those girls were hot messes and drama magnets. Both of them were dirty. Both of them were loud and stayed up late. One of them was border-line crazy and the other one was absolutely 150% bat shit crazy!! And neither of them got along with each other or with Dee and her original roommate. Oh, Lord, the stories Dee would tell!! I simultaneously laughed so hard I'd be crying AND felt so guilty and so bad that Dee was living in those conditions. For example, the bat shit crazy one would literally walk into their barracks room, spray Lysol all over everything in the room and the bathroom, not heeding where Dee or anyone else was sitting or what they were doing. Then she would leave. Just like that. And not come back for another hour or two.

When we were not on duty during the week, I remember bowling and playing a lot of pool with Jack. Sean, Dee, and other classmates would join sometimes, especially if we were bowling. Sometimes I would hang out with CW or her classmates. On the weekends, we'd go all over the place. Dee and I both had cars and some of us would go to the movies, out to eat, to see the redwoods, to baseball games.

We also volunteered. There were a couple local events that we helped with set up and take down. Almost everyone in our class volunteered. One day, there was an organization that had purchased a bunch of houses for families that fostered kids. The day we volunteered, all the furniture for the houses was being delivered. We moved it all in. It was very hard, very rewarding work. I remember being very proud to be a part of it.

August 4th is the Coast Guard's birthday. To celebrate that year, the base had gotten free tickets to Six Flags and Marine World. I remember going on the rollercoasters and doing the 75-foot bungee jump/free fall/swing thing. Sean, Dee, and I rode an elephant. We walked around and saw all the animals. The sea lions put on a show for all of us . . . not a PG show, either, if you catch my drift.

The next day Ed, Dee, and I all went to Alcatraz and hung out in San Francisco.

For the first couple months, A-School was similar to the station. We worked hard and did well during class. Then we played hard. We did not call ourselves a family, but I had a new group of friends that were all around my age. I still kept in touch with my Texas Family, too. Overall, I was happy . . .

FUTURE SKS

After Basic Comms, we started Advanced Comms and SAR. Our class was divided into districts (like the regular Coast Guard) and every student was assigned a sector within that district. Two instructors would work together in each district. One instructor would be on the radio talking to a student acting like the object of the SAR lesson for the day, such as a Coast Guard asset, or a vessel in distress, another mariner or a Good Samaritan. The other instructor would be with the students evaluating how they were responding and playing the role of a supervisor in a command center.

Dee, Sean, Ed, and I were in the same district along with the roommate that Jack didn't like and another person, I think, but I can't remember. Both of our instructors were retired military but working as civilians under contract. The Royal One was prior Navy who openly admitted he had never worked a single SAR case in his entire career. He joked that he had *been* a couple of SAR cases . . . but he had never worked one. He had, however, worked with radios and in the intelligence field. He was from the East Coast and didn't have any tact at all. He was very knowledgeable and quickly earned our respect. He joked around that his goal was to get under his students' skin and push their buttons. Well, this was sort of a joke. It was also true. He enjoyed it, but he did it for a reason. No matter what happens during a SAR case, no matter how the mariner is acting, the Coast Guard has to remain calm. If he didn't try to get under our skin, how would he know if we could do the job or not?

I want to say the other one was a Marine. He was certainly

built like a Marine. He was over six feet tall and he was jacked! I got along with him all right, but I liked and respected the Royal One a lot more.

Jack's instructor was Mr. H, a retired Coast Guard Commander who had helped build some of the radios/high sites, had extensive knowledge on communications, had worked some SAR, and had worked in the intelligence field. I don't know who Jack's other instructor was or if Mr. H was the only one. I didn't have a relationship with Mr. H when I was in A-School. I only knew him because of Jack. He was still instructing when I returned as an instructor and he remembered me. We became close then and I keep in touch with him now.

I loved every minute of being on the radio. I loved the basics, just talking to mariners or taking radio guards, and I loved SAR. This is what I had done at the station, but more extensive and the correct way. This is why I decided to go OS. I was beyond excited.

The Royal One never got under my skin. In fact, at the end of SAR, he did a quick debrief with all of us and told us pros and cons and when he got to me, he was like "and Herby, Herby annoyed me. I tried to get under Herby's skin, but Herby talks to a distressed mariner like she would talk to her grandma on the phone."

I treated every case like it was a real case. I had something to learn and I wanted to learn it. I knew they were fake cases; no one's life was truly in danger. I even got to the point where I could watch the clock and know that they had to end the case soon because it was either close to lunch or the end of the day. So, I would know exactly when the case was at its worst point and when it would have to start wrapping up. You can call that cheating if you want to, but I never panicked in real life during real SAR cases, either, so at the end of the day, it didn't matter.

Jack, on the other hand, was really struggling. Jack did great on the radio. I don't think Mr. H. ever really got under his skin, but Jack was not very organized. His paperwork was a mess, and his radio logs were awful.

Just before this SAR unit and maybe during this unit, too, Jack had something going on back at home, too, that he was really worried about.

While I was doing well in class, I was broke. I don't know what I had going on besides the car accident or maybe that was the only reason, but I overdrew my checking account twice— which I had never done before. And eventually I was car-less since it was totaled.

SAR started to take a toll on everyone. We had been in class for a while now. We were tired of our roommates. We were tired of all the rules. We were tired of the endless paper- work and homework long after being on the radio (if we only knew back then what the real world was like . . .). Being from the fleet, we all hated marching, the room inspections, the uniform inspections, duty, and the other rules. We knew that most of that stuff was not enforced in the fleet. TRACEN Petaluma is out in the middle of nowhere which was a prob- lem in of itself, but cell phone reception sucked on base, too.

I don't want to rate bash in this book; however, this did become a running joke in our class. Storekeepers (SK) are the people in the Coast Guard that order supplies for units. Their A-School was eight weeks long, half the time of OS A-School. Compared to talking to someone dying on the radio, how vital could ordering pens be? OS screws up, someone dies. SK screws up; you use red ink instead of blue. It didn't take long for our class, especially Jack, to begin saying, "I should have gone SK."

END OF SAR

Towards the end of SAR, both classes were done. We were tired of the endless paperwork, we were tired of the rules, we were tired of each other, and we were ready to go into the fleet to do something else. The instructors knew this. This wasn't any of their first rodeos, so they decided to let us have a little fun the last week.

The last week of SAR, the instructors let us give each other practice cases. I randomly drew Sean as the person I would give my case to. I decided to be a little girl on the radio. I started screaming that I thought my parents were dead. In SAR, we have very strict radio procedures and scripts. You can, of course, deviate from them here and there depending on the mariner you are talking to, especially if it is a little kid, but we were not trained for that. Sean had not worked SAR "in real life" before so, without skipping a beat, Sean keyed up the radio and said, "Roger, your parents are dead. What is your position? Over."

Our entire district had a really good laugh at Sean's expense. I really put him through the wringer during that case, too. At one point he told me the Coast Guard would get there in thirty minutes. I told him I couldn't tell time and asked him how many *Sesame Streets* that was. Sean didn't key up the microphone, but I could hear him from across the room "Uhhh, I don't know."

He keyed up and said, "Allison, (my character) that is two *Sesame Streets*."

I felt bad for Sean after the case was over. I had meant for it to be funny, but it was more stressful than funny to him. It was funny for the rest of us. I wished I had given that stressful case to Jack's roommate so we could have all laughed at him instead. Then again, Sean stayed patient throughout the whole case, as trained, but Jack's roommate would have freaked out. He kicked the sides of the cubicles on a regular basis. The Royal One really got under his skin.

Jack, after struggling through most of SAR, did finally figure out how to organize his paperwork and ended up doing very well. His district and he got a good laugh during the student given cases, too. Dee's slightly crazy roommate gave Jack a case. Jack asked her what the height of the seas was. She replied, "Seas are calm."

Not two minutes later, though, when Jack asked another question about the weather, she replied, "Seas are eight feet." That's calm?!? The vessel in distress was twelve feet long!

Ed also had played a very memorable character: Hans Gruber on the radio. This Hans was not a terrorist, though, he was on a German boat and he wanted to go disco dancing!! Ed's accent was great! I don't remember what the actual SAR was or maybe if Hans was a Good Samaritan, but we all laughed extremely hard. And Hans ended up being a repeat character!

August 18, 2006 was our last day of SAR. Jack and I could not have been more thrilled. Our entire class had made it through! We were all excited. As if the end of SAR was not enough good news, our class was also presented with our billets (the list of places we could choose to go after A-School).

BILLETS, TATTOOS, AND FUTURE BOOK STUFF

OS1/Sabrina was shocked! I had talked about my station over and over again during A-School. I rocked SAR. SAR and the fact that I got seasick were the reasons I put my name on the Operations Specialist school list in the first place! But when I handed in my billet sheet, I had "cutters" on the top of my list for my next billet. Did someone threaten me?!?

At that time, I was not sure if I wanted to be career Coast Guard. I was only 22 years old and single. In order to make chief as an OS (at that time), you had to have at least three years of rated sea time. I figured I should take a cutter, while one was available, and get the sea time out of the way in case I did decide to make it a career. I wasn't married; I didn't have kids who would miss me while I was at sea. It was a smart move for my future. OS1/Sabrina agreed, but was still really surprised.

To celebrate making it through SAR, Jack took me out for a nice dinner. He told me he would pay for everything but asked me to go easy on the drinks. We took the liberty van, driven by one of the duty personnel, into town. We started at one restaurant, but the liberty van was not around when we were done. So, we went to another restaurant for dessert, and I had another drink. We were having a lot of fun, so we went to a third restaurant after that. By then, I had started paying for

myself. It was a really fun night. It was also a nice way to celebrate the end of SAR. On August 21, 2006, our class received
our billet assignments. I was going to the Coast Guard Cutter
Mellon, my first choice.

Jack had also been talking about getting a tattoo. He kept
saying he wanted a compass rose and I kept looking at him
funny. A compass rose is on a sea chart and is basically three
circles marked with true north and magnetic variation. It's
large and usually purple. I couldn't picture anyone wanting
that, but I figured he knew what he was talking about.

I'm not sure why I wanted a tattoo. I had never thought of
getting one before. My Stepsister had one on her lower back. I
liked it but wasn't in love with it or envious of it. I did look up
to her but didn't feel the need to be like her in that way. I also
knew my mom would disapprove. She was very upset when
she found out about my Stepsister's tattoo. Of course, part of
that could have been that my Stepsister hid it from her for
three years. Mom found out about it when my Stepsister was
trying on wedding dresses.

I think I wanted a tattoo because I was so proud of being in
the Coast Guard, and I loved being an OS so much. I was still
thinking about writing a book. I still couldn't believe all the
great stuff that was happening to me.

I went with Jack to meet the tattoo artist. We had checked
out the shop; it had a good reputation. We had checked out
the artist's portfolio; he was amazing. Jack told him what he
wanted, and then I told him what I wanted.

On the front of our binders for SAR class there was a quote
from *The Perfect Storm*: "For many a mariner, the measured
voice of a Coast Guard marine radio operator is literally the
answer to prayer."

That quote was from the movie which changed my life,
talking about the job I wanted to do. But I didn't want words
tattooed on me. I told the artist I wanted a picture tattoo for
that quote.

Dee took Jack and me to get our tattoos. I asked if I could

go first. I was worried about the pain, and if I didn't go first, I'd wimp out. Jack agreed. The tattoo artist showed me the picture he drew. Two hands praying with rosary beads wrapped around them and hanging from the rosary beads was the OS rate symbol. It was absolutely perfect! It summarized the quote perfectly. I got it on the outside of my left ankle. I loved it!!

Jack got a badass compass (not a compass rose) on his thigh. It was wicked sick! He was so happy. We loved each other's tattoo. We told each other that if either of us wanted to copy the other's tattoo, it would be fine. No one else could copy us, though! Except maybe Dee. Since she was with us, but not even really her.

Later in class when we started doing navigation, Jack saw what a compass rose really was and realized that is what I thought he wanted. He finally understood my confusion.

September 1, we went to the Russian River for our class trip. Jack and another guy rented a canoe. OS1/Sabrina and some other guys grilled hamburgers and hot dogs. Classmates were swimming. I waded a little bit because my tattoo was still new enough that I was afraid I'd ruin it. Later that night, Ed, Dee, and I went to a Josh Gracin concert. Josh was in the military before he became a famous singer and gave the military free tickets. We were so excited!! Dee and I bought matching concert shirts. It was an awesome show! It was one more thing to put in my future book. (Follow your dreams...)

On September 5, Jack and I went to check out a car. There was a Petty Officer at a nearby unit selling a Chrysler Concorde. He wanted $3,000 for it and agreed to let me make payments. It was an ugly green color and as big as a boat. I hated it, but it was in good condition and I needed a car. I just needed it to get to Seattle, and then I'd be underway half the year; it would be perfect. I bought it.

Sept 20, the Coast Guard-sponsored NASCAR® came to Training Center Petaluma. We all got to meet the driver, Kevin Harvick, and take pictures with the car!! How cool was that?!?

I'm not into race cars, but I still got to do something that most people do not get to do! This definitely had to go in my future book, too!

Later that night, Jack and I went to the Oakland A's baseball game at the Alameda County Stadium for military appreciation night. I LOVE baseball (I played softball forever, remember?) and am a huge Cub's fan. Jack is, obviously, a Red Sox fan. We were both excited to go to the game, except we had to wear our dress uniform. Not the dressiest one; not our Bravos, thankfully, but our Tropical Blues. I don't remember who the A's were playing or who won, but I do remember having a fun time. Visiting every baseball stadium in the US is on my bucket list and I could now check off one more.

I think Jack actually won the A's tickets. Jack is one of the luckiest people I know. If there is a drawing, his name will be pulled. Every. Single. Time. If he did not win the tickets to the game, I know for sure he won tickets for us to see a preview for the movie, *The Guardian*. Jack, Dee, and I went to see it in the theater on base.

The Guardian was being filmed while I was at the Station in Sabine Pass, Texas. Some of the reservists who drilled there were actually extras in the film. I remembered them talking about how Kevin Costner and Ashton Kutcher had attended part of our rescue swimmer training and were both honorary rescue swimmers. Word on the street was that they were both extremely nice, too.

The sneak preview was more than we bargained for. It was an unedited, uncut version of the film! We could see the microphones hanging from the ceiling in some of the scenes! It was so funny.

The movie is somewhat accurate; mostly Hollywoodized. We were excited because we recognized some of the Mayday calls they played in the movie. The *Bow Mariner* was a real tanker that literally blew up off the East coast. They played the calls for us in class and clips of the calls were also played in *The Guardian*. Jack joked around that when we asked future

Coasties why they joined, their reply would be, "I saw *The Guardian*." Maybe that's a better movie than *The Perfect Storm*? I don't know.

We were nearing graduation, but then the command threw a plot twist at us. We were in school June-October. We had the 4th of July, Coast Guard Day, and one other holiday off school. For some unknown reason, the command decided that the classes onboard who missed those days of school would have to make them up. We had been scheduled to graduate October 6. The new graduation date was October 11.

We had three reservists in our class, though, including Jack. Unlike the rest of us who would be going out into the Coast Guard fleet, these three had "real life" jobs to get back to. The three of them ended up graduating before all the rest of us.

Jack had told me throughout A-School that he was a very out of sight, out of mind kind of guy. If I was ever in Boston, I was more than welcome to visit him. His parents would love it. But otherwise, he was not going to keep in touch. That was just who he was. It wasn't personal.

I was not having that. I'm not like that at all. Early in our A-School days, OS1/Sabrina had told us that it would be important for us to check our emails throughout our Coast Guard careers. She wanted us to start checking them often in A-School. We didn't really listen to her, though, so she started sending emails to the class saying, "If you get this, reply 'Roger, out.'" Those who did not reply got in trouble. Jack and I ended up making a deal that once a month he would have to send me an email. The email could say anything. It could say, "Dear Herby, I'm alive. Jack." or it could simply say, "Roger, out."

Before Jack graduated, I had worked on scrapbooks for my A-School friends, too. In the beginning of the scrapbook, I had a picture of each of us with our nicknames. It was very similar to the scrapbooks I had made for my Texas Family. For these scrapbooks, along with our nicknames, I also had our famous quotes.

I was The Band Camp Geek. And my quote was, "And one

time, at my station..." Of course.

Jack's was the Jack of All Trades. His quote was, "I should've been an SK."

Dee's was The Texas Taxi Driver, since she drove us around most of the time. Her quote stemmed from our Coast Guard Day trip and was "About those sea lions..."

Sean's was the Idaho Tree Hugger and his quote was, of course, "Roger. Your parents are dead. What is your position? Over."

Ed's was the Iowa Football Star and his quote was, "Yea, Coast Guard, this is the German U-boat, Das Boot. Hans speaking."

After our pictures, I had a page of random quotes that were said throughout our A-School course, followed by a list of dates. This list of dates, however, was done in message format, since I was about to be an OS now. (Which is again, how I have dates in this section of the book. The Mellon section and everything after starts to get hazy...) I made up silly A-School rules, like I did for the station. Then I had pages imitating the Master Card commercials:

Gas: $10

Praying Hands with OS designation: $100

Compass: $150

Best Tattoos Ever: Priceless

Tickets: Free

Gas: $10

Shirts: $25

Josh Gracin Concert: Priceless

After that, I again asked everyone to write me a note or letter. On the top of Dee's letter, she included a list of her own rules!! #5 says "You can make a hit list off your roommates alone!"

Right before the reservists graduated, our entire class had to weigh in. You cannot graduate A-School if you do not meet Coast Guard weight standards. I was three pounds over...

Jack and the other two reservists graduated. Dee and I took

Jack to the airport. We drove back to base and I wondered what was going to happen to me ...

OVERSTUFFED

I was only over a few pounds, but I was over. If I didn't lose the weight by graduation, I was not going to graduate. I was really freaking out. I had been working out throughout A-School. Dee and I ran. I participated in our class workouts. Sometimes I'd go to the gym and use the elliptical. I had cut back on drinking. I could have eaten a little better, but I wasn't crazy. What was I going to do? How was I going to lose those pounds in a week? I couldn't go back to the Station. Lee had worked so hard to get me to pick a rate and move on. If I got kicked out of the Coast Guard, I couldn't go back home. Everyone there knew that I had worked hard to lose weight to join the Coast Guard. How could I go home and tell them that I had put it back on? I could forget about writing a book. I couldn't write about following my dreams if my dreams only lasted for a year and a half.

Sometime after I was weighed, I had to be taped. Two female YN measure and tape different body parts while you are half-naked. In A-School I think they were still doing wrist, waist, and butt. You read that right. The Coast Guard determined Body Mass Index (BMI) by measuring your wrist, waist, and butt. It changed later, but it still doesn't make any sense. No other organization, no nutritionist, no dietician, no doctor, no personal trainer, NO ONE measurers BMI using this "method."

If your weight and BMI are determined to both be over, you are officially put on the fat boy weight program, so you have to get a medical screening; a complete waste of fucking time. They take your vital signs. They ask if you have any injury which is pretty pointless because if you do, you are still on the weight program. The entire point of the medical screening is to see if you can work out. Even if you can't work out, you are still penalized for being overweight.

I remember my screening in A-School, too, because the doctor specifically told me, "If you're having trouble with your weight now, you will always have trouble with your weight."

He wasn't wrong, but please tell me what the point of telling me that was?!? He didn't offer any helpful tips. He didn't do any medical tests to tell me why I'd have trouble with it. It was a blanket statement that offered nothing but irritation. And maybe that was his point? Maybe he wanted to motivate me to work out harder? I don't know, but he wouldn't be the only doctor to be so careless with his words . . .

After that I saw a nutritionist. Some units skip this step but Tracen Petaluma actually did this right. It wasn't very helpful, though. She didn't tell me anything I hadn't already learned at camp. Sabrina/OS1 is also a dietician so we talked about diet throughout A-School. I knew how to eat healthy and usually did.

My last week at A-School, I went to the gym early every morning. Since I only had a week to lose the weight, I started starving myself. After class, I'd walk or run with Dee. The day before my weigh in, I didn't drink any water. The morning before I weighed in, I went to the sauna to sweat for a long time. I also did not eat any breakfast. I weighed in, four pounds under! I was so happy! I was also exhausted, sore, and dehydrated. None of that mattered now. I could graduate!!!

It didn't matter to me at the time. It never mattered to me at any time while I was in the Coast Guard, but let me point out, for the sake of the rest of this book, that healthy weight loss is a half- to one pound per week. I lost seven pounds in one week. No one at that time, including myself, thought anything of it. No one was concerned for my health. Everyone was thrilled that I was able to graduate!

Lee had transferred to the Coast Guard Cutter *Aspen* in

Northern California while I was in A-School. I really wanted him to attend my graduation and pin me (put my collar devices on). Unfortunately, he was underway when I graduated.

OS1/Sabrina had been a great class advisor. I really looked up to her and appreciated her dedication to our class. She agreed to pin me instead.

Our class voted for the class Honor Graduate. There was a reservist that we all loved so I voted for him. OS1/Sabrina later told me that he won, ahead of me by one vote. A part of me was a little disappointed, but a part of me was very relieved. The Honor Graduate was given an award that I did not get, but the Honor Graduate also had to give a speech at graduation. I did not want any part of that!! I was that one vote. I did not vote for myself; I voted for him.

Ironically, since the reservists graduated early, the Honor Graduate wrote the speech and Ed ended up reading it during graduation.

I did get an award for the amount of volunteer work I did during A-School. I really enjoyed volunteering and was happy to be recognized for it. I also vowed to look for more opportunities to volunteer as I continued my career.

A commander (CDR) was our guest speaker. Before graduation he shook my hand and told me how happy he was to hear that I had lost the weight and was graduating. While I was happy that he was supportive and complimented my hard work, I was embarrassed that he was just one more person who knew. The fat boy weight program is not anonymous.

THE WANNABE

After A-School, I stayed with Lee and his wife for a week. His wife didn't have a job at the time, so I hung out with her. She was artsy and liked scrapbooking. I remember going through her craft stuff. I showed her the scrapbooks I had made for my A-School friends and she gave me some paper and more ideas for future scrapbooks. I had a good time. It was a nice break after A-School.

After staying with Lee and his wife, I drove up to Seattle to report onboard the Coast Guard Cutter (CGC) *Mellon*. It was in dry dock in Bellingham, Washington, for repairs. I was given ten days for house hunting, so I was trying to find a place in Seattle, where the cutter was usually homeported. I didn't have much money in or after A-school. Whenever you move in the CG, you usually pay for most everything upfront. Later, after filing a travel claim, the CG pays you back. I was in a new city, trying to find a place. The cutter was in Bellingham. I didn't really know anyone, and then, my cell phone completely died. I had to replace it.

I found a two-bedroom apartment in West Seattle on 35th Ave SW. I had to come up with my deposit and first month's rent. After I was somewhat settled, it was time to go to work. The schedule was very strange while my ship was in dry dock. We'd work a string of three to four days, having duty (24 hours, can't leave the boat, much like A-School) one of those days. Then we'd have two to three days off. Break-ins (Like me, new people to the boat trying to get qualified in whatever position they were going to fill.) usually stood duty every three days, but I don't remember having to do that in dry dock. It was really bizarre trying to figure out my new world, job, and role in a setting that was not normal. I spent most of my days confused.

One night I was driving from Seattle to Bellingham and got stuck in traffic from a football game for literally hours. It was late and snowing. After the traffic jam finally broke, I wanted to get to the cutter and to bed. Being from Illinois, I had experience driving in snow. I guess it was arrogance that made me drive too fast. I hit a patch of black ice and went spinning into a guard rail. For a split second I felt relieved. I hadn't hit anyone. I could regain control and keep going. But the car didn't stop. I bounced off the guard rail and, to my horror, hit a minivan with kids inside. I still thank God that no one was hurt. The lady got out and tore me a new one. I don't blame her. I was stupid. It was also really late, it was still snowing, and we were all shook up. I apologized as best as I could, made sure no one was injured, and called 911.

That is how I first met the Wannabe. I had worked with her a few times, but there are a lot of people on a cutter, and I really didn't know anyone that well, yet. The police officer arranged for a tow truck and took me to a diner. I called the cutter and my Chief sent the Wannabe (another OS3) to get me. She was tired and annoyed but nice to me anyway. She took me back to the cutter. A few days later, she took me to my car at a mechanic's shop.

The shop was in the middle of nowhere. My car was not in drivable condition and I asked how much repairs would be. First the mechanic told me that I'd have to pay for the tow. He would not make any repairs to my car until the tow company was paid. I didn't have any money in A-School. I had bought a new cell phone. I had just moved. I had paid first month's rent and deposit. I didn't have any money to pay the tow company.

I called my mom. Payday was less than a week away so I promised I would pay her back. She was kind of cool until she heard how much the tow was. Then she started lecturing me about how I should have gone with another tow company. The police officer called for the tow. It was in the middle of the night. I had just been in an accident. I didn't ask for the yellow pages. She finally agreed to help me out. She paid for the tow over the phone with her credit card. She was mad about that, too. Paying over the phone with credit cards at that time wasn't normal so she was worried they would keep her information or steal her identity or something. I just let her lecture me and am thankful she paid it.

Then it was time to discuss the repairs quote. When I bought the car, I was paying a person, not a bank, so I decided to simply get liability insurance instead of full coverage to save money. The car accident was my fault. The insurance company was not going to help me pay for repairs on my car. What was I going to do? My mom was already mad at me. I didn't think anyone else in my family could help me out. I didn't know anyone in Seattle. Just as I was about to panic, I thought of a person I could call.

Jack had consistently offered to lend me money in A-School and I consistently turned him down. In spite of my doubts, Jack actually kept in touch with me. His emails always said more than "Roger Out" as well. I hated having to ask him for money and wasn't sure if he even had the money since he was in the "real world" now. I couldn't think of any other options.

I called Jack. The phone rang a few times and I was worried he was not going to answer. To my relief, he answered. I started telling him what all had happened, and Jack quickly picked up on why I was calling. Jack asked me how much money I needed. I was thinking out loud and trying to do the math. The mechanic had given me a quote and I knew I had to buy food and stuff. But I didn't want to ask for anything more than I actually needed. I didn't want to take advantage of my friend and I didn't know how much money he had, either.

Jack finally said, "I'm going to send you $xxx."

I thanked him profusely, promised to pay him back as soon as I could, and hung up. I had stepped outside, at first to breathe and try to figure out what to do, and then stayed outside while I talked to Jack.

I went back inside and told the mechanic to make only the repairs necessary for my car to run and be street legal. I did not want him to fix anything cosmetic at all. I didn't care if I had to drive around a dented, beat up car, I just needed a car. The mechanic wrote up another quote and then the Wannabe took me to a rental car place.

The Wannabe was a couple years older than I and had been on the *Mellon* for about a year. She was outgoing and friendly. We spent a lot of time in the car together, so we were able to get to know one another. She was engaged to an ET3 who was stationed at base Seattle, if I remember correctly, and they had a small apartment. We ended up getting along great. After the whole car debacle, she helped me with cutter stuff, and we started hanging out after work. She introduced me to the show *Nip Tuck*, and we would watch it together whenever I would go to the apartment. I was excited to have a new friend.

There was also another OS3 that I went to the gym with and hung out with. She was also a couple years older than I and had been on the cutter for a little while. I was excited to have friends and was eager to learn all about cutter life.

It didn't take too long, however, for the Wannabe to begin pulling me aside and lecturing me for all sorts of random things. There was a female OS2 in our shop, CIC/Combat, who was always really rude. She was slightly older than I, intelligent, fully qualified, and along with two other female OS2s, basically ran the shop. She was the crudest person I have ever met. She absolutely loved to disgust people. She would frequently talk about things like period farts or period shits. She acted like she was better than everyone else and didn't have the time of day to get to know anyone new. Needless to say, we did not hit it off.

The Wannabe kept telling me that OS2 asked her to speak to me about my behavior. I was never where I was supposed to be. I never did what I was supposed to do. I had said or done something that was rude or disrespectful to someone and OS2 wanted me to lose my attitude. The "lectures" became a nightly thing and it really started to take a toll on me. Most of the things I was supposedly doing wrong were never explained to me. I didn't know where I was supposed to be or when. The cutter was in dry dock. The schedule was different. The "jobs" were different than a "normal" in-port. I didn't know what to volunteer for or how to help. The times when I was supposedly rude or disrespectful, I was only asking questions to try to get more clarification on what I was supposed to be doing. I couldn't figure out what OS2 wanted from me. My previous units I was a rock star. I left the station with a Bravo Zulu and kept in touch with my Mentor and friends. My Mentor was the one who insisted on me going to A-School. In A-School I got along with Sabrina/OS1 really well. She pinned me. My uniform was perfect for a couple of inspections. I got an award for volunteering. Now on the cutter I couldn't do anything right. I was always in trouble. What had changed? When did I become a shit bag?

One night the Wannabe pulled me aside and told me that the OS2 wanted her to talk to me about showering. I lost my mind. No one saw me shower because I did it at the gym after I worked out versus on the boat. I started to get really defensive.

"You ought to be glad I'm talking to you. If you're not going to be nice to me, I'll let OS2 talk to you, instead," she threatened.

I didn't want things to escalate but I was still mad. I asked, "Do I stink?"

"No," she said.

"Is my hair greasy?"

"No," she said.

"Then tell OS2 that obviously I'm showering!"

I'd like to say the issue was dropped, but it wasn't. Once we got underway, the Wannabe accused me of not showering again. I was standing watch double mids (12-4 in both afternoon and morning). I would shower after watch at 4-4:30 am.

No one saw me. I guess if no one sees you, then it isn't happening. I started making an effort to shower before my watch (around 11 pm) instead of after so more girls would know that I showered!

You would think all of this would have warned me that the Wannabe was a terrible human. But OS2 was rude to me (and others) on several occasions, so I really thought the Wannabe was either trying to make things better for me or being forced to be in the middle. The few times I lost my temper with her, I actually felt bad. I did not want to kill the messenger and I certainly did not want things to escalate. I was so, so incredibly naïve. I would pay for that later.

THE 3 CLAMS

While we were in dry dock I got as qualified as I could. I had all my in-port skills done in our workspace (CIC/Combat). I had some Damage Control skills signed off, but the cutter was being worked on in several places during dry dock and there wasn't any training or drills. (Damage Control is where you learn about the cutter and how to respond in an emergency, such as a fire or flooding.) I can't remember if I broke in Gangway Petty Officer of the Watch (GPOW) while we were in dry dock or not. (GPOW is the first person you usually see or salute when you walk onto a cutter. The GPOW answers the cutter's phone, makes announcements, and sounds the alarm in an emergency, amongst other things.) I might have when I was on duty. I know I didn't stand one in three, which was the normal break in schedule.

To advance to E5/OS2/Petty Officer Second Class, there were certain tasks that needed to be complete before February 1st in order to take the Service-Wide Exam (SWE) in May or to complete before August 1st in order to take the SWE in November. Success on the SWE was required for advancement. These tasks are designed to help the member learn more about their rate and upcoming job (should they advance) and to learn more about the Coast Guard.

Regardless, I did everything I could do. If there was something I could be learning or could get signed off, I did it. I did not, however, have any underway things signed off. This was not something I could control. Some things must be done when the cutter is underway. There is no way around that. There are other things that are normally done underway, but they can still be taught dockside if you turn on the equipment and "play around" with it. Since we were in dry dock and there were several repairs being made to the cutter, we could not turn on most of our equipment. I could not learn any under-way stuff nor have any of it signed off. Despite these circum-stances, I was not allowed to test to advance (promote). This really bothered me.

It bothered me so much that I talked to the OS1 about it. It was not my fault that we were in dry dock when I reported. I had shown I was pro-active and motivated. I had all of the in-port stuff signed off. I should be allowed to take the test. The OS1 let me make my arguments, but he did not change his mind. The standing rule was you had to be fully qualified to test and I wasn't fully qualified. No exceptions.

If we had been underway, I could have easily been qualified and completed all the tasks before February 1st. Once we were underway, I could have qualified before the SWE in May. I was not allowed to complete the tasks, though. I had to focus on getting qualified first. I couldn't get qualified or do anything more to get qualified until we got underway. But I couldn't work on the tasks in the meantime. It didn't make sense and it wasn't fair. I was very upset.

We got out of dry dock and did a winter Alaska Patrol (Alpat). We went up along the coast to Kodiak and picked up a helicopter and crew. We also had to go to "fish school" to learn about the laws for fishing in international and US waters that we would be enforcing. After we left Kodiak, we headed into the Bering Sea. I was sicker than a dog. You could time it. Every hour, on the hour, I was puking my brains out. For motion sickness medicine to work, you have to take it before you get sick. The medicine has to be in your actual system, not just sitting in your tummy. Otherwise, you just puke up the medi-cine along with everything else. I didn't think to take medi-cine before we left. There wasn't any medicine in my system. There wasn't anything I could do except wait to grow sea legs or until the next port of call to take medicine while we were on dry land.

Including the OS2 I talked about in the previous chapter, there were two other female OS2s in CIC/Combat and the three of them were known as (and were extremely proud of this) the "Clams" in Combat. One of them was young. She was smart, really knew her job, but she was really, really mouthy. She started as an OS in Radio, but the first classes and chief didn't want to put up with her over there, so the Combat Chief agreed to let her move. Back then Radio OSs and Combat OSs were like the "Bloods" and the "Crips": no one cross qualified. She was the exception, though. The Radio OS1 and Chief couldn't handle her or earn her respect. The Combat Chief liked her. She reminded him of his daughter or wife or something. He thought she was funny or something, I don't know, but he didn't think she was rude or disrespectful. That or because she was smart and sometimes right, he didn't care if she was rude or disrespectful. Other chiefs and officers on the cutter would tell him about things she said to them and he would promise to take care of it. He never did. She mouthed off to everyone.

The other female OS2/Clam was older. She wasn't that intelligent, and she wasn't that good at her job. She was also a true spaz. She freaked out over everything. Anytime we got busy or there was a somewhat stressful situation, she would pace around CIC/Combat and bark orders at everyone. She would get flustered and start making mistakes and then get even more flustered.

The ITs and ETs worked in our space, too. They were friendly so they would talk to us while we all worked. The Spaz Clam would tell them to shut up. If they didn't shut up or if she was especially stressed out, she would just flat out tell them to get out of her space. Usually they left. Every once in a while, there was actually work that had to be done and they wouldn't leave. If they were lower in rank, the Spaz Clam would nag them until they couldn't work anyway, so they would leave. If the IT or ET was higher in rank and wouldn't leave, she would get extremely passive aggressive. Sometimes I think the higher-ranking people stayed just to rile her up more. They were well aware of the rules and when they did and did not actually have to leave. They were not going to let her push them around. It was extremely awkward for me because she was in charge of me and expected me to be on her side. For the ITs and ETs, it was either really funny or really frustrating or both.

I don't know if the Clams got together and discussed this or if it just kind of happened naturally, but they all took turns being the bad cop. So, one of them would play the bad cop and the other two would pretend to be nice to you and help you out—but report back to the bad cop everything you said and did. My friend, Brett, another OS3, was always in trouble with the Young Clam, but the other two were nice to him.

Since I was an "insignificant" OS3, my job was to watch the radar. That was it. Just sit and stare at the radar and report contacts to the bridge. Oh, and plot the cutter's position on the chart every thirty minutes. CIC/Combat is back-up navigation for the bridge unless it is super foggy or bad weather and then we become primary navigation. CIC/Combat definitely served its purpose and we had other jobs and responsibilities. During the day and good weather, we were pointlessly on the radar. Of course, people on the bridge of the boat with eyes on the actual ocean and other boats could spot contacts before us on the radar. But that didn't stop the Clams from yelling at us when the bridge spotted a contact first.

CIC/Combat was always freeeeeeezing cold!! Supposedly they had to chill all the equipment and computers in there so they wouldn't overheat. I'd sit in the chair in front of the radar, shivering. I wore my uniform, a coat, a hat, the hood over the hat, and gloves. I'd report a contact on the radar or plot a position on the chart, puke in a little bag, go throw it over the side of the cutter, come back down to CIC/Combat, plot another position, puke, rinse, wash, and repeat for four hours straight, two times a day.

In between my watches, I had to go to Damage Control training, any E4, and below, duty (usually cleaning or trash call), and participate in all drills. Since I was breaking in, I was standing double mid-watches (12-16 and midnight-04). With everything going on and everywhere I was supposed to be, I hardly slept at all. I sleep very, very soundly. Since I was lacking so much sleep, when I did actually sleep on the cutter, I slept even more soundly. Sometimes I missed a pipe and did not show up for cleaning or another responsibility. The Clams found out every single time and the Bad Cop Clam or the Wannabe would always lecture me. They told me that it was good that I couldn't qualify to take May's SWE, and November's SWE was looking less promising, too. I slept even less.

We had little mailboxes where we were supposed to keep our stuff to keep the area clean. I knew it was a huge no-no to leave anything lying around. One watch, however, I was getting things signed off to get qualified and I left my watch packet on the chart table after I left CIC/Combat. It was an easy mistake to make. I was exhausted. The OS3 who was relieving me came down. I told him everything going on, and I left. I had forgotten we were going over signoffs and that my packet was on the chart table. The Bad Cop Clam found it and I'm almost positive she shredded it.

I discovered my packet was missing on my next watch and immediately felt sick to my stomach. I knew I had made the grave mistake of leaving it on the chart table. I apologized until I was blue in the face. I begged and begged and begged the Bad Cop Clam to give it back to me. I was almost in tears a few times, but I held them back. I told her I learned my lesson and that it would never happen again. She just laughed at me and told me that I knew the rules. She never told me what I would have to do to get my packet back. There was no method to resolve the issue. My packet was gone, and I'd have to deal with it.

So, I had to start all over on my qualification process. Luckily the Young Clam was annoyed by it too, because she had signed a lot of stuff off for me. Luckily, she helped me find a new packet and after I printed it, she just signed a lot off all at once. But I still had to re-do a lot of stuff I had already done, and it still took me longer to get qualified. Remember that I was standing the double mids and I couldn't advance because I was not qualified. The Bad Cop Clam shredding my qualification packet was a huge deal and negatively affected my quality of life. She thought the entire thing was funny.

One day I was talking to Brett about everything that was happening and said something about how I wished the Bad Cop Clam would stop using the Wannabe to lecture me. Brett started laughing. Brett told me that the Wannabe would come down to CIC/Combat in her free time and tell the Bad Cop Clam everything. She'd tell her what I said, how upset I was over my qualification packet, the times I missed sweepers (cleaning the boat because I slept through the pipe) and that I wasn't showering. Brett said the Wannabe wasn't protecting me or being forced to lecture me; she was instigating everything trying to impress the Clams. I was so hurt and betrayed. At my first two units everyone looked out for each other. I don't remember anyone telling the command anything. If someone did something stupid and got caught, fine. But if they didn't get caught, no one turned them in. And no one made up any lies or intentionally tried to get someone in trouble. I couldn't believe anyone would do that; let alone someone I considered a friend. I tried to argue with Brett, but what he was saying made too much sense. He knew about things that he couldn't have known unless he had heard the Wannabe talking about me. I stopped arguing with him. I was numb.

On top of being betrayed, lectured, denied the opportunity to test for advancement, and having my packet shredded, internet was also slow and sometimes out altogether due to being on a cutter in the middle of the ocean in winter. The Spaz Clam and Young Clam would let me check my email on watch sometimes, but not often. The Bad Cop Clam never did. I was sick, tired, in trouble, and completely cut off from my friends and family. I felt incredibly isolated. I wondered if this was how prisoners felt. I wondered if being underway was the same as going to prison: I didn't have much personal space, I was told where to be and when at almost all times, the other prisoners were mean just for sport, I couldn't get out, and I was denied visitation. How did all of this happen? How did I go from being a rock star at my first two units to being a prisoner? Had something in me changed? Did I not realize I wasn't working as hard as I used to? What could I do to show I was still serious about being in the Coast Guard?

I didn't know what to do. I didn't think anyone was in my corner / had my back. I didn't know how to get qualified faster. Yes, it was my fault for leaving my packet on the chart table, but the punishment did not fit the crime. I didn't know how to get on the Bad Cop Clam's good side. Was I ever on her good side to begin with? And what had I done to the Wannabe? Why was she mad at me? Why did she want to get me in trouble? The Wannabe's betrayal did something to me that I cannot describe. And because of her betrayal, I ended up betraying others later. I can't blame her for the entire thing, I did have a choice. I do take responsibility for my actions. But my actions were based on my experience. And in my experience, loyalty didn't exist on the Coast Guard Cutter *Mellon*.

The OS1 was nice but when I went to him about testing for advancement, he had told me no. It was the standing rule that you had to be qualified. Standing watch, participating in drills, clean ups, and other miscellaneous things were also standard rules. I was breaking them. He wouldn't be able to help me. It was also very clear that the Clams ran CIC/Combat and he did not. If I told him about the packet, would he punish them? Would I be able to get qualified faster somehow if he knew about that? If he couldn't or didn't do anything and Clams found out I snitched, I figured my life would get a hell of a lot worse. After asking to advance, I never asked or told OS1 anything else.

The chief let the Clams control combat. He knew what they

were like. He knew the Young Clam was mouthy. Other chiefs talked to him all the time. But as said, he never did anything about it. I figured he knew what was happening to me, too, and didn't care.

It didn't take long for me to become extremely depressed. I really thought I was in prison and really didn't know how I ended up there or what I did to deserve to be there. I started thinking the death penalty was definitely more humane than a life sentence. The death penalty was instant and not extremely painful. Being imprisoned was painful. Worse than the pain, was the knowledge that my Coast Guard career was over. I was going to eventually be masted (Coast Guard's version of court) for all the mistakes I was making and be reduced in rank instead of advancing. I was tired of being a failure. I was tired of serving my sentence. It was time for death.

The few emails I sent home really worried my mom. I don't remember what I wrote. I'm fairly certain I didn't say I wanted to die but she could tell I wasn't myself and I wasn't doing well. But what was she supposed to do?

In hindsight I should have said something to someone. The cutter was bigger and had more people than the OSs. But after the Wannabe betrayed me, I really had no idea who I could trust or who cared. As an OS3, I really didn't understand the concept of the command master chief. I think I knew who the clergy was. I remember one patrol attending church services, but I don't think it was my first patrol. The "clergy" wasn't really a pastor or priest or anything, he was just a Gunner's Mate (GM) on the boat that volunteered to lead the church services underway. So even if he did have the confidentiality thing, I didn't know it. And if Work Life existed back then, I didn't know what it was, either. And I could NOT go to Doc. Doc would be forced to report that I wanted to hurt myself. I had a friend in high school who attempted suicide. I knew the hell he went through after that. That was worse than the hell I was in already. I had heard that if you were depressed or suicidal in the Coast Guard, you would lose your security clearance. If I lost that, I couldn't be an OS. And then what would happen? Would I get kicked out of the Coast Guard? After working so hard for so long to get in? What would my family and friends think? So, I kept quiet and secretly planned my death.

SUICIDE MISSION

Between two and four AM
In the darkness I will hide
While I work up the courage
To Jump over the side
On the off chance I am discovered
There is no way I'll be recovered
Before hypothermia sets in
And death begins
The Bering Sea will swallow me
It will be quick; I'll go peacefully
And maybe, I'll be free

Poem By: Hillary Herbst

SECURITY CLEARANCE LIES

Once upon a time, was it actually true?
Or was it told to many but only applied to few?
Would a diagnosis be interference?
Would you actually lose your security clearance?
If you tried to get help, would your situation be worse?
So many people living under this rumored curse.
All of them wondering if they could survive hell.
All of them needing help but would never tell.

Poem By: Hillary Herbst

TACT, MBL, AND TRANSFERS

I obviously did not kill myself. I didn't because I didn't want the Clams to win. I knew that they wouldn't feel guilty over anything if I actually did it. I could picture them laughing at me, saying things like "She was weak," or "She couldn't hack it," instead of mourning my death or saying anything nice about me at all. They had control over my career, but something in me would not let them have control over my life or death.

Despite the Bad Cop Clam shredding my qualification packet, I did get qualified as a CIC/Combat Watch Stander on the Alaska patrol. After I was qualified, I stood one six-hour watch a day instead of the double mids. I was still working on my Damage Control qualification.

Toward the end of the patrol and during our in-port period, I started making some friends on the cutter, outside of the OSs. A lot of the non-rates, especially my boat hubby (a later story), helped me with my Damage Control qualifying stuff. They were the ones that had been on the cutter the longest and knew a lot about it. My boat hubby was trying to strike Boatswain's Mate, along with a lot of others. Non-rates on cutters work really hard and, in general, are not treated very well. Some of them legitimately wanted to be a BM. I think my boat hubby fell into that category. Others were just striking it so they would be treated slightly better.

I also became friends with a female machinery technician (MK3) and was introduced to some of the other engineers due to her. She was really nice and a lot of fun to hang out with, but she wasn't always reliable. It was always 50/50 if she would show up when we made plans. One of the times she came through was while we were in port in Seattle. We went hiking in northern Washington. I think the goal was to see the Mt. St. Helen's volcano, but we got lost. We ended up hiking random trails on the side of the road and seeing a small waterfall. It was a fun day.

The Alaska patrol was approximately three months long, and then we were back in Seattle for about the same amount of time. That is the "normal" routine for 378s, which was the Mellon's classification.

We got underway again in May 2007 and headed to San Diego for Tailored Annual Cutter Training (TACT). TACT is exercises performed "for" the Afloat Training Group (ATG) which test the cutter crew's ability to respond to a variety of mishaps or dangerous situations such as fire, flooding, or other damage to the cutter. Before a cutter goes through TACT, the cutter is also supposed to do Common Assessment Reporting Tool (CART). This is usually done dockside for a few days and the ATG looks at all the departments' training programs and records, ensures the cutter has all the required and updated manuals, and much more. The ATG did check all of these things while we were in San Diego, but for some reason the cutter did not actually do the formal process of CART in Seattle before we came down to San Diego.

The OSC and OS1 told me that it was good for me to go through TACT while I was still breaking in for Damage Control. I would learn a lot from ATG about how things were supposed to be done so I could finish my qualification. At the same time, if I made any mistakes, the cutter would not be "punished" for them because I was not qualified yet. They were right about all those things. I finished up my qualification by the end of the patrol.

Side Note My Damage Control qualification was very similar to my Boat Crew qualification. I did well on the oral board, but my performance was terrible. I never did don the fire suit and SCBA in under a minute. I tried and tried and tried. The ET1 testing me finally gave up on me. He tried to help me set it all up and show me how to do it. He could tell I was really trying, but every single time I got all the straps from the fire suit mixed up with the straps from the SCBA. The faster I tried to go, the worse it was. I struggled with a few other things, too. The ET1 finally said that he would just make sure I was given a different job so that I would never be on the fire team itself. He signed off my qualification. For the rest of my time on the Mellon, I was either part of the P6 (dewatering) team or a boundary man. Neither of those jobs required wearing the full fire suit, and it never took me long to don the SCBA by itself.

I believe TACT was three weeks long. We were in and out of port in San Diego for that time. If we were in port or dockside and were not on duty, we were allowed to check out the area. Sea World was free for military so a bunch of us decided to do that one day. That is when I first met Calvin. He was one of the non-rates that transferred to the cutter early in the transfer season of 2007. Calvin was from the East Coast and is a few years younger than I am. His real name is very common, and a lot of the guys on the cutter already had that name. I was bold enough to tell him he could no longer use his common name, even though I barely knew him. I told him it was getting too hard to keep track of all the others, plus him, so he would need a nickname instead. Luckily, he found humor in this, so we agreed on Calvin. After that, not only did I call him Calvin, but everyone on the cutter called him that--to the point that some people argued with him over his real name!! My nickname during my time in the Coast Guard was Herby, and to this day, there are still people who don't know Calvin or my real first names.

Calvin brought a nice camera to our Sea World adventure and had been taking pictures all day. I asked to look at it for a minute and then handed it back to him. I thought he had it and so I let go. He didn't, and it dropped to the ground. I freaked out. I felt so bad. I must have apologized 100 times and told him I'd replace it. He was not upset nor even mildly concerned. He kept telling me it would be fine. I didn't believe him, and I was dying inside. But somehow, magically, it turned out to be just fine, like he said. Later that day the camera turned back on and started working again. Out of the blue, for no reason. We became really good friends that day and hung out all the time.

San Diego was a lot of fun. After I met Calvin at Sea World, a bunch of us went to a Padres' Game (One more stadium down!) and checked out the Gas Lamp District. I think that was the trip I also saw Third Eye Blind at House of Blues. We went to San Diego a couple more times during my tour on the *Mellon*. Third Eye Blind is one of my top three favorite bands and that show, whenever I saw it, was amazing!! When I was not on the cutter, not doing drills, and not around the Clams, I was really enjoying myself. I also found out how many other people hated the Clams, as well, and that made me feel better. Although, I could never figure out how everyone could know about them, everyone could hate them, but no one could do anything to stop them. Maybe I was just weak and couldn't hack cutter life.

The cutter did well during TACT, but we did not earn the Battle E. Battle E is an award ribbon given to the officers and crew of any Coast Guard cutter which earns the Operational Excellence Award during annual refresher training. Since our cutter did not officially do CART, the crew was told that we could not earn the Battle E. If we had officially completed CART, we would have supposedly earned it. The crew was relieved to be done but upset that we didn't earn the award.

Immediately after San Diego, we headed to Alaska for another patrol. Just like the first patrol, we went to Kodiak first to bring a helicopter and aviation team with us. We also picked up a Russian interpreter. He was a Marine and was very nice. I loved it when he was working in CIC/Combat with us. He taught us some Russian. I used to half jokingly, half seriously, tell the MK3 "You're dead to me!" when she would blow me off. True to her nature, she had blown me off on a port call during that patrol.

I asked the Russian interpreter how to say, "You're dead to me!" in Russian. Later I saw her in the berthing area and said "Ты мертв для меня!"

She looked at me and was like, "That's either 'I love you,' or 'You're dead to me!'"

I started laughing and was like, "Well, ya just blew me off so which one do you think?"

She laughed and said, "You're dead to me." At the end of the patrol I traded the Russian interpreter a Coast Guard flask for his Marine Cover/Hat. I still have that.

We got underway from Kodiak and headed toward the Maritime Boundary Line (MBL); the imaginary line in the ocean between US waters and Russian waters. This patrol we would not be monitoring fisheries, like we had (or were supposed to) on the winter Alpat. This patrol our job was to literally drive back and forth on that line to ensure US fishing boats stayed in US waters and Russian fishing boats stayed in Russian waters. If a boat crossed the line by so many yards, we had to do incursion drills, which included plotting their position every minute to keep paperwork if the case ever went to court. That is why we had the Russian interpreter with us. He was supposed to help if we boarded a Russian vessel in US waters.

I took medication before we got underway, so I did not get nearly as seasick as the first patrol. I wanted to get qualified as a Watch Supervisor. If Spaz Clam could do it, I knew I could. It wasn't really that hard. I was low man on the totem pole and the Clams would never give up power, so that was a hard NO. Just like the first patrol, I sat on the radar all watch, and froze to death. Now I was a qualified watch stander, so I was allowed to work on the things required to advance and my schedule was better. The Clams treated me with a tiny bit more respect. I also avoided the Wannabe as much as possible.

At some point during the patrol, Combat got a new OS Chief.

Chief G was an RD and switched over to OS when the rates changed. He was very, very different from the Chief before him. He did not have the same philosophy of "get your work done and then hide" that the old Chief had. He was also in CIC/Combat ALL the time. Part of that was because he wanted to learn his new shop and get to know his new people. Part of that was just him, though, and never changed. Chief G had endless energy; I don't think he ever slept, and some people thought he was insane. He still is indeed insane, but I love him. Chief G saw through the Clams and didn't allow much of their shit anymore, but the old Chief hadn't left just yet, so some of it continued. I still had to wait to break in Watch Supervisor.

Young Clam transferred off the cutter after TACT, and a new OS2, Ramona, took her place. Ramona is a little bit older than I. She had been in the Coast Guard longer. She's very pretty. Looks isn't all she has: she is very intelligent, as well. The two remaining Clams hated her guts. They hated her more than they hated me. I liked her, at first. I have pictures of us hanging out in Dutch Harbor, Alaska, during a port call. The Clams did everything they could to drive a wedge between us. Later, others did, too, and that made our friendship difficult to maintain, ultimately ending it for a time.

Life was starting to get better. I was happy the Young Clam was gone but at the same time, she was the nicer one, so I wished the others had left instead. At night, if I didn't have watch, I would play Dominoes or Catch Phrase in the mess deck (galley) with my boat hubby, Calvin, and other non-rates. I would also watch movies, read, or catch up on emails—if there was an available computer. Just as I gave up my idea to jump over the side of the cutter in the middle of the night, though, I think some of the rest of the crew was starting to consider it ...

The Captain onboard was a terrible leader and Captain. I don't know of anyone who liked or respected him. He had a lawyer background, so he never took any risks at all. The small boats and helicopter could not be launched unless the weather was clear blue and 72. The three could never, ever be launched at the same time. Plus, he had a terrible temper. If you made one mistake, he'd pull your qualification without a moment's hesitation. The Jr Officers were so scared, they were literally incapable of making decisions. And their boat driving skills were "eh." Morale was already low ...

The MBL, while sounding exciting at first, was anything but. We were literally playing cat and mouse with a bunch of fishermen. All we did all day and all night was patrol that line. If we were on the north end, then all the Russian boats on the south end would cross the line into the US waters. As we would turn around, they'd head back, and the US boats would cross into Russian waters. We were close to a few and did numerous incursion drills. All those fishermen knew exactly what they were doing and what the laws were, though. So, after plotting them every minute on the minute, for five to seven minutes, they would cross back over into their waters. Our crew was becoming stir-crazy.

The Aviation Team we picked up in Kodiak was awesome. The LT/Pilot was extremely talented and very down to earth. The rest of the guys were goofy, fun, down to earth, and talented as well. For a while on the patrol they were really the only source of morale. They did silly things like having a hot dog eating contest in the galley. Even they had their limits. They were tired of the Captain "grounding" them every day. The LT/Pilot was willing to fly in almost any weather; that was what he trained for after all! He wanted to participate in the incursion drills or maybe catch a boat in the wrong waters by flying on the opposite end of the cutter. But when everyone came down to CIC/Combat for the briefs, the Captain always found a reason they couldn't fly.

As said earlier, most of our patrols were about three months long and this one was scheduled for about the same. I think it might have been scheduled to be slightly shorter because we had included San Diego with it. The cutter out of Hawaii that was supposed to relieve us, broke down, so we were extended for two weeks. Then the other relief cutter broke down, and we were extended for another two weeks. Morale took a hit both times.

We were close to the International Date Line and everyone onboard wanted to cross it. Those who had crossed it before and had gone through the ceremony were known as Golden Dragons. Those of us who had not were Wogs. Certain lines in the ocean and places have these traditions: the equator, the Panama Canal, the Arctic Ocean, the Mediterranean Sea, etc. The ceremonies used to be straight up hazing, but that was no longer allowed. Now, the ceremonies were just practical jokes and obstacle courses around the cutter. Once you became a Golden Dragon, you got a big, beautifully framed certificate and a smaller one for your wallet. At least, that is what the *Mellon* did. That is one thing the cutter was good at, I guess. Some of my friends did the ceremonies and don't have any certificates.

The Captain, however, would not allow us to cross. We were underway to do a job, not to have fun. Morale on the cutter slowly decreased until it was nonexistent. I had mostly overcome the Clams and had made some friends, only to encounter this situation. Everyone on the cutter hated everyone else. You could hear a pin drop on the mess deck floor during meals. There weren't anymore "game nights." Everyone was afraid of the Captain's wrath or just wanted to be home. It was awful.

Thankfully, it was transfer season!! The cutter was supposed to get a new Captain. The Change of Command Ceremony was supposed to take place in Seattle after we returned from the MBL patrol; however, since we got extended twice, the new Captain ended up meeting us in Dutch Harbor, Alaska. The Change of Command Ceremony took place around the end of July 2007, in Dutch Harbor, Alaska, at the grade school.

Once we got back underway, the new Captain could tell how low the morale was. I mean, anyone with a brain could. The tension was so thick you could cut it with a knife. He got with the Chiefs and asked them if there was one thing he could do to immediately improve morale. The Chiefs told him to let us cross the line. The new Captain immediately ordered the cutter to head toward the International Date Line! Morale immediately improved and on August 4, 2007 (Coast Guard Day), I went through all the traditions and ceremonies and became a Golden Dragon.

That was not the only thing the new Captain did, though. On most patrols the only day that the crew relaxed was Sunday. On Sundays the only "work" the crew had to do was stand required duties. The Captain extended that to Saturdays, as well. The new Captain did not have a lawyer background, either, so was not so cautious. We began launching the small boats and helicopter on a regular basis. The aviation crew was thrilled. They were even sent on a SAR case while we were in port Dutch Harbor. A boat had sunk and there were people on the life raft. We were the nearest unit. The aviation crew went to the cutter, suited up, and got airborne. They found and saved the people on the raft! We still didn't catch any fishermen, but at least our routine wasn't as boring and mundane anymore, well for everyone except the Russian Interpreter.

Somehow, the entire crew and I survived that endless patrol . . . I'm not sure we would have without the transfers.

SHELLBACKS & TARANTULAS

We returned to Seattle sometime in August or September of 2007. Upon our arrival, the Captain gave us a long stand-down period: we didn't have to come to work unless we were on duty. "Normal" in-port routines for OSs are phenomenally brief. The majority of our work is done underway, so in port we can enjoy a lot of time off. Once liberty is called at the end of a workday, the OSs are usually the first across the brow, ready to go home. A normal workday is 0700-1300, also known as trop hours. The in-port workdays are short because the crew works 24/7 when the cutter is underway.

For non-rates and other rates, in-port routines are not that easy. Storekeepers (SKs), for example, find it hard to order supplies while underway with limited or no internet connectivity so the majority of their work is done in port. The BMs and Seamen (non-rates) paint and do repairs to their areas of the boat that they cannot do while underway. The MKs and firemen (also non-rates) repair the engines and other parts of the cutter, as well. They do not always cross the brow at 1300 as their work must be done before the cutter is underway.

There were two in ports, though, that I remember the OSs had to assist with big cutter projects and did not cross the brow at 1300, either. All the non-skid (the "floor" on the outside of the boat, bumpy grey material to prevent slipping/sliding/falling) had to be replaced on all the decks. To save some money, the Captain decided that the crew of the cutter could at least tear up the old non-skid by themselves. A contractor might be hired to lay down the new non-skid. (A contractor WAS used for the flight deck because it ended up being so messed up when the crew attempted it.) The constant noise of needle gunning and hammering on the decks filled the entire in-port period while all the non-skid was pulled up. Hearing protection was used while we were actually doing the work, but I don't remember using hearing protection while inside the skin of the cutter. I'm sure the average reader can figure out that the entire cutter is metal, so no matter where you were, it was LOUD. It wasn't "hard work" *per se*. I mean, all you had to do was hammer until the non-skid broke in pieces, but you were also sitting or kneeling in uncomfortable positions for hours at a time, swinging that same hammer or holding that same pounding needle gun. We all had blisters on our hands plus sore muscles. In the beginning of the project, a few of us did get kind of creative and would carve out our names or "draw" pictures before we chipped all the non-skid away. Towards the end, we just wanted to be done.

The base in Seattle is small and a lot of units share the space. Parking is limited. I would normally get to the base early, work out, get to the cutter, shower, and then begin the workday. I always lost weight while in port. I worked out some underway—that is actually how the joke with my boat hubby started—but it was difficult when the seas were rough and with our busy schedules. Not only did I work out more in port, but I also had a normal sleep routine and I could eat whatever I wanted—not the extremely unhealthy food that was served while underway. Yes, underway, there was a small salad bar and, yes, I partook of it. But selections were slim and got worse the longer we were underway. I always gained weight while underway.

On the *Mellon*, I had been able to weigh in under my max allowable weight. It was always a struggle, and I was always right on the dot, but I made it. Somehow, in port I could lose the weight that I had gained underway. In October of 2007, however, that changed. I weighed in four pounds over my max allowable weight. I was also over my BMI (I was never under this, for the record. Never. Not even when I weighed in at 138 at MEPS) so I was put on the "fat boy" program again. There is a note on my paperwork that says my thyroid was checked. I never heard back from medical, so I'm assuming it was "normal." I wish I knew back then what I know now. I'm curious if it was actually normal. They probably just checked my TSH levels and not my T3 or T4. But it doesn't matter. Let's say it was normal.

I was sent to the Swedish Nutrition Clinic, as was procedure. Again, they did not tell me anything I did not already know from having attended the weight loss camp before the Coast Guard. They also did not have any tips for how to eat healthier or how to get more sleep while I was underway, either, but I filled out all their forms and talked with them, as procedure dictated.

I was very concerned that I would not be allowed to take the SWE since I was on the weight management program. After being screwed over in February, I was finally allowed to get everything done, but now this. I felt I was never going to advance to E5 or have a career in the Coast Guard. I put the *Mellon* on the top of my list for billets in A-School in order to make Chief and make the Coast Guard a career. Now I wasn't even going to make E5. I know this all sounds very dramatic, but it is how I felt. These were all the things going through my head. I was terrified.

Now the Clams had something new to give me shit for. They had finally started showing me some respect. There had even been talk about my getting qualified as Watch Supervisor and taking over Electronic Warfare (EW). Now, I was fat. Why did I put the *Mellon* towards the top of my list in A-School? This was the worst unit ever and was going to be the end of my career!!

It was only four pounds, but it was October. So, Halloween, Thanksgiving, and Christmas were right around the corner. As an added bonus, my birthday is the beginning of January.

I don't remember how long it took me to lose the weight

and get off the program. I do remember Calvin being very supportive of me. Non-rates are required to live on board the cutter until they are fully qualified and sometimes even longer. Calvin was older and was used to living on his own. He hated being stuck on the boat. He also loved to cook. I hate cooking. So I "let" Calvin come over to my apartment whenever he wanted on the condition he would cook dinner for me. He would make dinner, and, while I cleaned up the kitchen, he'd watch TV, especially on football game nights. Sometimes he'd go back to the cutter; sometimes he would sleep in my spare room. It was a really nice arrangement for both of us. He got the freedom he was used to having, and I got a personal chef. Sometimes we'd invite other non-rates over, too, so they could have a nice meal or watch the football game with us.

Calvin introduced me to orange roughy. It is a fish that does not taste like fish. I normally do not like fish, but I loved that. It was very healthy and very low calorie. This was his way of helping me lose the weight I needed to lose.

If left on my own, I prefer cardio, but I remember working out with my boat hubby and Chief G, especially on the patrol following October weigh-ins. Both of them encouraged me to do more weightlifting and spotted me as I did. I also remember doing sit-ups while tossing a medicine ball to my boat hubby. I actually enjoyed working out with both of them.

I did get the weight off and was allowed to take the SWE. Thanksgiving and Christmas were very hard for me, though. Now my weight was on my mind again, and I did not want to put any back on. I must have really been watching what I ate or talking Calvin's ears off or both because I remember Calvin's mom sent me a Christmas card with a nice message in it wishing me luck and sympathizing with my weight-loss efforts. Calvin apologized to me profusely for telling his mom "my secret." I was not mad at all. First off, anyone can tell their mom anything and I knew Calvin and his mom were very close. Secondly, I was a combination of flattered and regretful that Calvin had that level of concern for me. How had my weight taken over my life, again?!?

We got underway just before Christmas. I remember this because of an inflatable snowman on the flight deck while we were moored up in San Diego. Yes, San Diego and not for TACT. This patrol we were finally heading down south!! Hello calm waters!! No more fisheries or MBL. Now we could chase drug runners! Our port calls were in San Diego, Puerto Vallarta, Mexico, and Panama!

Of course, the crew was upset about missing Christmas with their families (not a problem for me), but morale was pretty high because we were going south. The FSs made a special meal for Christmas with the DC Chief and one of the Jr Officers dressed up as Santa and Mrs. Claus.

On my birthday we headed across the Equator!! I went through another ceremony and became a Shellback.

The patrol was awesome, although we did not catch any drug runners. I actually had a good time and have a lot of good memories. I also have an incredibly funny, but both bad and sad, memory...

On Dec 27, 2007, I decided to hang out with a couple of the non-rates that I did not know very well. We were in Puerto Vallarta, Mexico. They were fluent in Spanish and despite three years of Spanish in high school, I was NOT. We decided to go on the Los Veranos Canopy Tour, zip lining in the "jungle." It was awesome!! I loved it, until the end...

At the end of the zip lines, they had animals that participants could pose with for pictures. One was a tarantula. We had been talking about it the entire time we were zip lining. I am terrified of snakes and was not going to play with any of those, but I thought maybe I could hold the tarantula or scorpion. I was with two guys and didn't want them to think I was a sissy. I wanted to be able to hang out with them in the future so I had to prove I could actually "hang" with them.

The tour guide asked us if we were interested and took out the tarantula. The guys looked at me and I reluctantly sat down. The guide put the tarantula on my head and it started crawling around. It tickled. I wasn't sure how to feel. It was cool but scary at the same time. The guys took a picture.

The tour guide saw them take the picture and said if we wanted a better picture, I had to "eat" the tarantula. I looked at him like he was crazy and said, "No, thank you!"

But the tour guide insisted that it would make a great picture and story for later. The guys I was with kept goading me on; they even offered to buy me drinks later. I kept saying "No," until Vince promised, "Come on Herby. If you do it, I'll do it, too."

That was all it took. Like the "double dog" dare in *The Christmas Story*, I couldn't refuse if Vince was going to do it after me. I sat down. The tour guide told me to open my mouth very wide and no matter what, I must not exhale. I opened my mouth. He started to insert the tarantula.

I could feel the hair on my tongue and roof of my mouth. I was freaking out. I had no idea what the tarantula was going to do. Then the guy told me to open my mouth a little wider. As I did, I made the grave mistake of exhaling. The next thing I knew, the tarantula was not in my mouth anymore, and the tour guide was seriously going crazy!

For readers uneducated about tarantulas (as was I at the time), the tour guide told me not to exhale because tarantula's skin is extremely sensitive to heat. When I exhaled, the tarantula literally jumped out of my mouth.

That doesn't sound like anything to worry about, though, right? Wrong. Tarantulas also have a spine similar to ours. When the tarantula jumped out of my mouth, it landed on the ground and literally broke its back. I had, without meaning to at all, just killed the tarantula.

The tour guide was so upset. He kept crying out over and over again, "I told you not to breathe! I told you not to breathe!"

He picked up the tarantula and was petting it like you would pet a dog. The guys and I were so lost. We were still trying to figure out what was going on. The guy finally explained to us about the skin and the back. Suddenly, I was like, "We need to leave!"

The tour guide, completely devastated, threw the tarantula in with another tarantula and the other tarantula started eating it!! I almost threw up. We paid for our tour and got the hell out of there!!

The guys were laughing so hard, I'm surprised they didn't pee their pants. I, on the other hand, was in complete shock. Why had the guy even attempted to let me "eat" the tarantula if they were that sensitive? Surely this was not the first time someone breathed! The image of one tarantula eating the other is permanently burned in my brain. Every time I think of it (including now as I type) my stomach starts churning.

I had "proved" myself to the two guys, but definitely not in the way I had hoped. Since the tarantula was dead, Vince could not keep his promise, so the guys just bought me extra drinks that night. Unfortunately, since I did not open wider, there is not a picture of the tarantula in my mouth, either. And it did not take long for "Herby's breath is so bad, it killed a tarantula!" jokes to start going around the cutter. I had finally convinced everyone that I really did shower, but now no one believed I brushed my teeth!!

SCALES AND SUCCESS

We left for the south patrol a week or so before Christmas and I think we pulled back into port in Seattle sometime in March. I had been working out with my boat hubby and Chief G underway and trying my best to watch my weight, but I wasn't having much success staying under. In port I continued to work out, but less weights and more cardio again. I remember Chief G encouraging the entire OS shop to run with me. There was one day that some of the OSs and I think some of the non-rates ran all the way down Alaskan Way from the base.

Despite all the working out, April weigh-ins came around and I was over the max allowable weight again. I can't find the paperwork in my files, so I don't know how much I was over. I don't think I went back to the nutritionist since I had just been in October. I don't know whether or not I had a medical screening, but I can't find anything in my records about one.

I know I was overweight for two reasons. One, I made the cut to advance to E5/OS2/Petty Officer Second Class after November's SWE, but when time to advance came around, I was still on the weight-loss program, so my advancement was put on hold. Two, I remember being told that if I didn't make the next weigh in, it would be strike three, and I would be kicked out of the Coast Guard.

I did not know what to do. I lost weight in port, but I could not figure out a magical solution for losing weight underway. Let's be real, underway a "normal sleep routine" was non-existent, patrols were extremely stressful, the food we were served was nowhere near healthy, and workouts had to be creative due to the seas and the small gym. I have several friends who say they lost weight while underway versus in port, for all the same reasons. I guess some people are stress-eaters and some are not. The friends who say they lost weight mostly say they didn't eat underway or they got really seasick or both. I also know some people have better metabolisms than others, and I'm sure a number of other factors play into it, as well.

One of the ET Chiefs had been doing a cleanse and had lost a lot of weight. He gave me some to try out. I followed the directions to a T and somehow managed to gain more weight!! I then tried Slim Fast. I had more success with that. That also became a good plan for underway because the cans were relatively small and did not have to be refrigerated. I could take them with me and not have to eat the food being served on the mess deck.

In the summer of 2008, we got underway and headed up to Alaska. Chief G was completely qualified or close to it and had taken over combat. The Clams hated Ramona, and the Clams knew that they were about to transfer. All of a sudden, all the doors were open for me. The Bad Cop Clam started showing me Electronic Warfare (EW) stuff. She had been on the Combat Systems Training Team (CSTT) and in charge of EW for most of her time on the boat. I had been part of the EW team and had participated in the drills during TACT. Now, I was supposed to take her spot on CSTT and be in charge of the drills the next TACT.

After the Young Clam transferred the previous year, I had taken over as the Training Petty Officer for all the OSs, Radio and CIC/Combat. I had done a little bit with the program, but Chief G encouraged me to do a lot more. I made Jeopardy games and invited Radio OSs to take on the CIC/Combat OSs in order to go over whatever topic we were supposed to be covering that month. I even found a buzzer online so we could have real teams, and people could buzz in with their answers. Once the buzzer was hit, a timer was set, too. It made my running the game training a lot easier. Everyone also enjoyed the more hands on, competitive approach, instead of just flat lectures.

At last, I was allowed to break in as CIC/Combat Watch Supervisor!! Finally, I did not have to sit on the radar for hours at a time plotting contacts. Ramona was an OS2, as well, and after she was qualified as a watch stander, she started breaking in watch supervisor. I remember being both happy and jealous. We needed another watch supervisor, so this was the way things were supposed to work, but it just didn't seem fair that I had to jump through a bunch of hoops to break in, and Ramona was just "handed" it.

Finally, after almost two years of fighting for more responsibilities, I was given ALL of them. At last, the Clams were being nice and training me. The Clams did not like Ramona, and both told me on numerous occasions that they were not happy that she was doing the same things as I. Both of them told me that they wanted me to take over the shop. Spaz Clam would "spaz" out trying to shove information down my throat trying to make that happen. Ramona had the Clams' numbers and knew how to "play their game." The more Ramona pissed them off, the more they treated me like royalty. I loved it. I was too young, too naïve, and too caught up in my own excitement to realize they were doing the same thing to Ramona that they did to me.

Along with taking on more responsibility in Combat/CIC, I also started helping some of the non-rates with their process to become BMs. Since Calvin, my boat hubby, and others had helped me with my DC qualification, worked out with me, and helped me lose weight, I thought this was a good trade off.

OS and BM have some things in common. I could not sign off any of the non-rates BM practical assignments since I was not an actual BM. However, I could teach all of them how to plot positions on a chart and how to do Moboards. At night, instead of playing Dominoes or Catch Phrase, I started holding training on the mess deck. Sometimes Chief G would join, too. If

Chief or I initialed something on the non-rates packet, the BMs would sign it off later for the non-rates, trusting Chief's and my judgement and saving work for themselves.

I could sign off the non-rates EPMEs for them. EPMEs are general military/Coast Guard knowledge and are the same for every rate. I also held training for and signed those off. I was not going to let anyone else have the same awful experience on the cutter that I had. If a non-rate was proactive and wanted to become a BM, I would be sure to help them get there.

The BM chiefs started to take notice of all the things I was doing to help the non-rates and the officers and captain started to take notice of all the things I was doing in CIC/Combat. I became a much-respected petty officer.

Chief G and I also got really competitive and started having Moboard races to see who could complete a Moboard the fastest while still being accurate. I don't remember ever winning, but I do remember it being very, very close. Standing watches was fun now. The cold didn't bother me anymore because I was not sitting in one place doing nothing, and I had figured out how to combat sea sickness.

Eventually the Slim Fast, salads, workouts, and last-minute starvation paid off and I made weight. On July 1, 2008, I finally advanced to Petty Officer Second Class/OS2!! Not only is this something to be very proud of, but E4 to E5 is one of the biggest pay raises in the Coast Guard. I was beyond happy to finally have made it. We were underway so I think Chief G and OS1 were the two who pinned me. Even if we had been in port, I'm pretty sure I would have still asked them to do it.

An admiral somewhere decided to send the *Mellon* on a mission to find out how much ice was in the Arctic Sea. Up until 2008, the only Coast Guard Cutters in the Arctic were the Polar Rollers (Ice Breakers). With pending global warming and the ice melting, though, this admiral wanted to find out if there was a fishing fleet up there and if 378s would need to start patrolling the area.

I don't know how it all came about, if it was the same admiral or the captain of the cutter or what, but an "outreach" port call was also arranged for Nome, Alaska.

On July 2, 2008, the Coast Guard Cutter *Mellon* anchored outside of Nome and BMs took turns driving everyone on the cutter into and out of Nome all day!!

Nome is an interesting place. There is a lot of history there. I have pictures of several of us under the sign for the End of Iditarod Sled Dog Race!! I also have a picture of me in front of the Anvil City Square sign. Several people on the cutter panned for gold.

However, Nome was also "undeveloped," for lack of a better description. Most of the roads were dirt. Most of the people did not own cars, but four-wheelers and snowmobiles instead. And almost ALL the shops "downtown" sold lottery pull tabs!! Pull tabs are similar to lottery scratch offs, but you pull back a cardboard tab instead of scratching something off. We purchased several. I don't remember winning much.

If that wasn't enough excitement, after we weighed anchor, we headed farther up north to do the Blue Nose Ceremony. Blue Nose is similar to Golden Dragon and Shellback. Some of the rituals and "hazing" was the same, but we had to swim in the Arctic Ocean to become a Blue Nose!

For Golden Dragon and Shellback there were plenty of people onboard who had gone through and completed the ceremonies before. Since Blue Nose takes place in the Arctic Ocean, there were several more Wogs onboard than actual Blue Noses. The Captain had to be creative with the rituals, but he and the Blue Noses in the crew pulled it off!

On July 4, 2008, I put on a Coast Guard Gumby Suit and jumped off the side of the cutter, swam around the stern to the other side, and attempted to climb the Jacob's ladder back up. Unfortunately, Gumby suits are "one size fits all." I'm 5'4 on a good day. There was at least a foot of "suit" beneath my actual foot, and I could not get a good "grip" on the ladder. The small boat had to come around, and the BMs had to lift me up into it.

From there, I was able to climb the Jacob's ladder.

Overall, I had a very good time. I remember being very impressed at how well the Gumby Suits worked. After we all took them off, we were still actually dry!! I was amazed at how that could be, when we all had jumped into the ocean and swam. The water was still very, very cold.

I was super embarrassed, though, about having to use the small boat. I had just made weight so I was scared that the BMs would not be able to lift my fat ass out of the water. I also remember thinking that everyone onboard would think I wasn't really working out because I was not strong enough to climb the ladder.

I don't remember seeing too many fishing boats up north. I don't know what the report back to the Admiral said, and I don't know what, if any effect, our going up there had for future cutters and patrols.

Back down "South" the Captain had us boarding Every. Single. Fishing. Vessel. In. The. Water. He had both small boats and the helicopter underway/airborne almost every single day. He divided all the qualified boarding team officers and members into three teams, and they took turns boarding all the boats. Down in Combat, it was our job to take the information the boarding teams passed us and determine if fishing boats were following the regulations. This was extremely difficult, though, as the regulations were based on numerous factors that constantly changed. Often, we would look in the materials we were given during "fish school training" and report back that a boat was in violation, only for the captain of the boat to pull out a memo updating what we had so the boat would be just fine.

Interestingly enough, all of those boats are competitors. So, after we had boarded a few, we no longer had to look for the "fleet." Most crews would throw other crews under the bus, telling us where they were fishing and suggesting who to board next.

At first the entire crew was happy to be doing boardings,

especially anyone who had been onboard during the last captain's reign. After a while, though, the crew, especially the boarding teams, was exhausted. Every single day we were boarding three to four boats at a time and the results were almost always negative. Everyone wanted a break.

Then we learned we were getting close to breaking the record for the most amount of boats boarded in one patrol. Everyone then wanted to meet the challenge, and we eventually did break the record!

I was the OS in charge of communications for the entire patrol. Well, technically OS1 was in charge, but he could see how much I loved it, and he was also transferring, so he let me do most of them. I was on the radio with all the Boarding Teams taking down the information they passed to Combat. I loved every minute of it. Finally, I was able to do my job!!

I thought I had kept all of my qualification letters for everything I did in the Coast Guard. For some reason, though, I either don't have or can't find my qualification letter for Watch Supervisor. I don't remember the exact date that I passed my board for Watch Supervisor, but I know it was during this patrol! And since this board was just knowledge-based stuff and no practical "hands on" stuff, I know I rocked it!! Dare I say that the Clams were proud of me?!? Or were they just happy I got qualified and Ramona wasn't yet? I don't know. It doesn't matter now.

In this one patrol, I advanced to OS2, qualified as EW CSTT, and qualified as CIC Watch Supervisor. I had the attention of almost all the Chiefs and Boarding Officers, the non-rates loved me, and I finally had the attention and recognition I was used to from previous units.

OS1 transferred sometime after that. I'm pretty sure it was when we pulled into Kodiak to offload the Russian Interpreter and the helicopter and crew, but it might have been in Juneau or after the entire patrol. It is really hard for me to remember exactly when each person came and left. Whenever OS1 left, he pulled four of us aside and specifically said goodbye only to us. He told us he was sorry about the Clams, and that he was proud of what we had done. That confirmed to me that he really didn't have control over the shop and had nothing to do with their meanness. It is also the main reason I kept in touch with him.

Yes, you did read correctly above when I said OS1 may have transferred in Juneau! On our way back to Seattle, the captain arranged a port call in Juneau, Alaska, so the crew could celebrate our victory of breaking the boardings record. This captain knew how to motivate his crew.

My boat hubby was a non-rate striking BM. He had been on the cutter longer than I and almost everyone knew who he was. He was fully qualified in every position he could be on the cutter. He had been consistently working out with me, he was on the bridge with me for almost every special sea detail (when we pulled into /out of ports), I had been assisting him with his BM practical's and EPMEs, and we hung out most port calls. It didn't take long for us to start "fighting" like husband and wife and for other people, especially Chief G, to start commenting on it and making jokes about it.

On our first couple days in Juneau, we went exploring. We went to the glacier and took the tram up the side of the mountain. We rented a car and tried to go whale watching. Juneau is gorgeous!! The glacier is so beautiful!! We had a really good time and got a lot of really gorgeous photos.

On our last day we decided to go into "town" and take it easy, drink a little, and do some shopping for souvenirs. There was a store in Juneau called Del Sol. It's actually a chain of stores, but this was the first time I had heard of it. Everything in the store is clear or black and white, but when taken out in the sunlight, it changes color. As we walked by Del Sol a salesman called out to us to come into the store. None of us were interested. The salesman then said that if we came in, he would give us all a free gift. We didn't have anything better to do nor anywhere to be, so we walked in.

The free gift was a small, clear, plastic ring with a sun on top. As with everything else in the store, it turned colors once you went outside. The thing must have cost a whole 50 cents and we all felt duped by our free gift, but the store was actually really cool, so we all looked around. I ended up buying some nail polish that went on clear but turned red when in the sun.

My boat hubby took the free gift ring we were given, got down on one knee, and proposed to me!! I guess the proposal just counted as the wedding, too, because after that we were "officially" husband and wife to anyone who knew us. July 12, 2008, I was "married."

We pulled back into Seattle shortly after that for another in-port period. Ramona and I had plans to attend two EW C-Schools. At some point the new OS1 transferred onto the cutter and most importantly, the two remaining Clams finally transferred off!! I was not at all sorry to see them go.

HALF A CLAM

I've been going back and forth about whether to write this chapter. It's not that I want to hide what a horrible person I might have been, but these stories are not fully mine. A part of me really wants to "tell all" so everyone has a full understanding of what happened, how, when, why. I want everyone to know the decisions I made and the consequences that I will live with for a long time. On the other hand, I've already done enough harm to these other people, so why do more? My compromise is to "tell all" but to be extremely vague about it. Hopefully, this is the right decision.

There were two people on the cutter who I considered to be good friends and were dating. This is a huge no-no on cutters. I understand the reasons it is not allowed. I also understand that we are underway for months at a time, away from our families, living, working, eating, fighting, loving, hating, and partying during port calls with the same people 24/7; sometimes, "Something's gotta give."

The right thing to do is to tell the command you've fallen for your shipmate as soon as it happens and before you get physical with them. The command will then send one of you to a new unit so you can continue dating. Imagine seeing someone, going on a date or two, and thinking you like them. Then you must decide if you really like them or not, right then, at that moment! If you decide you like them, after two dates, your relationship immediately becomes a long-distance relationship. Since you both are already trained for a cutter, one is usually sent to another cutter. Sometimes they are sent to the sister cutter. When the sister cutter is underway, the other is in port and vice versa. If you are sent to another cutter, not the sister cutter, it is often in a different state. This is not true all of the time. Some of my readers may be thinking, "If it's meant to be . . ." I understand all of that. I just want to explain the process and all the "what ifs" that potential couples must consider. Some couples choose to hide their relationship rather than risk the separation.

Sometimes, couples aren't at all serious but are looking for some "fun." These people just hope and pray they don't get caught.

My two friends had actually been dating for a while and the command had caught on. They had been given several warnings to stay away from each other. I don't know why they chose to keep on "secretly" seeing each other, but they did.

I didn't care. I liked both of them. They were both nice to me and fun to hang out with. After all I had been through, I wasn't about to avoid people who were kind to me, even if they did break some rules. If perfection was the criteria for friends, I wouldn't have had any at all.

One of the other girls, who coincidentally was sleeping around on the cutter, caught my friends together and turned them in. I don't know why she decided to go after them. It wasn't because she believed that the rule should be followed. I'm assuming, at one point, one of them pissed her off. The inner workings of people's minds, especially in that environment, are insane.

The Executive Officer (XO), second highest in command on the cutter, like the vice president of the cutter, made an announcement. He would be investigating the two of them and their relationship. His investigation would include interviewing almost everyone on the cutter. If anyone knew anything and lied to him, they would be punished, too.

I didn't know what to do. I had never been part of a Coast Guard investigation before. I didn't know what the investigator could ask for or demand to see. I didn't know what the Coast Guard's version of a "warrant" was or if they even needed one. I didn't know who knew about my friends' relationship and who didn't. If someone else talked and my name was mentioned, I'd be in big trouble. I had pictures of the two of them hanging out. If the XO could demand to see my camera or computer, I'd be in big trouble. I was about to make second class and I had worked very, very hard for that. I worked hard for my entire Coast Guard career in general. They knew what they were doing. They were stupid for getting caught. I had to tell the XO what I knew. I had to.

At the same time, they were good friends. And if the XO couldn't demand to see my pictures or computer, then he wouldn't know I hung out with them. And if other people didn't talk, my name wouldn't come up. Snitches get stitches.

I went back and forth in my mind for days. I had no idea what the "right" thing to do was. I tried to ask other people what they were going to do or what I should do. No one would say "I'm going to talk," or "I'm not going to say a word."

The Spaz Clam somehow knew I was friends with them, pulled me aside, and told me I had better talk. That should have been reason enough not to talk. Whatever advice she gave, I should have done the opposite. But, would she tell the XO I was friends with them? I wouldn't put that past her, either.

One of the OS's in radio told me to say something. He was friends with (and I suspect sleeping with) the girl who turned them in, though, so he might have wanted to support her.

I made myself sick trying to figure out what to do, but finally decided if the XO asked me, I would say something. I told my friend (the girl) that I was going to talk. I had hoped she would beg me not to, but to her credit, she looked at me and just said, "Do what you think you need to do."

I prayed that the XO would never interview me. If he didn't interview me, then I wouldn't have to tell him anything. Maybe he didn't know we were friends. Of course, he interviewed me. I did tell him what I knew.

The two of them were sent before the Captain's Mast, a type

of military court. I did not go to the mast, but heard they denied everything, argued with the witnesses, and argued with the Captain. Both of them were given the max punishment, which included brig time. I felt sick to my stomach.

Chief G was the mast rep (lawyer) for one of them. Chief G said over and over, "I kept telling them to shut up, but they wouldn't. They pissed the Captain off."

Hearing Chief G say that and hearing everything about the mast and them arguing made me feel better. They were responsible for their own behavior, so they earned their punishment. I was not in trouble. I did not have to worry about the XO going through my things or my being knocked down in rank. I could continue training and doing what I needed to do to advance to OS1/Petty Officer 1st Class/E6.

After the couple's time in the brig, they returned to the cutter. The girl never talked to me again. The guy would talk to me from time to time on the rec deck, so I thought we were friends. I was happy. But then one night, I asked him something, and he replied with, "Why do you keep talking to me as if we are friends? We are not friends."

I was taken so off guard, I didn't know what to say. I asked him why we weren't friends and he looked at me like I was stupid, saying something to the same effect. After going back and forth a little I said, "I told her I was going to talk. She knew I was going to say something."

He then very angrily told me, "Yeah and you were the only one. Your statement (written testimony) was the only one. No one else (besides the girl who turned them in) said anything. If you had kept quiet, the XO would not have had any proof of what we did. WE WERE SENT TO THE BRIG BECAUSE OF YOU!"

I nearly threw up on the spot. I was the only one. No one else talked. Apparently outside the OS shop, there was loyalty on the cutter. Apparently not everyone was like the Wannabe. My friends did "hard time" because of me. I was doing everything I could to make everyone's lives better on the cutter because of how bad mine was and I turned in my friends.

I apologized profusely. I asked him why he even talked to me in the first place. I told him that was why I thought we were still friends. He told me it was too rude to just outright ignore me, but that he was purposely short with me and had hoped I got the hint. I apologized more. I tried to explain that I didn't know any better. I tried to justify what I did. But hearing my own voice, I knew I was guilty. I hated myself.

I don't know if he said it to get rid of me or if he saw how sincere I was and really meant it, but that same night, he did say he forgave me. We did talk a little after that, but it was never the same. We never hung out again. As said, she hated my guts. She did purposely avoid me. All I kept thinking was, "Why didn't you tell me to keep my mouth shut? Why didn't you tell me your friends were actual friends and not like the Wannabe?"

After that, things were strange. I thought my boat hubby and Calvin would hate me and never trust me again. I vaguely remember talking to Calvin about it once, but I have no idea what he actually said. He didn't hate me, though. He continued to be my friend, as well as my boat hubby.

The couple eventually transferred. They got married and to my knowledge, are still married and have kids now. I hope they are both doing well.

I know my readers at this point are probably a hung jury. Some of you are probably thinking they brought it all on themselves and if they were real friends, they wouldn't have put me (or anyone else) in that position. The rest of you are thinking that if I were your "friend" I'd be in the hospital. Snitches get stitches. What was I thinking?

My inner self is a hung jury, as well. They were in the wrong. They got caught. They argued. They deserved their punishment. Ok. But I didn't have to provide the rope that hung them.

In ways I learned from that "mistake" and in other ways I did not. I tried hard not to do the same thing again, but I did a couple of similar things instead...

Later on in my cutter days, one of the Radio OS3s accused Ramona of having an inappropriate relationship. This time I didn't have any rope to give to anyone, but that did not stop me from doing everything I possibly could to try to help get Ramona busted. The seeds that the Clams had planted were watered by others and then budded into hate flowers. I was convinced that Ramona was a huge threat to CIC/Combat, our readiness, and our mission. She was destroying our shop. If this was the only way to take her down, well, I was onboard with it.

Now I realize that she was only a perceived threat to me. She was not destroying our shop. I should not have tried to take her down. While I did not have any real control over what happened to her, I should have stayed out of that entire situation.

I thought that her guy and she had gotten in trouble, but Ramona said that there was never any proof of anything and that she never did get in trouble. Up until that point Ramona and I were frenemies. After that, we were enemies. I didn't care about our friendship, but I was really scared that she was going to try to get revenge since she did have some dirt on me. She is either a better person than I am, or she didn't have proof or both because she didn't try.

Ramona is married now with two kids. A couple years after we were both off the cutter, she found me on Communicator. We started talking and she forgave me for everything. We have been good friends ever since. I even got to see her when she came out to Petaluma for Chief's Academy!! We had dinner one night at one of my favorite restaurants to celebrate!

But as said, I repeated the "mistake" a few more times . . . I mean, the third time really is the charm. Right?!?

A few years later, at another unit, another friend was having an inappropriate relationship. Theirs was a little different, though, because she was enlisted and single, dating a married officer.

Again, I didn't care. In general, what people do behind

closed doors does not bother me. I really only care about how you treat me. And this friend treated me very well. We hung out all the time. I had met her family. I loved them all.

The command started to figure things out, though, and one of the "big dogs" pulled me aside one day and asked me what I knew. I was not going to make the same mistakes as I made on the cutter. I was not going to get another friend in trouble. The command could not trick me again. I replied, "I know she is a good friend and I won't get her in trouble."

This "big dog" was clever. This "big dog" tried a different tactic. This "big dog" told me everything he thought he knew. He didn't have any proof, but everything he told me was accurate. He told me that he was going to keep investigating. He told me that if he found proof, he was going to take my friend and her partner both down. He told me that if I saved him the time and trouble, though, he would make sure my friend would not go down.

I repeated, "She is a good friend. I will not write a statement. I will not get her in trouble."

The "big dog" replied by sweetening the pot a little bit, "Just point my investigation in the right direction. Just tell me where to look. I promise they will not find out you talked. I know you two are good friends. After her partner gets in trouble, she will need a shoulder to cry on. I will not take your shoulder away from her."

I believed him. I told him where to start looking. And then the more we talked the more details I gave him. I honestly thought I was helping my friend out. He told me that she would not get in trouble, and he told me that she would never know he got his information from me. I didn't tell him everything, but I did more than tell him where to look.

And he lied to me. Well, not 100%. Some of what he said was true. My friend got a slap on the wrist, so that was kind of good. She could have gotten in a lot more trouble. But at my friend's partner's mast (trial), my statement was read. What? Yes, my statement. The "big dog" wrote down everything I said. I didn't write a statement or sign anything. That was part of my refusal to help. "I will not get my friend in trouble; I will not write a statement." Little did I know that I did not actually have to physically write a statement to write a statement.

Since the accused has a right to face their accuser, my statement was read at his mast. And of course, he told my friend that I was, once again, the one who gave his command the rope to hang him.

My friend didn't even give me a chance to explain myself. She told me she knew what I had done and that what hurt her most was that I didn't even give her a head's up that I had betrayed her. I didn't even have the courtesy of telling her they were about to be slapped across the face. She honestly thought, upon first hearing everything, that someone else had betrayed her. She never thought that I, of all people, would do that to her.

I couldn't defend myself, even if she had given me a chance. How could I say, "You weren't supposed to find out it was me?" That's not really a defense. I tried to apologize, and she replied with something to the effect of, "I will never trust you again."

What just happened? How did I let this happen a third time? How did I take down another friend? Well, I didn't take her down. She got a slap on the wrist. She didn't even lose rank. But that didn't matter to her. I still betrayed her. Her partner still got in a lot of trouble. And she no longer trusted me.

I told another friend about it at the time. I was both angry that my friend couldn't see that I had saved her from more trouble, and I felt sick to my stomach that I betrayed her trust. I was looking for reassurance that I had made the right decision and I was still a good person. He told me that in the Mafia, people were killed for less.

Later he tried to take that back. Later he told me that it wasn't right for the "big dog" to take advantage of me and lie to me the way he did. He then told me that it was not my fault that I was so easily manipulated. I guess that makes me a good person?

In case you are wondering, I did finally learn my lesson. I did have the chance to actually sink someone's career. This person was actually a major piece of shit. He was actually guilty of quite a few crimes, but he was just sneaky enough to get away with them all. I knew some of the crimes. I was friends with people he had committed the acts with and he kind of admitted to them, although he blamed my friends for most everything.

There were other people over the years (Yes, years.) who accused him of other things (always similar but somewhat different), but they came forward anonymously or through emails and it was all circumstantial. There was never, ever definitive proof of anything.

Most of the people we worked with were convinced that the command had an agenda against him. Most of the people we worked with liked him and didn't think he was guilty of anything.

This person actually harassed me. I had told the command a few things that I saw and each time they very passively aggressively retaliated. None of it was too serious or caused much harm. All of it was against the Uniform Code of Military Justice (UCMJ). And again, most of the people we worked with thought I was over-reacting. None of them saw what I saw or knew what I knew. I was just, for some reason, trying to help the command build a case that just wasn't there. I needed to admit I hated him and just get over it instead of trying to get him in trouble.

The command was eager to take him down especially after a transfer season and a new person took over. The new person in command wanted me to tell him everything. I could write a statement and the new person in command would guarantee he would be masted. If he was found guilty, the new person in command would make sure he would not retire.

In this case I did not care about the guy himself. Our friendship was never really a friendship, and I didn't care if he hated me or not. I cared about everyone else we worked with. I didn't want anyone else to ever think I was a Snitch ever again. I didn't want anyone else to think I was easily manipulated, or that I had an agenda or was vengeful. I didn't need to repeat a mistake a fourth time!!

I told the new person in the command that I was not going to write a statement. I said if he was that stupid, if he had done that many things, if the command was that close to catching him, then they did not need me to be the one to give them the rope. I said that he would eventually hang himself and then everyone would know the truth.

He was told to never speak to me again. To his credit, this time, he didn't. He also stayed under the radar for just long enough to retire. You read that right. He retired. He never hung himself. He is out now and enjoying a nice pension. And everyone we worked with was happy for him. And even now, if they are reading this, they are still on his side and still think I'm crazy.

I know that in three of the four events written about above, I was trying to do the right thing. Sometimes it is incredibly hard to know what the right thing is. At the end of the day, I either lost a lot of trust which took years to rebuild, or I lost friendships altogether. It doesn't really matter if they were actually good friends or not. At the time, losing them or their trust hurt like hell. And on the one hand, I have forgiven myself and I am doing my best to move forward. On the other hand, though, I sometimes feel like half a Clam.

GROWTH AND COMPASSION

After I had written some of the chapters of my book, I asked if any of my friends, especially Coasties, wanted to read it and edit it for me. One of the people who agreed to edit the book for me was an LT who I was stationed with in Mobile. After he read the *Mellon* chapters, he wrote and asked if any of the Clams were still in the Coast Guard. He was enraged with how they treated me. He remembered his time on a cutter and how bad he had it. He didn't like to read that I experienced something similar. He was especially upset that I was suicidal. He told me he would be happy to help me exact revenge on the Clams if they were still in.

After the Young Clam transferred, I never heard from her again. Rumor had it she fell in love with another Coastie, got married, moved to Alaska, and got out of the Coast Guard.

The Spaz Clam is the only one still in the Coast Guard. The Spaz Clam claimed we were good friends, even trying to hang out with me on a couple of her last port calls. She swore up and down she wasn't like "the other two." I guess that was her version of an apology to me. She said she really liked me and promised to keep in touch. She didn't and I was fine by that.

In 2017, she somehow got recommended to be an OS A-School instructor and I ended up being her sponsor. She called me from her unit in Alaska and did officially apologize to me. She told me that she had changed since her days on the *Mellon*. When she got to Petaluma, she just wanted to focus on getting qualified and being the best instructor that she could be. She asked if I would help her out.

I forgave her. Hell, I had changed a lot in ten years, so I figured she had, too. Regardless, we had to work together again, so there was no reason to hold a grudge or invite drama into my life. I helped her look for houses, going so far as to visit a few, ask questions of the owners, and take pictures of the houses and notes of the neighborhoods.

Another good friend of mine, Dee from A-School, transferred the same year. I was her sponsor, as well. The Spaz Clam, Dee, and I had made plans to go to a Cubs vs Giants game and run the Superhero 5K at Six Flags.

The Spaz Clam reported, and everything was fine for a little while. She backed out of the baseball game and run, but I didn't really care. Then there was a mess with the phone lines, and she blamed me for it. I think that is what made her mad. I'm not really sure. The only other thing I did was back out of helping her with a chart lesson. I don't remember where I had to be, but I had to go somewhere else. I arranged for another instructor to help her, too. If something else happened, I honestly don't know what it was. She never told me. She never officially told me she was mad at me, period. It became very obvious that she was, so Spaz Clam was still Spaz Clam. Unfortunately for her, though, I was no longer an OS3 who she could push around. We were both the same rank now. I was fully qualified, and she was not. She became very passive aggressive, so I killed her with kindness. I didn't even intentionally "kill her." I was just over all the bullshit and drama. I knew she could no longer hurt me, so I just didn't need to give her the time of day. She did nothing to negatively affect my reputation, and she did everything to negatively affect hers.

The Bad Cop Clam never officially apologized to me. She told me she was proud of me and to do her proud in taking over the shop and EW. I guess you could say when she transferred we were on good terms. A few years later she found me on communicator (the Coast Guard version of AOL instant messenger) and we talked a little bit. She eventually fell in love with another OS at one of her units, got out, and got married. We're friends on Facebook and Instagram now, although I'm not sure why. We never like or comment on each other's statuses or pictures. However, **yesterday** I actually saw someone else posted a video of her with the status, "I'm so proud of my friend. It's been so awesome to be part of her story. Her story is another example that a simple step in faith can completely change one's life!"

The timing of that post is absolutely crazy. I had actually rewritten other chapters in this book for other reasons that I will explain in just a minute. After I rewrote them, I discussed some concerns and fears that I had with Elad, my therapist. He, as always, gave me some great advice. As I was debating how to follow his advice, I saw that Facebook post. This entire chapter is a combination of the LT asking the revenge question, the Facebook post, my chapter re-writes, Elad's advice, and my growth.

I was really happy to see that post yesterday. I did not watch the video. For some reason, that I'm sure Elad and I will discuss later, I can't bring myself to watch the video. I've grown a lot, but I still have more work to do. At the same time, I really hope it is true. I hope she has found God. I hope she has found something that makes her happy. I hope she is a better person now. I was flattered that the LT was enraged, and he offered to help me get revenge. (I am also slightly concerned he has some unresolved issues of his own.) I immediately turned him down and for the same reason: I am hopeful that the Bad Cop Clam has found God and happiness. I don't know her story. If she wrote her own book, what would she write? Was her childhood a good one? Were her parents loving and caring for her? Did she enjoy school? It doesn't sound like she went to church, but I don't know. What was her Coast Guard career like? What examples did she have of good leadership? What does she think happened while we were stationed together? Did she realize how much of a negative impact she had on me? Was it really intentional?

Those same questions apply to the other two Clams, as well, and the Wannabe. Was the Wannabe just as young and insecure as I was? Was she just trying to stay on the Clam's good side? Maybe she was considering killing herself, too, and telling on me made her situation better. It doesn't excuse her behavior, but I can understand that.

Everyone is fighting a battle. Whether they are fighting with a mental illness, an addiction, a physical illness, a loved one's illness or death, everyone is fighting a battle. Almost everyone has dealt with some sort of trauma in their life. I've been in therapy for 2.5 years now and this one of the biggest things I've started to realize. I'm beginning to understand (I'm not completely there yet, but I'm beginning) that most of what people do to me or others is not actually personal. Just as it was not personal back before I joined the Coast Guard when Nate blew me off running. Sometimes people are just not capable of being "good people" or doing the right thing. Sometimes anxiety lies to you and confuses you as to what is real and what is not. Sometimes depression or grief makes you lash out. I'm sure there are plenty more examples, but I only really know about my medical issues, not all medical issues.

What good would come out of me asking the LT to help me get revenge on the Clams? Would it change what happened? Would it be likely to help them become better people? It wouldn't help me heal. It might temporarily make me feel better, but, in the long run, it would not help me heal.

No, I don't want revenge on the Clams. I don't hate them. I'm not mad at them. Whatever demons they are battling, I hope they are winning. Because if they are winning and they are changing, that means they are not hurting more people, which means everyone wins. And if we could all have compassion for our enemies, I think this world would be a better place. I know that is very idealistic, and I know it is easier said than done, especially when the wound is really fresh. You can't build on a negative. You can only build on a positive. Revenge is negative. Compassion is positive.

While I'm writing about having compassion for your enemies, though, I also still need to learn how to have compassion for myself. Along with asking if anyone wanted to edit my
book, I also sent very specific chapters to specific friends. As
said in the previous chapter, some of the stories in this book
are not just my story. I want to write about everything that
happened, but I do not want to disrespect anyone or write
more details or dirt than I have to write. Ramona is one of the
people I sent chapters to.

After Ramona read everything that I wrote, she had a lot of
feedback for me. Some of my dates were wrong, which I already knew. She remembered some of the correct ones, so I
was able to fix some of it. As said in the previous chapter, I
thought she got in trouble for her relationship, but she told
me that they actually didn't get in trouble. The biggest "flaw"
she saw in the book was that I was being too hard on myself.
I had written a lot about how she and I were enemies and I
didn't treat her well. I thought I was being very honest about
how I behaved, but Ramona told me that I was making the
situation sound a lot worse than it really was. Ramona said
that we were friends up until I tried to help get her in trouble.
She reminded me that the Clams were really upset after we
came back from our C-Schools because they had tried so hard
to cause a war between us and we had gotten along really
well. She reminded me of times we laughed at the Spaz Clam,
especially during pass downs and of times I let her sleep in
and relieve the watch later if she was up all night because of a
mission. She told me her version of how and when everything
took place and said I didn't have to rewrite the book, but it
wasn't accurate, either.

I changed the dates and rewrote some of the stories. I kept
some of the stories the same though because this is my book
and my perspective, not Ramona's. Then I asked Elad about it.
I asked him what I should and shouldn't change when Ramona
and I have such different memories. Elad agreed with me

that it was my book, and I should write it how I remember everything happening; however, Elad also reminded me that it is normal for me to be really critical of myself. I spend so much time regretting things that I have done in the past and beating myself up over them. Elad said, "Ramona didn't feel that way. She didn't think you were that bad. Perhaps other people don't remember you being that bad, either. Part of the reason you are writing your book is to show the possibility of transformation. Maybe you should write your book from that perspective."

I apologize a lot in this book. I apologized more before this "epiphany." I'm writing this book so people can understand how and why I made the decisions I made. I'm writing this book to show the causes and effects in my life and to bring awareness to some serious issues in not just the Coast Guard, but in our society. I'm writing about how unhealthy I had become and how much better I am doing now. (Better. Not completely healed. It's a journey.) I'm hoping that I will inspire others who may need help to seek it out. I'm hoping that I will inspire others who are battling demons to keep fighting another day. Originally, I was hoping for some sort of forgiveness, too. I was hoping that the people I may have hurt may pick up this book and understand why I did what I did. I was hoping that maybe they would call me, and we would become friends again. I was hoping that *they* would have compassion, but as Ramona and Elad pointed out, *I* did not have any compassion for myself. I made the best decisions that I could, at the time, with the information I had. And while some of those decisions were not good decisions and they did have a negative impact; they probably were not as bad as I have replayed them in my head for the past however many years. It's almost as if someone brought me a movie of my life and I was like, "Add more drama. Drama sells. This movie is not dramatic enough." And that movie became my story instead of my real one.

I'd still like forgiveness, but if I don't get it from the people who I hurt, I just gave it to myself. I went through a lot. I did what I felt I needed to do to survive. Good and bad came out of that but no amount of regrets is going to change what happened. So, while I'm giving my enemies compassion, it is time that I give myself some, too. I re-wrote what Ramona asked me to re-write and it's no longer from my perspective or from her perspective, but a perspective of compassion for what we both went through. And I will try to keep that perspective in the rest of this book. And I urge you, Dear Reader, to think about the amount of compassion you have in your life, for both your enemies and yourself.

MEDICAL ISSUES

I had some trouble with my plantar fasciitis while on the *Mellon*. I'm not sure why, but wearing my boots never really bothered me too much. Our dress uniform shoes were really, really bad, though. If I had to wear those for any length of time, it would become hard for me to walk.

I don't know if it was having to wear my dress uniform shoes while on GPOW (the person on the quarterdeck of the cutter that greets everyone coming on and makes announcements and answers phones), gaining some weight, walking on the cutter—especially all the ladders or when we were in high seas, or something completely different that made me start having problems again, but I did.

The first year or so that I was on the cutter, I would take a tennis ball underway and try to "massage" my feet every night or when they hurt. I still had my orthotics from before boot camp and I "hid" them in my boots. I purchased and wore braces on my feet and lower legs at night when we were in port, so no one would know. I kept the pain to a minimum and never, ever said anything to Doc about it.

One of the SKs said she had plantar fasciitis and that the Coast Guard provided her with orthotics. She encouraged me several times to say something. I thought she was crazy. I had to jump through hoops to join because of plantar fasciitis. I didn't know how she managed to get away with it. Maybe hers wasn't a pre-existing condition. At any rate, I wasn't willing to take the chance of getting kicked out over a little bit of foot pain.

One in-port period I got a flyer in the mail for a massage

therapist near my house. I called her to make an appointment. I've gotten massages for as long as I can remember. I love them. However, back then, most massage therapists had not heard of plantar fasciitis. When I would meet them and they'd ask about problem areas, I would always say I had plantar fasciitis and they would look at me cross eyed. I would try to explain and eventually they would say, "So you want me to focus on your feet this massage?" I'd reply yes.

As a result, some massages helped my feet and the plantar fasciitis, but most did not. I still went to get massages for the rest of my body, but I gave up on telling them I had plantar fasciitis or asking them to focus on my feet.

When I first met Tierza, she had the same standard "medical" form and asked the same questions about problem areas. I'm not sure why I decided to take another chance and tell her I had plantar fasciitis, but something in me told me to tell her. As soon as I did, she replied, "Oh, then you don't want a deep tissue massage, you want myofascial release."

I want what? Say that again. Myo…what? Tierza explained that everyone has fascia. If you picture raw chicken, you can see the thin, white layer of "slime" on top of it. People have that "slime" too. That is fascia. And fascia is supposed to be thin and flimsy like that "slime" on the raw chicken. My fascia, though, in my feet, was probably like stale saltwater taffy. That was probably the cause of my plantar fasciitis. Myofascial release is a massage that breaks up the stale saltwater taffy and makes it flimsy again like chicken. She explained the massage would be different than what I was used to, and it would hurt, but that it would help my feet. She asked if I wanted to try it.

I was so excited and said yes. She was not lying. That massage hurt like hell!! I was squirming and trying hard to breathe the entire time she was on my feet. In all the massages I had ever had, I had never felt this technique before, and I did not like it!! Until …

After my massage, I got off the table and got dressed. It did not hurt to stand up. And when I started walking around a little bit, the middle of my foot did not feel like it was being ripped in half. What the . . .?

Tierza had a deal: if you purchased massages in bulk, they cost less. It became my routine to purchase 5-10 massages every in-port. I'd go every 2-3 weeks. My feet would feel great. I loved it. The massages didn't hurt as much, either. Then we would get underway for three months or so. I'd do all the things mentioned above (tennis ball, stretching, and orthotics). My feet would do well for the first month or six weeks, and then they'd start hurting again. We'd pull back in port, I'd purchase more massages. The first couple would hurt like hell, and then I'd feel better again. Wash, rinse, repeat.

Sometime in 2007, I was also diagnosed with two other medical conditions. The Spaz Clam actually told me what one of them was before I went to see the Doc, so I think it was spring/summer 2007 I was diagnosed with acid reflux. We were underway and I started having bad pains after I ate. I'd get hiccups often and burp. Sometimes when I burped, I'd throw up a little in my mouth. I didn't know what it was, but it hurt, and it was gross. Spaz Clam was on watch with me and told me it was probably acid reflux. When I went to see Doc, he confirmed it and put me on Prilosec. That worked great for several years.

I don't know if it was the same appointment or earlier or later in 2007, but I was also diagnosed with premenstrual dysphoric disorder (PMDD). PMDD is a severe, sometimes disabling extension of premenstrual syndrome (PMS) or as I like to say, it is PMS on steroids.

My periods have always been heavy, and I remember cramping in high school. Occasionally, I would come home "sick" because I either sprang an embarrassing leak, or I was in a ton of pain. As I got older, though, I learned to just take an aspirin the first day or two and I was fine. In 2007, though, not only had aspirin stopped working, but I also had more symptoms. The week before my period I did not sleep at all. If I did sleep, I had bad nightmares. I didn't put it together at first, that it was the week before my period and probably hormones. I stopped watching some of my favorite shows, such as *Law and Order* and stopped reading before bed to try to curb the nightmares. Neither of those things worked.

I also got extremely depressed the first day or so of my period. I know I wrote earlier that I was suicidal. This was different. I knew why I was suicidal. I knew all the bad stuff going on in my life, and I didn't see a way out of it. But this, this was waking up in the morning crying. Crying over nothing. The day hadn't even started yet. Why was I sad? I didn't know.

My mom had always been against birth control. My mom is an herbalist, so growing up we saw the doctor sometimes, but most of the time my mom had other herbal remedies. She swore by peppermint tea for my female issues in high school. I tried that and sometimes it worked, but the aspirin worked a lot better. I also hated the taste of peppermint tea.

Other friends were 50/50 on birth control. It had helped some of them and some of them said it made them a lot worse. My main concern was my weight. I was already struggling; I didn't need to gain more.

Doc put me on Yasmin. I did not gain nor lose any weight. Within a couple of months, all of my symptoms improved except for the sleep thing. Even with all the medications I'm on now (2019) and with therapy, I still don't sleep during my period . . . or very much at all in general. I swore by birth control. I told every female who asked, or said they had any issues at all, that birth control was helping me out tremendously. I swore by it for seven to ten years. Now I wish I hadn't. Now I hope all those other females sought out other treatments . . .

ELECTRONIC AND ALL OUT WARFARE

While stationed aboard the USCG Cutter *Mellon,* in August 2008, Ramona and I went to Electronic Warfare (EW) Threat Recognition C-School in Jacksonville, FL. We stayed in the hotel on the Navy base and Ramona managed to get a rental car for us.

Around that same time, the Coast Guard changed from metal crows (collar devices) to sew-on patches. Ramona accidentally packed the wrong uniform and did not have necessary collar devices. We looked in both exchanges, but we were on a Navy base and couldn't find Coast Guard collar devices. Ramona wasn't sure what to do.

Thankfully, a Coast Guard 210-foot cutter happened to be moored at one of the piers on the Navy base. Unfortunately, it was behind a locked fence. Ramona and I were trying to find a clever way to get over or around the fence when one of the guys I knew from Station Sabine walked over. We went onto the 210 and one of the first class petty officers gave Ramona a set of crows.

We told that story to our class later, and the Navy guys couldn't believe it! According to them, they can't just "walk onto" any Navy ship they want whenever they want. They also claimed that no one in the Navy would just give collar devices to another person who forgot theirs or didn't have them. Well, boys, this is one of many reasons why the Coast Guard is better than the Navy.

EW schools are hard!! Everything is classified, so you cannot take notes in class. You cannot bring "home" study material. You have to memorize everything.

EW in the Navy is an actual job rate. Ramona and I were the only two Coasties in our class and EW for us was a collateral job that we really only used once a year when we had to go through TACT.

Threat Recognition meant that we had to learn all the ships, subs, aircraft, the weapons systems they have on board, the missiles for those systems, and the emitters on those missiles, and much more, for almost every country, We were straight-up memorizing letter and number combinations. It was horrible. At the same time, Ramona and I did better on almost all of our tests than the Navy guys did. (I told you Ramona was intelligent. I can hold my own.)

Ramona and I got along great! We had an awesome time in Jacksonville. We're both German. We found a little hole-in-the-wall German restaurant, owned and operated by Germans, with real authentic German food. It was delicious!! Ramona showed off a little by ordering in German and talking to them about where she was from in Germany.

We also went to a cool sports bar and restaurant, Sneakers. Before we had left for school, one of the OS3s told us we had to go there. She worked there before she joined the Coast Guard and wanted us to bring her back a T-Shirt. She also said the food was good.

She wasn't lying. The food was great. And the atmosphere was nice, too. Ramona and I watched the summer Olympics. Ramona almost got our asses kicked because she was rooting for Germany in some of the events!! Luckily, she redeemed us by rooting for Michael Phelps in the swimming competition.

Hurricane Flo cut our C-School short. They closed down the base for a day or two to prepare for her. Ramona and I were supposed to stay, but we had had enough. Ramona drove us to the airport. We had to turn around twice because a couple bridges were out. We didn't think we'd get a flight out, but miraculously we did. We made Flo jokes for a long time after!

EW Journeyman C-School was the end of September through the beginning of October 2008, in San Diego, CA. That school was a little better. The information we had to memorize was "normal" information instead of number-letter combinations. The concepts were easier to grasp, as well. Ramona packed the right uniforms this time, so we didn't have to roam all over God's green earth to find her some. And Ramona and I kicked our Navy counterparts' butts in class again!

Ramona and I did get along with Lamb, one of the Navy guys in our class, and we hung out with him after class. I don't remember everywhere we went, but I do specifically remember going through two haunted houses. I'm usually a big baby and don't enjoy haunted houses. Ramona happens to be worse than I am. Maybe she was just more verbal about it before I was. The first haunted house wasn't too scary. Ramona hates clowns, though, so she jumped when a couple popped out.

After the first house, there was a radio station asking trivia questions. If you answered the trivia question, they gave you tickets to a second haunted house. I think Lamb answered it. Maybe Ramona did. I don't remember except that I didn't.

I don't know why Ramona agreed to go. She really didn't want to. Maybe it was just because Lamb and I wanted to go, and she was being a good sport. If that was the case, that bit her in the ass!!

The second haunted house wasn't a house, but an outdoor maze with some buildings in it. One of the people who ran the maze must have heard Lamb and me making fun of Ramona in line before the maze. We started walking through and there were zombies and clowns everywhere. The first building we entered, "creatures" were banging on the walls. Normally this would have scared the hell out of me, and I would have been clinging to Lamb. Ramona, however, was so scared that her fear actually calmed me down to the point where I started finding everything incredibly funny. Then, all of a sudden, the creatures started calling out, "Ramona, Ramona, where are you? We are coming for you, Ramona!"

That sealed the deal. Ramona was completely terrified, and my fear of haunted houses was completely cured!! Lamb and I walked through the rest of it laughing so hard we were crying, and Ramona ran through it just trying to get to the end.

Both C-Schools were a lot of fun. Ramona and I got along very well. We had a lot of inside jokes and stories. I think I even sent some emails, telling the above stories. Ramona told me how good a writer I am and that I should write a book some-day … (Hmmm … seemed to be a common theme …) Ramona and I even confided in each other a little bit. Nothing too serious, but we talked, as friends. We were friends at that time.

We returned to Seattle. I starved myself after Ramona and I returned from San Diego, so I managed to make weight during weigh-ins. I had to. If I hadn't, that would have been strike three, and I would have been kicked out of the Coast Guard. Ramona and I did work out during both C-Schools, but I'd be lying to say I ate healthy. That German restaurant alone killed me. That is why I had to starve myself. Again, starvation was "normal" for "fatties" to try to make weight, and no one batted an eye that I was doing it.

Middle or end of October 2008 we got back underway. We were going back down south! Morale was high, and the entire cutter wanted a drug bust. The new OS1 was working hard to get to know the shop and break in watch stander and eventually watch supervisor. I initially liked him, but that quickly changed. I had gotten qualified as a watch supervisor at the end of the previous patrol, and Ramona was ready for her board to get qualified at the beginning of this patrol. Ramona did well on her board, but I was still upset at how "easy" it was for her to just jump right into EW and watch supervisor when it had taken me so long. Instead of being happy that the process was working as it was supposed to, I was jealous and mad. So instead of acknowledging what Ramona knew when it came time to decide whether she was qualified, I pointed out all the things she fumbled or did not know. I thought she should have to break in longer. The OS1 talked me down, even though he was not qualified as a watch supervisor yet, and she passed her board.

Initially, I was happy that the OS1 had talked me down. Ramona, Chief G, and I were the only qualified watch supervisors. If she had not passed her board, my schedule would have been awful. Since she did pass, we each had one eight-hour shift per day. It worked out well because we all preferred the shifts we took, too, so we were all happy . . .

I don't know if it is normal for everyone to just complain. I think it often is. I think every duty section believes they get stuck with all the holidays. Every rate feels they work the hardest. Every individual gets screwed the most. I think that is just human nature.

My OS3s started complaining to me how much they hated standing watch with Ramona. They accused her of doing some things that were against the rules, and then they just complained about her over-all watch style. This enraged me. My mind immediately took be back to being an OS3, stuck on the radar, freezing, sick, and not even being allowed to check my email. There was no way in hell I was going to let Ramona treat these OS3s this way. This was the reason she should have had to wait to become qualified! She was not ready to be in charge yet!

I told the OS1 about it, and he kind of blew me off. He thought I was being petty (Looking back, I probably was.). He didn't want to deal with it. Since OS1 didn't help me, I went to Chief G. Chief G took me more seriously and asked the OS3s about it. Suddenly, the OS3s didn't have any problems with Ramona at all. They didn't repeat anything they had said to me, or if they did, it wasn't serious enough to involve Chief G. He told me that the OS3s were happy. I was furious with them for not telling Chief G the truth. When I was in that situation, I didn't have the chance to tell my chief what had gone on with the Clams. I never spoke up because I was too afraid. But these guys had the chance. Chief G and I were on their side. What the hell was wrong with them?

I think they stopped complaining to me after that. Things apparently weren't that bad; Chief G didn't need to be involved. The OS3s must have realized how seriously I took them and stopped complaining.

The seeds the "Clams" had planted, though, were now watered by the OS3s' complaining that Ramona was not a good watch supervisor. Eventually, the Radio OS3 provided sunshine and a hate flower bloomed.

I vaguely remember doing marks in Texas. The Coast Guard, like most jobs, evaluates employees on a semi-annual basis. There were several categories at the time, with one the lowest mark and seven the highest you could receive in each category. As I have previously said, when it comes time to advance, Coast Guard members take the Service Wide Exam (SWE). The SWE score is combined with marks, award points, time in, and other factors to give the member their final score. All members are then put on a list in order and are advanced as needed. Those needed are "above the cut." Those not needed may make a second cut or most likely have to test again.

In Texas I vaguely remember BM2/Lee sitting down with me one day and telling me what I was doing well, and what I needed to improve, and I signed a sheet of paper. A-School is a school, so marks were not done during this period. On the cutter, with the first OSC and OS1, I did not have to provide supporting bullets for what I had done. In fact, I very specifically remember the first OSC being insulted when I handed him some, saying that if he didn't know what was going on in his shop with his people, then he was not doing his job.

Ironically, with all the shit going on with the Clams and with all the "trouble" I had been in, my marks with the first OSC and OS1 were always good. Which, thinking about it, meant the OSC did know how hard I was working and what I had accomplished, but he did not know what was going on in his shop at all. Or worse, he did know and did not care about the hazing.

This patrol, however, with Chief G and the new OS1, my

marks were terrible! (They were average, really, but I was pissed!) I made OS2, EW CSTT, and Watch Supervisor in the same patrol! I had done all the communications with all the small boats and boarding teams when we broke the record. I had more responsibility on the cutter now than I had ever had. How were my marks lower?!?

I hadn't written supporting bullets, though. The new OS1 claimed he didn't know I had done all that. (In all fairness, he probably didn't). He claimed he marked me based on what he saw. (He probably did.) I was beyond mad at him. How dare he try to screw me?

I appealed my marks. I remember having to eat lunch with the captain of the cutter!! Luckily, it was the new captain; the good leader. He went through my marks and raised a couple of them. OSs are fortunate in the fact that we work hand in hand with the command. It is easier for us to be recognized and rewarded because of this while members in other rates must find other ways of getting the command's attention. In this case, the captain knew most of what I did in CIC/Combat because he was directly involved in those missions, too. I didn't have to fight very hard for him to raise some of my marks. However, the higher marks also came with a lecture on how to properly write supporting bullets. The captain told me that if I wanted proper numbers in the future, I would need to advocate for myself. He acted as if I should have known this, as did the new OS1. I think writing bullets or doing marks was actually a requirement for advancement, so I did practice it, once. Maybe I should have known that was how things were supposed to be done, but the former OSC ripped my fucking head off when I wrote them, so I was taken off-guard by the captain's remarks. OS1 had already listened to Ramona's EW ideas, ignored my complaints about her being a bad watch supervisor, and had now given me bad marks. My hate seeds for him were planted and watered now, too.

Along with San Diego, our port calls for this patrol were Panama and Costa Rica! Costa Rica is one of my top three favorite places on Earth! I loved every minute we spent there. There was a bar called Samoas built in a large sailboat. In the middle was the stand for the cash register and a large sail, among other things. At the bottom of the sail were covers (hats) from all different Navy and Coast Guard units that had come through. If you gave the bartender a cover, you were given a free drink. The entire bar was covered by a large canopy. On the poles of the canopy were life rings from different Navy and Coast Guard units. The bar was part of a hotel and also had a pool. At some point everyone from the cutter ended up there. The pool was closed at night, but they opened it for us. I hung out with Calvin, my boat hubby, and some of the OS3s from Combat and Radio.

We included Shinedown, another non-rate who had transferred that summer. He was good friends with Calvin, and we went bowling a lot while in port. He had a manual shift car, so Calvin and he taught me how to drive a manual. I would drive it to or from base and the bowling alley. At Samoas, Shinedown and I split the best pina colada ever! Not only did it taste great, but it was poured into a large hollowed-out pineapple instead of a cup! It was great!

The next day a bunch of us went on a horseback tour in the jungle. Calvin didn't initially want to go, mainly because he couldn't afford it. I was a little afraid of going, and I found out one of the non-rates that I didn't like was, too. I begged Calvin to go, even offering to pay for him. He agreed. I was freaking out the next morning on the bus, as he made it at the very last second because he was hung over from the bar and pool party the night before!

We rode horses to a tent in the middle of the jungle and ate a traditional lunch. Then we went on a couple of zip lines. One of the non-rates actually hit a tree!! She wasn't hurt so it was funny as hell! The zip lines ended at a beautiful waterfall. We were given time to swim underneath it. That was a dream comes true for me! Sunsets and waterfalls are my favorite things on earth.

One of the junior officers climbed up one of the sides to jump down into the waterfall. For some reason unknown to me, I wanted to do the same thing. I'm not strong at all, so I struggled to climb. I was so excited that I made it up. The officer helped me. I got to the edge and wanted a picture. As I went to jump, my foot slipped, and I fell into the water fall instead. Ahhh, good memories.

Calvin and a couple of the other non-rates climbed up a different side where there was a little stream and smaller waterfall. They lay down in the middle of that and were taking pictures. We all swam there for quite a while, none of us having a care in the world.

Finally, the tour guide said it was time for us to go. We hopped in a van and were taken back to the cutter. Calvin and I were both excited that he went. I will never forget that day. I hope to make it back to Costa Rica again sometime.

There was a rule on the cutter that you could only hang out with people within one rank of you, lower or higher. It was very loosely enforced. I think it was primarily for the chiefs and officers. It also made sense for the BMs and MKs because they had non-rates that actually worked for them so not hanging out with your boss was probably appropriate.

I had come to the cutter as a 3rd class. The non-rates helped me with all my DC stuff and were my first friends. It took me a long time to make good friends on the cutter and to not want to kill myself. I absolutely refused to stop hanging out with my boat hubby and Calvin. I loved them and they were there for me when literally no one else was. I had made OS2 in July, which put me two ranks ahead of them. I did not care. The new OS1, however, cared. He "counseled" me several times, warning me not to hang out with them. After Costa Rica, I walked into Combat and OS1 was waiting for me. He started asking me what I did during the port call and who I hung out with. I was preparing for a fight when Chief G walked in and said, "Hey Herby, I just saw your boat hubby. He says, 'Hi!'" OS1 angrily walked away.

OS1 continued lecturing me, trying to keep me from hanging out with the non-rates who were my friends. It was the last straw for him. I officially hated him, and I'm pretty sure he had had enough of me, too. But Chief G knew how much of an asset I was to CIC/Combat. He also knew how much I was helping the non-rates with stuff for advancement and how much the BMs appreciated me. Chief G had a crazy ability to read people, too, so even though I never told him, I think he knew that I battled some demons, too. Whatever his reasons, OS1 was going to have to find some hard-core dirt on me to actually be able to take me down, and he knew that. To his credit, I don't think he actually had a vendetta against me. I think he was just trying to keep peace and order in his shop. He did speak highly of me, too, when talking about my accomplishments. A part of me did understand that at the time. A part of me knew he was just doing his job. Another part of me couldn't stand him.

I don't know exactly when or how, but I had transformed. I was no longer going to be pushed around on that cutter. I went from a shy, timid, suicidal third class to an obnoxious, smart, hardworking, OS2 with a "fuck you and pound sand" attitude. I guess you could say I became a Clam myself, but really my anger was only directed towards Ramona and OS1. They were the only two I thought were getting in my way and holding me back. I had decided that with Chief G on my side, I was never going to be told "No" on that cutter ever again. And somehow, mostly with Chief G on my side, I never was. Until I transferred.

RANDOM EVENTS AND PEOPLE

There were so many significant events that happened while I was on the cutter, it is impossible to remember exactly when they all happened, even with Ramona's help. A lot happened in a short amount of time and she doesn't remember everything, either. It is also hard to decide what is and isn't relevant to the main point and focus of my book. Keeping those things in mind, I'll just include these few extra events.

Shortly after the first patrol, I paid Jack back for paying for my car repairs. One of the best things about being underway is the amount of money you save! I also went to visit him twice. I think the first time was in 2007. I remember Jack picking me up at the airport and immediately upon my getting in his car, he told me that I had a choice. We could either do tourist shit the entire time I was in Boston, or we could do cool shit that real Bostonians do. He could take me to the *Cheers'* bar for a beer, if I was dying to go, but he knew several other bars that had better beer, better atmospheres, and cost less. He'd rather show me shit that real Bostonians do, but it was my vacation, so I needed to choose right then. How did I want to spend my vacation? I chose the second option with the exception that I wanted one day of tourist shit so I could buy some souvenirs. He agreed. Jack and his family are some of the best hosts I have ever stayed with and that trip is one of my favorite trips of all time. True to his word, Jack took me to a bunch of spots that he enjoyed as a child and adult. He introduced me to some of his friends. One day, he took me to Faneuil Hall so I could buy souvenirs. He even admitted that that part of town was kind of cool. The second time was in April of 2009. My cousin had moved to Boston, too, so I stayed with my cousin one week and Jack the second week. I also saw the first OS1 from the *Mellon*. We went to a Red Sox game together.

My younger sister, after doing a couple of years in college on a softball scholarship, became bored and joined the Marines. After boot camp and her A-School, she became an Aviation Ordnance Technician and was stationed in Iwakuni, Japan. In March of 2008, I went to visit her for three weeks. Japan is beautiful and she took me to some really nice places and we had some fun. We also got in some pretty big fights at the hotel.

I don't remember the date we went through TACT again or what patrol it was part of, but the *Mellon* earned the Battle E! If that wasn't good news on its own, my training records were immaculate and the ATG asked if they could use them as examples for other departments on the *Mellon* and other cutters on the west coast. They also took some "charts" I had made for EW to give to other cutters! Not only had I taken over the jobs after the Clams left, but I did them better than the Clams did!! I was so proud of myself.

I told the story earlier of one of the in-port periods we all had to tear up the non-skid on the boat. The other in-port period where it was all hands-on-deck: the entire crew had to go into all the bilges and along the bottom of the cutter and scrape off all the paint so the metal of the hull could be inspected. One of the other Coast Guard cutters had a hole in its hull and was in dry dock so the Coast Guard wanted to inspect the rest of the fleet, fixing anything before it became a major issue. Once the cutter was inspected and deemed seaworthy, the crew then had to re-prime and re-paint all of those same areas.

When we were not working in port, Calvin and I went to a lot of concerts. Some of the other OSs or non-rates would join us depending on who we were seeing. A huge group of us went to see Hinder. A much smaller group wanted to see Brad Paisley. I guess there weren't too many country fans on the cutter. Seattle has a phenomenal music scene. Amongst many other bands, I saw Matchbox 20, Alanis Morrissett, Hollywood Undead, Cage the Elephant, Evanescence, Seether, The Killers, Dierks Bentley, Rascal Flatts, and Taylor Swift. I listen to just about everything, as you can tell.

We also went to a lot of baseball games. Everyone on the cutter enjoyed this as the stadium is literally two blocks from the base so we parked on base and walked to the games. The Pyramid Ale House was also right down the road, so sometimes we ate dinner or grabbed a few drinks there before the game.

I also found time to volunteer. The Coast Guard teams up with local schools in certain areas of the country in a program called Partners in Education (PIE). Members at the local unit volunteer in classrooms to help mentor specific students or just assist the teacher with whatever they need. Since the cutter's schedule was so sporadic, instead of volunteering in a classroom, I volunteered in the library instead. When we were in port I helped the librarian put books away, set up book fairs, and read to students.

In late March of 2009, Chief G and I participated in The Big Climb. "At 788 feet of vertical elevation, The Columbia Center in downtown Seattle is the tallest building in the Pacific Northwest. It takes 69 flights of stairs, or 1311 steps, to reach the sky view observatory . . . The Leukemia and Lymphoma Society's Big Climb event raises money through individual and team fundraising."

I remember firefighters from all over not only participated in the climb, but raced to see which department was fastest. Some departments started early in the day and did the climb multiple times to see who could climb the most, too. I remember seeing them and having a tremendous amount of respect for them and their job.

Chief G and I, on the other hand, nearly died. 69 flights of stairs is a lot of stairs!! I was absolutely determined to get to the top, though. Sean, from A-School, had given me a list of things to do in Seattle when I got my orders to the cutter. If I remember correctly, he was stationed there before A-School, and he had insider tips on the best places to go and things to do. One of the things he told me was that the Space Needle was all right, but there was another building in Seattle that was actually taller and had a better view of the city. He said that it was normally cheaper if you could find someone who let you go to the top so he recommended I do that instead of the Space Needle. Now was my chance to take Sean's advice and see the amazing view of the city. I had my camera and I was going to do this! Chief G couldn't let me out-climb him so both of us climbed all 69 flights of stairs! Completely out of breath and with shaking legs, I reached the top. Sean was right; the view was absolutely phenomenal. I'd write that it was breath taking, but I don't know, because my breath was already taken by the climb!

There are also so many more people that I became friends with and keep in touch with to this day. In port, I attended a little church in West Seattle. The pastor was prior Navy and one of the members was a former Coastie. Both of them understood patrols and random schedules and made me feel at home. The former Coastie was also happy to have someone else on his side for the Navy versus Coast Guard "rivalry" the Pastor and he had. The church was a smaller Baptist church. I like smaller churches. I want to know the pastor, and for the pastor to know and remember me. It feels more like family that way. Bigger mega churches feel more like a business. I don't want to "make an appointment" to see the pastor if I have a major life event. I want the pastor to already know I'm struggling, and the church to step in and help out. I stayed with the former Coastie and his wife for a week before I left Seattle and still keep in touch with them to this day.

Shinedown really should have been mentioned more than he was, but he will be mentioned again. There were various

OS's that came and went that I did actually get along with in both Radio and Combat and I keep in touch with them. I was good friends with an FS3 who married an ET3. I was the witness at their wedding and was the first non-family member to hold their baby. Calvin was the second, I think. The first Doc on the cutter, Hammer, was really cool and will be mentioned again. Some of the ETs ended up being instructors in Petaluma at the same time I was. One of the BM2s on the *Mellon* was the BM1 in charge of the barracks when I first reported in Petaluma. A couple of the non-rates that I was "friends" (maybe more acquaintances) with on the *Mellon* are chiefs now and were both in Petaluma during my time there. It was crazy to see how far they had come. I'm extremely proud of and happy for both of them. One of the ETs almost got me killed in Mexico taking a "short cut" back to the cutter and then telling drug dealers that we were Coasties. In her defense, she was drunk, but still. I'm sure I'm forgetting someone and I'm really sorry. After the first six months, I made friends and many of them I keep in touch with to this day. I hated the cutter, but I'm glad I met these friends.

ONE LAST F YOU

We went on another Alaska Patrol in 2009. That might have been when we went through TACT again; I don't remember. There might have been two patrols in 2009; I don't know. The south patrol at the end of 2008 or one of the patrols in 2009 was when the Radio OS3 and I went after Ramona. Seeds had been planted by the Clams and watered by the CIC/Combat OS3s. I became friends with other people on the cutter who provided sunshine, and my hate flower for Ramona bloomed. I don't have an excuse, just the story that I have written thus far. I'm extremely happy Ramona has forgiven me, and we are friends now.

I took the SWE for OS1/Petty Officer First Class/E6 in October of 2008 and was above the cut to make it. I got orders to transfer to Sector Mobile, Alabama. I reenlisted on the 41-foot boat from Station Seattle. One of the BM1s on the cutter had advanced to chief and transferred there. Chief G got in touch with him to ask if they could arrange something for me since I was at a station as a non-rate, and the 41 was the first boat I was qualified on. He agreed. The BMC let me get the 41 underway from station. We went to the middle of the Puget Sound, in front of the Space Needle, and I raised my hand to add more years to my Coast Guard career. The station 25s had just finished an escort so I have a picture of me on the back of the 41 with my hand raised, and the 25s and Space Needle in the background. That was a really special day. It was also the one and only time I took advantage of being able to reenlist anywhere I wanted.

Mobile, Alabama, was my first choice of places to transfer,

and I was very happy. During the summers in high school, I visited my friend, Krystal, in Biloxi, Mississippi. One summer her parents took us over to Mobile to see the USS Alabama. I remembered that, and I love the South. I thought Mobile would be perfect.

I spent my last five months on the cutter trying to hand off all my jobs in CIC/Combat to the OSs staying and hanging out with my friends every chance I could get.

I had two going-away parties that I specifically remember. Chief G, some other friends, and I went to a Mariners baseball game. It was the Mariners 10-Year Anniversary Celebration, and they were giving away toy trucks to the first however many people into the stadium. I wanted one really badly. I ended up with four of them! "We love ya, Herbie! OSC G" is written on the one he gave me.

"Herby, thanks for being the amazing person you are! Haha Take Care. Love Shine Down"

Someone else (I'm pretty sure it was Shine Down's best friend and the non-rate that I paid to shine my boots. Yes, I paid him to shine my boots. I ironed uniforms in boot camp; I suck at shining boots. He was very good at it and needed money!) carved their initials and I (heart) you in the cardboard of theirs and then wrote, "My knife made this."

The last one says "Good Luck" with a signature I can't read.

I have two Mariners' tickets in the bag with the trucks, so the game was either May 19, 2009 or June 5, 2009. I don't remember who went to the other game with me, but as I've repeatedly said in this book, I love baseball!!

The second going-away party, Chief G took all the OSs, my boat hubby, and Calvin (yes, Chief invited non-rates. Gasp!) to the top of the Space Needle for lunch one day. That was my official going away party. Sean was right when he told me the view from the other location was better, and the Space Needle was expensive. I'm very happy I participated in The Big Climb and took pictures from up there. However, having lunch at the Space Needle was also very special. The restaurant literally rotates very slowly as you eat, and you get a 360-degree view of the city. The food was good, as well. I appreciated Chief G very much for making that happen.

Remember when I said I wasn't told "no" on the cutter again until I transferred? Well, Chief G had written me up for an Achievement Medal, having cited my accomplishments as CIC Watch Stander and Watch Supervisor, EW CSTT, OS Training Petty Officer, and most importantly, ATG using my training program and EW stuff as training aids for other departments on the *Mellon* and for other cutters on the West Coast. These were more than enough to meet the criteria according to the manual to earn an Achievement Medal. Chief G very proudly wrote the award and the Division Officer and Operations Boss very proudly signed off on it. (Both of whom were very awesome people! Again, both of them should have been given more mention in this book, but there just isn't space. The Division Officer was the one who climbed the waterfall in Costa Rica.) The award made it to the XO, though, and he bumped it down to a Letter of Commendation. This is not an award to just shrug off; however, I deserved an Achievement Medal. The XO claimed that I was not an example of a good second-class petty officer because I had struggled with my weight so much. That was the reason he gave for bumping down my award. Negatives shouldn't outweigh positives when getting awards. They are two separate things. What he did was not right at all. But he was the XO of the cutter, so it didn't matter how hard Chief G, or the division officer fought for me, I was given a Letter of Commendation instead of the Achievement Medal upon departing the Cutter *Mellon*. It was one last "Fuck you!" from the absolutely worst unit in the entire Coast Guard. I could not have been happier to leave.

SECTOR MOBILE

I reported into Sector Mobile in June or July of 2009. I was a second class (OS2) but above the cut to make first class (OS1). I arrived at sector the same day the new senior chief did. I was introduced to some people and then told to take my 10 days house-hunting leave.

I ended up renting a 3-bedroom, 2-bath house in west Mobile over by Government and Knollwood. A BM1 at the sector had gotten married and moved into his wife's house. I was renting his former house. Since we were both in the CG, he did not ask me for a deposit. Rent would be $850 a month.

After I got settled in, I went back to work. The LT at the time was one of the smartest people I have ever met. Prior enlisted Army and now an LT in the CG, he not only knew Search & Rescue, but he also knew the "M" side, as well. (Most people are only familiar or an expert with one.) I don't know what little birdie whispered in his ear, but he knew changes were coming to command centers, and I was going to be his guinea pig. Of course, he didn't tell me this. He presented it to me in a different way.

Every sector varies a little, despite command center school's best efforts, but typically there are four jobs or desks at a sector. The Communications Unit Watch Stander (CU) listens to the radios all day long. They are responsible for taking guards with Coast Guard small boats, cutters, and aircraft, as well as auxiliary and some other local government agencies. The CU monitors classified emails and message traffic. And their main job is listening for and responding to distress calls. This job is usually performed by an E3 (SNOS) or E4 (OS3).

The Situational Unit Watch Stander (SU) is the most varied

desk among sectors. At Sector Mobile, this desk worked very closely with the Prevention department. The SU monitored large vessels arriving and departing from our ports, responded to pollution incidents, responded to non-Search & Rescue related Marine Casualties (for example, a barge hitting a railroad bridge—no train on bridge at time of impact, no injuries), and was responsible for keeping Maritime Domain Awareness. This job is usually performed by a highly motivated, proactive OS3 or an OS2. Occasionally for various reasons, an OS1 will do it.

The Operational Unit Watch Stander (OU) used to be referred to as the Search and Rescue (SAR) Controller. This desk is in charge of all Law Enforcement, Fisheries, and SAR cases. For SAR, this desk runs the computer program SAROPS that calculates the drift in the water and comes up with search areas. The OU then dispatches units to respond. This job is usually performed by a highly motivated, proactive OS2 or an OS1.

The fourth desk is the Command Duty Officer (CDO). The CDO has overall oversight of the entire watch. The CDO assists all the watch standers with all cases and helps coordinate units and assets if there is more than one incident happening within a specific area. The CDO also briefs the SMC (SAR Mission Controller), captain, and district. If there is an incident that might be of national interest, the CDO is responsible for calling the 800 number to notify headquarters and the Commandant. This job is usually performed by chiefs and officers. Every once in a blue moon, if the command is supportive and the OS1 is very motivated and proactive, an OS1 will fill the position. This is not very common, but I know someone who achieved it . . .

Since I reported to Sector Mobile as an OS2 above the cut to make OS1, I should have been breaking in at the OU desk. The LT, however, asked me if I would break in as a CU. Rescue 21 (the radio system) was not around when I went through A-School. I had never used it before. The OU doesn't need to know the ins and outs of Rescue 21; however, they do stand by for the CU when the CU takes a break so they should know the basics. They should also be familiar with all the equipment in the command center, in general. The LT said he'd like me to get qualified and to learn how to use Rescue 21. It would also help me become familiar with Sector Mobile's tri-state Area of Responsibility (AOR). I agreed.

Breaking in CU was fun. I got to know a lot of the OS3s who I would be standing watch with later. It allowed me to build a rapport with them before I became an OU and started running cases. It also allowed me to see what it was like to be in a room by myself for twelve hours, having nothing to do but listen to the radio. I gained some compassion for later on.

I also remember one of my very first cases. A boat was about to capsize. There were six people onboard. One of our 87-foot cutters was going to respond. I was working with Micah, but I was doing the majority of the comms. One of the females on board the distress vessel ran back inside the cabin to get something. Unfortunately, the vessel capsized, and she got trapped. We rescued the other five people onboard. I was proud of everything I did; I know that I followed all protocol. Later I even received a compliment from the captain of the 87. I was also bummed that I lost someone. Why did she run back inside? What was so important? Why did the other people let her?

I took my CU board a week or so later and became a qualified CU. Another OS3 took emergency leave to take care of her mother who had unfortunately had a stroke. I agreed to stand watch at the CU desk until she returned.

To become an OU, you must go to Yorktown, Virginia, for SAR School. It is four weeks long and you learn all the SAR policies and how to run SAROPS (computer program that calculates the drift). There was a wait for the school, so the LT asked me if I would break in at the SU desk before moving to OU. He said it would give me the opportunity to see what they did and to continue learning the tri-state AOR. I agreed.

In December of 2009, a critical message came out from the Coast Guard Cutter *Dallas* in Charleston, South Carolina. They needed an OS to go on patrol with them to train their combat OS's because they had been in a long dry dock. I had just come from the *Mellon* and was qualified as a CIC/Combat Watch Supervisor and EW CSTT. Since I was not qualified SU or OU yet, my LT asked if I wanted to go. I agreed. (More on that next chapter)

I returned to Sector Mobile in January and got qualified at the SU desk. That desk is no joke. You don't learn anything SU related in OS A-School. In fact, you become part MST standing watch at that desk due to all the pollution incidents you respond to and monitoring incoming vessel traffic. It took me three or four months to get qualified and that board was the hardest board I took while at Sector Mobile, including the elusive board that most OS1s don't ever take . . .

I stood watch at the SU desk for a month or so and then I went to SAR School. I came back and broke in and became qualified as an OU! I finally made it! This was the job that I had wanted since OS A-School. I was finally running SAR cases. I was very excited and very nervous.

Including the patrol with the *Dallas*, I got qualified at all three desks in less than a year at Sector Mobile. The first couple months of standing OU, I also continued to stand two watches a month at the SU desk (the minimum amount of watches per month required to maintain your qualification). The LT wrote me up for and I received a Letter of Commendation (LOC) for this feat. It was a great first year!

A few years later it became a requirement to get qualified at all the desks in order. In other words, you were not considered qualified as an OU unless you had already obtained CU and SU. If you did not have all the desks, you could not be promoted. All the sectors were encouraged to have their SUs and OUs dually qualified for standing both watches. Good thing the LT asked me to stand all the desks my first year at the command center. I took the next SWE to advance without any issues. It was as if he knew these changes were going to be made ... Like he wanted to see how it would work at his sector...

COAST GUARD CUTTER DALLAS

In December 2009, I went to South Carolina to do a short training patrol with the Coast Guard Cutter *Dallas*. My LT asked me if I wanted to volunteer to fill the critical solicitation since I was not yet qualified at Sector Mobile, and I had just come off the *Mellon*. I agreed.

When I got to the Cutter *Dallas* and crossed the brow, I immediately regretted my decision. My stomach dropped. I couldn't believe I had agreed to get back underway. After everything that had happened on the *Mellon*. After making my mom save emails, I sent her to prevent this from happening again, I volunteered to go! I felt so sick.

My mom and I had talked before I went. I told her I would be a first class instead of a third class. I told her that it was only for a couple weeks. She was shocked I had volunteered but agreed that the patrol would not be bad.

I dropped my stuff off on board the cutter, came back to the pier, and called a friend of mine from A-School. I was mid-panic attack. How could I back out of this patrol? I did not want to get back underway. What was I thinking volunteering for this? Cutters were evil places with evil people. My friend calmed me down. He told me all the same things I told my mom. He reminded me that first classes are basically gods on-board cutters. He said that I would have a fun time. I calmed down and that night went out to eat with some of the OSs and hung out in downtown Charleston. I thought they were all nice and had a good time.

The next day we got underway and I met the rest of the CIC watch standers. There was also a chief who volunteered to get underway to help train the OSs. He was really nice and very knowledgeable. We stood opposite watches to ensure that we got plenty of sleep and all the Combat/CIC OSs on board the Cutter *Dallas* received training.

The Combat/CIC OSs on the *Dallas* got along very well. The shop hung out with each other. They were, dare I say, friends. The atmosphere was so different from the *Mellon*. The chief in charge of CIC gave me the run down. He told me who was qualified and who wasn't. He was thrilled that I was EW CSTT and asked if I could train one of the other OS1s on how to run EW during a General Quarters (GQ) drill. I'm not sure if they were initially planning to conduct a GQ drill on the patrol, but we ended up conducting one. I did show the OS1 how to run EW.

When I was not on watch or training, I could basically do whatever I wanted. I hung out in the "elusive" first class lounge. I watched movies. No one bothered me. Well, except for a yeoman chief (YNC). She gave me a hard time because I never went outside. Apparently, when underway, you should go out on the boat decks at least once a day and get some sun (provided it is nice weather). She even gave the OSC a hard time about keeping me down in CIC too much. She was right. Going outside was nice. I should have done that more when I was on the *Mellon*.

We had two port calls on our two-week training patrol. The first one was in Jacksonville, Florida. I was familiar with the area due to the EW schools I had attended. We went to Sneakers for dinner and played Bingo, I think. I know we played a game while we ate. All the CIC OSs were there. We all had a good time. I couldn't believe these people worked together and hung out on port calls. No one was out for blood. No one was trying to turn anyone in for anything. It was so strange, but so cool. I wondered that if the people on the *Mellon* had been that way, I would have actually enjoyed my time on a cutter.

The second port call was Dry Tortugas, a small group of islands located in the Gulf of Mexico at the end of the Florida Keys. Dry Tortugas is most known for the historic Fort Jefferson, a prison during the Civil War, and where Dr. Samuel Mudd, who helped Lincoln's assassin, was imprisoned.

Along with the OSs, I became friends with a few girls in the berthing. I also ran into Kat, a non-rate I was stationed with in Texas! This was her last patrol on the *Dallas* and her last unit in the Coast Guard. It was great seeing her again.

The girls in the berthing and I hung out at the fort and on the island all day. We took all sorts of pictures. We also went swimming. I had such an amazing time. I was so excited to be able to add another cool place to all the places the Coast Guard had sent me.

The two weeks I was on the *Dallas* flew by. I trained a lot of watch standers in CIC. I assisted the OS1 with EW training. I read an entire book, *Suzanne's Diary for Nicholas* by James Patterson, and I watched *The Hangover*.

Upon my arrival at Sector Mobile, I received a Bravo Zulu (a letter of recognition) from the captain and crew of the *Dallas*. I knew the OSC had a large part in that, and I thanked him for it. He thanked me for helping out his people.

I met a lot of great people. I still never wanted to get underway ever again, but I could see why some people actually preferred that life. Much like everywhere else in the Coast Guard, the people you are stationed with and your chain of command can really make or break the unit, and you. I didn't find any Clams on the Coast Guard Cutter *Dallas*.

SAR SCHOOL

In order to become an OU, you must attend a four-week school in Yorktown, VA. Yorktown is most famous as the site of the siege and subsequent surrender of British General Cornwallis to General Washington during the Revolutionary War. It was also a major port during the Civil War. If you are a history buff or love running, Yorktown is a must-go place. If not, Yorktown is tolerable.

It is approximately a 14-hour drive from Mobile. Several people had told me that the base was out in the middle of nowhere and that I'd want a car. You also usually make more money driving than flying, so I made the long drive.

My roommate was another female OS1. She was nice. She wasn't around too much, so I basically had the room to myself. That was really nice.

The first week of school was death by PowerPoint®. All the instructors took turns going over all the policies in the SAR addendum. The last three weeks were spent learning SAROPS, the computer program that calculates the drift of the water and plans searches. Policy is also covered during this time. I loved the material we were learning but caught on very quickly and was bored most of the time. I was paired with a couple of officers for some projects: a CDR, if I remember correctly and a LTJG. The JG was having trouble, having never been in a command center before, and I tried to help her out as much as possible. Later the CDR emailed my LT telling him what a joy it was to meet me and how well I did in the school, helping my classmates, including the JG. That was really nice of him and completely unexpected.

Yorktown isn't too far from Washington, DC. I had never been. One of my classmates, an officer if I remember correctly, told me that his mom lived out there so I could stay with her. It was slightly awkward, but free is free. One Friday after class I drove out, spent the night at her house, and took the train into DC the next day. I spent all day going to all the monuments. I tried to find the Holocaust Museum but got lost. I went to the Spy Museum instead. In OS A-School we learned how to guard, receive, and destroy classified material. Part of our lessons included learning about spies. Some of those same spies were mentioned at the Spy Museum and although I'm not much into history, I really enjoyed all of that. I took the train back and spent another night at the officer's mom's house and then drove home to Virginia Sunday morning. I had a really good weekend. (Later when I told my best friend about it, they could not believe that I would actually stay with a stranger. They would have gotten a hotel. It was not a matter of safety for them it was just too strange. My only consideration was whether I would be safe or not. I thought I would be and went for it. I was safe and free is free!)

The most exciting part of SAR School, though, was running into Shinedown again! The base at Yorktown is a Training Center, just like Petaluma. While OS students go to Petaluma to become OSs, other rates, such as BMs, go to Yorktown. Shinedown was one of the non-rates I was friends with on the *Mellon*. He was the one who helped me learn how to drive a manual car and one of the people who went to the Mariners going-away game with Chief G and me. He should have been mentioned more in the *Mellon* chapters, but I really don't remember the exact year he transferred or how we started hanging out. I also don't have a funny story about dropping his camera at Sea World, so I just didn't know how to include him more. Shinedown is a few years younger than I, and he is one of the nicest, most genuine people I have ever met. While the *Mellon* was mostly full of egotistical, out for blood, selfish Clams, Shinedown was the exact opposite of all of that. I don't want to make him sound cheesy or "less manly" or be all corny, but Shinedown was just so pure and innocent and I love him so much for it, especially in that environment after all I had been through. He was a true breath of fresh air.

Shinedown had transferred to BM A-School from the *Mellon* and was going to graduate while I was in SAR School. I was excited for him as I remembered helping him learn how to plot positions on a chart and do Moboards. I was proud that he had made it off the cutter and that he was going to advance and move on with his career! I was also excited to see him and to be able to hang out with him again. As if those weren't reasons enough to be happy, Shinedown asked me if I wanted to "pin him" (put his third-class crows/insignia on his collars) at his graduation!!

He had previously asked Calvin if he wanted to pin him. Calvin agreed and was going to drive out. Calvin had made BM on the cutter and had transferred to South Carolina. Shinedown and he had kept in touch and since Calvin was a BM, as well, and a good friend, it made sense for him to be the one who pinned Shinedown. I was excited to see Calvin again. Calvin and I had not kept in touch too much since the *Mellon*. We texted every now and then, but overall our friendship had kind of faded. I was excited to hang out again, like the "old days." Shinedown had no way of knowing I would be in Virginia when he graduated. I told him to just leave it be and let Calvin pin him. But Shinedown remembered me helping him out and would not have it. Shinedown said Calvin could pin one side and I could pin the other. I was beyond humbled and honored. I said as long as I could get out of class, I would definitely do it.

The SAR School instructors were unsure when I first asked them to go to Shinedown's graduation, but it ended up working out. The instructors at SAR School pack as much in as they can in the four weeks you are there so there isn't much down time or room for you to miss class. I was fortunate, though, as Shinedown's graduation was towards the end of SAR School.

The morning of Shinedown's graduation, I took my SAROPS assessment at 0700 and was ready to pin Shinedown at 1000.

Calvin and Hammer drove out and so did Shinedown's family. Hammer was the Doc on the *Mellon* when I first reported. I think he transferred early in the transfer season in 2007. We didn't hang out too often, but I do remember going to his house one time when the power was out. He had a fireplace, so a lot of us went over there to stay warm. I also remember his going away party. I have group pictures with him in San Diego, but I don't remember him standing out too much. I didn't know him that well, but I did like him. Calvin, Hammer, Shinedown, Shinedown's family, and I all went out for dinner the night before Shinedown's graduation. It was so great to be reunited with some of my best friends from the *Mellon*. I was in heaven. We were goofy as hell at dinner and took several pictures. After dinner, Shinedown went with his family and Calvin, Hammer, and I went back to a hotel. I caught up with both of them and had a lot of fun!

The next day, Calvin and I proudly pinned Shinedown as he graduated and advanced to BM3! We took several pictures afterward. Shinedown was the first person I had ever pinned, and I could not be happier about that! I cannot think of a more noteworthy or deserving person to "pop my (pinning) cherry." (Did you just cringe, Mindy? ☺)

*Side Story: As I was preparing to go to SAR School, I was debating whether or not to take my Trops (dress uniform). I knew most people would be flying versus driving and packing would be limited. It did not say anywhere in our orders that we would need our dress uniform. The uniform of the day for school was our working uniform. My best friend told me to take my Trops, just in case. They said I'd be driving, so I had room and there was no reason not to take them, but I didn't. When Shinedown asked me to pin him, I needed my Trops!! My best friend had to UPS overnight them to me!! I didn't live that down for a long time!

That same day or maybe the next day, I graduated from SAR School. I then returned to Sector Mobile to start breaking in at the OU desk. I was qualified at the OU desk in the summer of 2010. As said in a previous chapter, I was able to qualify at three of the four desks in Mobile in under a year.

After pinning Shinedown, Calvin's and my friendship re-ignited. We started keeping in touch again, and when I came back out to Virginia for Command Center School and SAROPS Train the Trainer School, I took extra leave and visited Calvin afterward. I went to South Carolina a couple other times and he came down to Mobile a couple times. The first time I went to Las Vegas was also with Calvin. We had a blast, but what happens in Vegas stays in Vegas so there won't be a chapter about that.

I visited Jack in Boston again in May of 2012, my third trip to Boston since A-School. Dee joined me for that visit, as well. It was an A-School reunion. Shinedown was stationed out there, and all of us met up and took the Samuel Adams tour together and had dinner. Shinedown and I have kept in touch since then, but that was the last time I actually saw him.

Hammer and I have been in and out of touch since York-town. He got out of the Coast Guard and lives in New York now. Since he was a Doc (and a good one at that) while he was in, I emailed him a couple times when I started to have medical problems in Petaluma. He helped me find current policy in the correct manuals. He was a true Godsend. In January of 2019, I went to New York for the first time. I stayed with someone else, but Hammer drove down and we spent an entire day together, going to Coney Island, walking across the Brooklyn Bridge, and seeing the Statue of Liberty. It was really good to see him again, and I hope he visits me in Alabama soon!

FAME AND GLORY

Most people, including myself, do not join the Coast Guard for fame or for extraordinary amounts of money. Most OUs (SAR Controllers) do not do the job so they can be publicly recognized on a regular basis. In fact, some are really happy to be behind the scenes and never be recognized at all. I did not want to be an OU for public recognition, either, but after I had been doing the job for a while, I was kind of bummed out that I had not gotten a "big case" yet and had not been in the newspaper. I understand how this sounds. My job was to assist or save people who were in danger. If I was not busy, that meant people were not in danger (hopefully!). But I had trained for a specific job, and I wanted to be able to perform that job. My LT told me to be patient. He told me that one day I would get a "big case" or be in the newspaper, although, he reminded me that was not a good reason to be doing the job.

That day came at the end of May in 2011. I had been qualified for around 11 months. I came in for day watch (Our watches were from 6-6, either day or night.) and the night watch stander had a long brief waiting for me. He had gotten a call from a worried wife the night before that her husband was not back on time from a fishing trip. The wife had limited information about the boat, who her husband was with, and where they had gone. Most of the time her husband and his friends went to a specific spot, but this outing they had decided to hire a professional fishing captain to go with them and show them some new spots. Throughout the night, the watch stander was able to find out who three of the four people on board were, more about the boat, and a little bit more about where they might be. He came up with a search area and had dispatched several units, but the four guys were still missing when I arrived in the morning.

Searching in the day is easier for several reasons. I had more resources available to me than the night watch stander did. I was able to reach out to businesses and marinas that had been closed the night before. I was able to launch more assets, not just Coast Guard assets, to search. I was also really proud of myself, though, for thinking outside of the box. I called Sector Mobile's fisheries' guy to try to find out who was the professional captain, the fourth guy, on the boat. The SU worked with the fisheries officer on a regular basis to enforce boating safety and other regulations. Calling the fisheries officer for help on a SAR case wasn't a "normal" SAR procedure or phone call. He came through for me, though, and learned the captain's name.

The searches the night watch stander had planned were nearing their end, and I was trying to come up with a new plan for how to proceed. I had set a few things up when I received a phone call from a Good Samaritan. A guy staying at a condo reported seeing a "small raft, going in circles, a couple miles offshore."

I will admit that when the phone call first came in, I was rather annoyed. Most reports from condos were not very accurate, and I did not have time to chase down something fake when I was busy with something very real. I did my job, though. No matter what I personally felt, I always did my job. It was a good thing, too, because when I plotted where this "small raft" might be, it was in the middle of where I was searching. Now I had a choice to make. Do I pull assets off of the current search for the new case? Or do I send someone else out for the new case? Is this the same case? Who do I send?

After consulting with the watch team, we called a local government agency that we worked with often, told them about the "small raft" and asked them to go out and look for it. I continued the other searches for the original case. After a little while, the other agency called and asked for more guidance on where the "small raft" was. My watch team directed them where to go.

After some time and confusion, we found out that the "small raft" was actually a capsized vessel and four guys were sitting on top of it. After more time and confusion (We had the four regular watch standers, plus the command day workers, plus a few people in training. There were a lot of phone calls from different agencies, Coast Guard units, family members, etc, being taken by all the people in the command center. It was organized chaos.) we found out that the capsized vessel was the boat that we had been searching for all night. The four guys needed some medical attention, but they were all alive and doing well under the circumstances.

I was very relieved. I was also proud of myself and the watch team at Sector Mobile. We had all worked well together and we were able to find and save the guys we were looking for. I thought outside of the box and used resources that were not usually used. Some of the information I gathered was not correct (I found out later) but I did find out who the captain was and during SAR cases, you have to adapt and be flexible to all information coming in. There were a lot of lessons to be learned, and they were discussed later, but overall, it was a great case with a happy ending.

I called the family and let them know the good news. I think they had already heard. I called the Good Samaritan and told him the good news. He was thrilled he was able to help. I stood the rest of the watch beaming. This is what I had trained for, and I had done well. I was partially responsible for saving four lives. This is why I joined the Coast Guard. I did a good job. My team did a good job.

The next day there was an article in the newspaper. I was excited for all of 30 seconds until I saw that the local government agency that we had directed to go search had taken credit for the entire case!!! I understand that when the press meets the boat at the pier, they see the people on scene. I understand that they will be the people in the pictures and they, of course, will be mentioned. What I could not understand was the interviews with them. They did not mention the Coast Guard one time. They literally had taken credit for receiving all the initial information, for responding, for searching, and for finding the four guys. How could they? My LT reminded me that I was not doing the job for the media attention. He also reminded me that I had done a good job the day before and, most importantly, the four guys were alive. He was right so I calmed down. I was on watch again and had a job to do. I needed to focus.

Later that morning, I received a phone call from the wife who had originally reported her husband missing. She had read the newspaper article, as well, and she was upset that the Coast Guard was not mentioned. She wanted me to tell her how the other agency had gotten involved and what happened. I followed the Coast Guard's public affairs rules and told her as much as I could about how all the events unfolded. The wife had no idea there was a Good Samaritan involved and she wanted to know his name and phone number. She wanted to call him and thank him. I told her that I could not give her his phone number, but with her permission, I would give him a call and let him know she wanted to talk to him and give him her phone number. She ageed, thanked me, and hung up.

I called the Good Samaritan and relayed that the family wanted to thank him. He took the wife's phone number and said he would call her. I was thankful that I could get them in touch with each other. The Good Samaritan deserved to be recognized for what he had done. I was also thankful that the wife wanted the Coast Guard to get some recognition, too. But I kept my LT's words in my head, stayed humble, and continued with my watch.

The following Saturday, the story made the front page of the local newspaper. The article was so long it carried over to another page. The wife had talked to everyone involved, including the four guys on board the boat. After she had everyone's stories, she called the newspaper. The new article included where the guys went, what they were doing, how and why the boat capsized, what was going through their heads, how all agencies involved were notified, all their efforts, and the Good Samaritan.

I called my mom. I bought a few copies of that newspaper, and my mom found the article online. Since she is a printer, she blew it up for me. It is still framed and proudly hanging on my wall today.

The headline of the article is "Sunken Boaters Relied on Faith." I was beyond amazed at how all the events of this case unfolded. It was my first big case. It was a successful case; all four guys lived. The watch team, including me, was inexperienced, but we all performed extremely well. A condo report was real. I had treated it like it was real, so nothing bad came out of that. There was a newspaper article and a corrected newspaper article. That never happens!! And the guys onboard were Christians. When I write my book on how God takes you through bad things to lead to good things and how hard work pays off, this story will have to be in it!!

Throughout the next three years, several of my cases made the newspaper. Most of them had good outcomes. A few were really tragic. Sometimes my name was mentioned; most of the time it was not. My actual picture was never in the paper. I was on television once. I was excited beforehand and extremely nervous during and after. The piece was covering an anniversary of a bad event. I hope that my short phrase did not upset anyone who lost anyone and only added to the narrative in an informative or positive way. I also never personally met anyone I "saved." Sometimes this takes a toll on people. I've heard 911 operators have been bummed out by it, as well. The way I always look at it is that I never pulled a dead body out of the water. I never held a child who was bleeding out. I never performed CPR on someone, to have them die in my arms. I wasn't on scene, by choice, for a reason. So, if I wasn't the first to get my picture taken or be recognized after, that was OK, too.

I printed out all the articles and still have a three-ring binder with them in it. I can't stress enough how proud I am for the work that I did while I was in the Coast Guard, especially in Mobile. I did not do the job for fame or fortune. There are several cases that were great that did not make the paper. But those articles are nice reminders of all I accomplished. I also used them for training aids when I taught in Petaluma and someday, maybe my grandchildren will read them and get to know me a little better. The fact that I was as successful as I was, and that I am as proud as I am of my record, makes the fact that I got discharged even more bittersweet.

COMMAND CENTER SCHOOL

My first couple of years in Mobile, there was an OS1 on the OU desk named Sam. Sam transferred to Virginia and became part of the Coast Guard Sector Standardization (STAN) Team. STAN is similar to TACT on a cutter. The STAN Team comes into the Command Center (Sector) and looks at all of the manuals, training records, and other admin things to ensure that they are all up to date and being used in the proper manner. After that, just like on the cutter, Sector personnel conduct drills. On the cutter, the drills were responding to fake emergencies, such as fires or flooding. At a Sector, the drills are fake SAR, pollution, fisheries, law enforcement, and other such cases. Sam told me shortly after reporting into Virginia that all personnel at command centers were going to be required to go to Command Center School. He said that as soon as that was made a requirement, everyone would be putting their name on the list to go so there would be a long wait to get into a class. Sam suggested I take his insider tip, so I put my name on the list to attend the school.

In February of 2011, I went back to Yorktown, VA, for three weeks for Command Center School. One of the civilians that worked with me at Sector Mobile was to be in the same class. We decided to "caravan" up: we left around the same time, stayed at the same hotel for a night, and then arrived in VA at around the same time. This was nice for me because I am normally a drive from point A to point B person and kill myself doing it. By driving up with the civilian, I was able to break the drive into two days, enjoy a nice hotel for a night, and ensure I was safe.

I had two roommates while I was in Command Center School, both of whom were OS3s. Stephanie was stationed in Michigan, and Sofia was stationed in Florida, I think. I don't think I got off on the right foot with the two of them. I didn't intend to be snobby, but I was kind of surprised that they put an E6 in a room with two E4s. I didn't think I was better than they and really didn't mind. I probably should have kept my mouth shut, but I was just surprised and said so aloud.

Despite sticking my foot in my mouth, I ended up getting along with them for the first week or so. After that, I'm not exactly sure what happened. Sofia just started acting really weird when I would hang out with Stephanie. Eventually she even told me she did not want me to hang out with Stephanie at all. Since I'm not 12 and since Stephanie did not care who I did and did not hang out with, I continued to hang out with Stephanie. This ended up causing a lot of tension in our room.

Our entire class went out to eat one night and one of the guys was talking about his girlfriend. Sofia had been giving people advice on and off the entire meal, but for some reason she decided to really jump on this guy about his relationship. I forget what was said, exactly, but at one point she started a sentence with, "If I were you . . ."

I was tired of listening to it all. Sofia fought with her husband on Skype almost every night. I looked at her and said, "If I were you, I'd stop giving other people advice when my relationship wasn't so good."

I should not have embarrassed her like that. It was not my "fight" and I should have stayed out of it. I had simply had enough, though. The entire class was out to dinner and she felt it necessary to grill this guy about his girlfriend. "Two wrongs don't make a right," but that is why I said what I said.

After that dinner, Command Center School berthing became just like A-School berthing, only now I wasn't caught in the middle of two girls fighting; I was part of the fight. That's not entirely accurate. Stephanie and I did not go out of our way to irritate Sofia. We did, however, find humor in how easy it was to achieve. Sofia was extremely passive aggressive. The last week of school, we invited the class to our room for pizza. Sofia decided to do laundry in the middle of the "party." It was what it was.

Command Center School is awful. I shouldn't write that. I know it has a purpose, and I suppose some people really gain a lot from it. I did gain a lot from it, but more indirectly. The goal of Command Center School is for all the Command Centers (Sectors) to be standard. In theory, if I left Mobile and went anywhere else in the country, I should be able to stand watch with little or no problem once I learned the new area of responsibility (AOR). In practice, however, a lot of things differ dramatically from Sector to Sector. For example, Michigan has ice; Alabama does not. Miami has a lot of immigration cases; Portland does not. Some Sectors are extremely busy; others are not. Every Sector has different local agencies and resources available to them. You cannot standardize things that are not standard. This is just my humble opinion, but since the school is still going today, obviously the people paid more than I do not agree.

The first week of Command Center School was similar to SAR School: death by PowerPoint®. Again, all the instructors took turns going over every Command Center policy. We had quizzes every morning. It was straight up boring as ****. This indirectly helped me, though, because at Sector Mobile's next STAN visit, I aced the test. Most of the questions were the same as the ones on our quizzes in Command Center. It is also very good to know policy. I don't disagree with that at all. I just don't agree with how it was presented to us.

After that, our class was divided into mock Sectors to practice cases. I don't even want to write about how big a mess I considered that to be. Maybe it really wasn't. Maybe I am too critical. I did not enjoy it, and I do not think I learned anything from it. That is all I will say.

The two biggest things I got out of Command Center School were, first, a larger network. I kept in touch with a lot of people from my class. One of the guys, "Happy Meal," was stationed in Charleston, South Carolina. We would chat on communicator when we stood watch together. If one of us had a case, and the other didn't, we would go into the system and read what the other one had going on. We were both very intelligent, and both very good at our jobs, so we rarely needed to help each other out. But once in a while, one of us would spot something and suggest it to the other. It was kind of nice having a third party look over your case and help you think outside the box. I also keep in touch with Stephanie to this day. She and I have both been through a lot, both as individuals, and together. I'm proud of us for continuing with our journeys. She is about to graduate college here soon, and I am so happy for her.

The second thing I got out of Command Center School was the ability and authority to break in as Command Duty Officer (CDO)—as an E6/OS1, upon my return to Sector Mobile. I had been back for a month or so and just started thinking about it one day. I was qualified on the three desks (CU, SU, and OU) and now I knew all the policy from Command Center School. If I wanted to make Senior Chief, I would need the CDO or an equivalent qualification. That was two advancements away, but I also didn't know if I would get another Sector after Mobile or if I'd be going to a unit with an equivalent qualification. I didn't really care one way or the other about the position itself; I just really thought it would open up more doors for me in the future if I had it. I emailed the LT, kind of expecting a "No." I didn't necessarily think he would flat out say "No"; I just thought there would be a catch or something else I'd have to do before he said "Yes." His email reply was, "You have Dirlauth to start breaking in CDO." I remember the "word" because I had to look it up. I had never heard the term before and did not know if he said "Yes" or "No." Someone finally told me that it meant Direct Launch Authority! I was excited!

In the summer of 2011 the LT transferred, along with a lot of other people in the Command Center. Transfer season is always crazy for several reasons, but mainly because the number of qualified watch standers is much less than the month before. Of course, losing your LT (the "boss") makes it even harder. I did not stop standing watches at the OU desk, but instead started going over stuff with the current CDOs when I had a slow watch. My break in process didn't really officially start until around Jan of 2012, I think. The new LT was unsure about it at first, but quickly learned it was Ok from the rest of the command and did not have any personal objections to it. It was a strange process due to everything going on, but in April of 2012, I passed my oral board and became Sector Mobile's first and only (at that time) E6 CDO.

5KS AND TRAINING

Sometime while I was in Mobile, the Coast Guard revamped the "fat boy" weight program. They came up with a new system for calculating your "maximum allowable weight" (MAW). Instead of having to weigh in at less than 148 pounds, I was now allowed to be less than 160 pounds.

The Coast Guard also came up with a new method for calculating BMI. Instead of the wrist, waist, hips method used while I was in A-School and on the *Mellon*, the new method was adding waist and the fattest part of the buttocks (Yes, that is the exact wording in the manual.) and subtracting the neck. So, they added the two fattest parts of my body together and then subtracted the smallest part. This was supposedly a huge improvement and allowed more people to be able to pass tape. It didn't help me out any.

Fortunately, I was never on the weight program while I was in Mobile. Part of it certainly had to do with the extra twelve pounds I was now allowed to have. The other part had to do with not being forced to eat Coast Guard food (as when at a Training Center or underway) and working out on a more routine basis. Although, my workout routine had to be very, very specific in order to stay within the Coast Guard standards...

The first two years I was in Mobile, I ran here and there. I ran on the treadmills at the gym on base while I was in SAR School in Virginia. I also, as mentioned above, could control what I ate and tried to stick to the routine that I had learned while I was in camp before the Coast Guard. The twelve extra pounds gave me some cushion room, but I was still very concerned about weigh-ins and being overweight. I was walking (and running!) a very thin line, and I knew it.

In 2011, I found a personal trainer. Lisa was married to a Coastie stationed at the Aviation Training Center in Mobile. She had been a personal trainer for over ten years and consistently took more classes and tried to learn more about the body, nutrition, and the latest work-out routines. Since we could work out on base, there wasn't a gym fee. She charged me $20 an hour and I started working out three times a week.

We would start the workout with a walk or run. Then we would do a lot of the same exercises they would do in CrossFit, but Lisa would never, ever time me. For one, I did not want to be timed. I refused to work out that way. The major reason I didn't want to be timed was to make sure I was doing all the exercises the proper way and not losing form because I was trying to beat the clock. So, Lisa did not force me to be timed,

I also lifted some weights and used TRX suspension training equipment. I really, really enjoyed TRX. Something about using my own body weight to do all the exercises really made me happy.

As I worked out with Lisa, my body started to change. I started losing inches all over. I lost some around my arms, chest, waist, hips, and thighs. I lost twelve inches in total. I started getting compliments at work and from strangers. My confidence started going up. I really liked Lisa and her style. I enjoyed talking to her and getting to know her. I enjoyed being able to lift heavier weights and do more repetitions. It was nice to see progress.

I also gained twelve pounds. Most people would not think much of this. Most people would assume that it was muscle weight. Or most people would just ignore it. My body was changing in such great ways, making a lot of progress. Most people could see all of these things as being good things and ignore the weight gain.

I was not most people, though. The Coast Guard said I had to weigh less than 160 pounds, but I now weighed around 170 pounds. And semiannual weigh-ins were right around the corner.

I had lost inches around my waist, hips, and butt, but not enough to be under the BMI for the Coast Guard. I have child-bearing hips!! And my neck is very small.

So, there I was, happy with a personal trainer and happy with my body, but not able to make Coast Guard weight standards. So, I stopped working out with Lisa, starved myself, and weighed in at exactly 160 pounds.

After weigh-ins, Lisa tried to modify our workouts. She tried to add more cardio and fewer weights. She also tried to incorporate more stretching, as I was always in a lot of pain after we worked out, and it took me a long time to recover from workouts. She did a lot of research. She wanted to know why I didn't have much energy, and why I was in so much pain and didn't recover after workouts. She frequently told me that I was one of her most dedicated clients, and I worked just as hard, if not harder than everyone else, for fewer results. It was a puzzle to her, and she didn't like it. She kept asking me if I had any health problems. As far as I knew, I just had PMDD and acid reflux, neither of which should have affected my weight or work outs, except maybe loss of energy during my period. Lisa was convinced that there was something else going on, but she wasn't a doctor and didn't know what it was. Lisa was used to being able to modify workouts and diets and helping her clients out. This was why she continuously took classes. She wanted to be the best. She was very disappointed that she could not figure out how to help me.

On top of the Coast Guard weight issue and everything else listed above, Lisa started having some health and personal problems of her own, so eventually I stopped working out with her. We have remained friends and have kept in touch, but I have never hired her to train me again.

Since Nate taught me how to run after high school, I've always really enjoyed it. A lot of people at Sector Mobile ran. A couple of the guys really enjoyed running 5Ks. I ran a 5K before the Coast Guard and had a lot of fun. My time was 29:30.

After I stopped working out with Lisa, I knew I had to do something to stay within Coast Guard weight standards. Since working out with Lisa didn't work out for Coast Guard weigh ins, I decided I should start running more again. One of the guys convinced me that running outside was more fun than running on the treadmill. It took me a while to give it a try, but he was right. It also helped more when running 5Ks because they are all outside. I couldn't run six miles every day anymore, like before the Coast Guard, but I found that running 2-3 miles every other day or so was very doable. I found a massage therapist in Mobile that also knew how to do myofascial release, so I was able to keep my plantar fasciitis in check. In 2012, I made it a goal of mine to run at least one 5K every month. I was running about 10 miles every week, trying to get my endurance up and keep my weight down while also taking care of my body and, especially, my feet. The first 5K I ran, I came in at around 45 minutes. My goal was to get back down to less than 30 minutes again. The guys on base told me about a website that listed all the 5Ks in the area every month. I did a couple 5Ks on my own, but most of the races the guys signed up for, too, and we went together. We never ran together once the race started because they all ran faster than I and earned medals. But most of the time we would carpool to the race and hang out after and get something to eat.

Towards the middle of the year, I had several T-Shirts. One of the guys actually had so many T-shirts he stopped "claiming" them at his races. Another guy gave them to his dog or donated them. I was so proud of myself for running that much. My time wasn't under 30 minutes just yet, but it was slowly improving. I also really liked some of the T-shirt designs, especially if the race was for a charity or cause that I really believed in, such as the Coast Guard's Run to Remember.

Right before I transferred off the *Mellon*, Calvin had made me a T-shirt quilt. I had a bunch of T-shirts from boot camp, A-school, all of our patrols, and from bands we saw in port. I didn't want to wear them because they were all from special events or meant something, and I didn't want to ruin them. I also didn't want to keep them hidden in a box somewhere. The solution was to make a quilt out of them, and Calvin knew how to sew.

Somewhere in the middle of the year, I decided that I would have a quilt made of my 5K shirts, too. I did not stop "claiming" mine. My dog did not get them. The new Command Center LT (the one that transferred in after the prior Army guy) was a great seamstress and made quilts all the time. She and I got along really well, and she knew how hard I was working to get under 30 minutes and to stay under 160 pounds. At the end of the year, I gave all my shirts to the LT, and she made me another quilt! Her sewing machine was fancy, so she included an embroidered square in the middle that says, "My Year of 5Ks (top of circle), Hillary Herbst (bottom of circle), 2012-2013 (middle of circle)."

I have one Facebook status that popped up in my memories recently. On April 1, 2013, my Facebook status was, "Today, for the first time in 8 years, I weighed in UNDER my max allowable weight without having to starve myself or any other shenanigans. Note that it is also the 1st of the month, not the 31st."

Weigh-ins for the Coast Guard occur every April and October. Some units have a designated day that everyone has to weigh in. Some units leave it up to you when you want to weigh in as long as you weigh in before the end of the month. Since I usually had to starve myself, I usually waited until the end of the month. In April of 2013, all the running and 5Ks paid off. I made weigh-ins without having to starve myself.

I continued to run, including 5Ks, the next two years in Mobile. I'm fairly certain April of 2013 was the only time I was able to weigh in on the 1st without issue, though. My weight also played a large role (no pun intended . . .) in why I wasn't eager to make Chief.

THOUGHTS ON CHIEF

When I first joined the Coast Guard, chief meant something. It was a rank with a lot of respect. The chief was the subject-matter expert, the role model, the one to be respected or feared, the one whose presence you could feel as soon as they entered the room. There is also a lot of tradition and history behind the chief rank and the chief's anchors and I was fascinated by all of it.

In A-School I put the cutter at the top of my list in order to get my sea time out of the way to make chief. In Mobile, the LT set me up for success by having me stand watch at all three desks so I could make chief. I advanced to first class petty officer/OS1/E6 in September of 2009. The SWE to advance to chief is only once a year instead of twice a year. In May of 2011 I was eligible, and I took my first SWE for chief. If I remember correctly, my score was just above average. I took the SWE to make chief every year after until I was discharged in 2018. I only studied for the exam two of those years, maybe three.

Besides the fact that I have incredibly poor study habits, I had reasons why I wanted to advance, and I had very specific reasons why I didn't. The reasons varied from year to year and from Mobile to Petaluma. I thought I would be more motivated to advance in Petaluma, but I was actually less motivated at that unit. At first the rank of chief scared me. All the qualities that chief represented, was I those things? Was I a subject-matter expert? A role model? Someone to be feared and respected? I spoke about it to one of the officers who stood CDO. In a former life, he had been an OS chief. He told me that he thought I was those things, but he also told me to think of everyone else I knew who was eligible to make chief. He told me that whether they were "qualified" or not, I could be sure that they were going to take the SWE. He asked me if I wanted to work with them or for them. That put things into perspective. That might have been one of the years I actually studied for the SWE.

I remember one year in Mobile, probably 2011, maybe 2012, there were four of us who were eligible to take the SWE. We all studied really hard and all four of us had scores between 80 and 85. Two of them advanced. The other guy and I were so far down on the advancement list, there was no hope for us whatsoever. As said before, the SWE score is not your final score for advancement. Your evaluations, time in service, sea time, award points, and other things are calculated in as well. When comparing those who made it to the two of us who didn't, the only real difference was the amount of time in service we all had. For me to advance, I would either need to score much higher to make up for my lack of time in or wait until I had more time in. I was pretty bitter after that and it became one reason that I lost interest in advancing.

Another reason I lost interest, especially in Petaluma, was because, in my humble opinion, chief stopped having those same meanings in the Coast Guard. Chiefs are no longer the subject-matter experts and they are no longer really allowed to be feared or respected. Even if they were allowed, most of them don't deserve it, and I don't see most of them as being good role models. Most of what I saw chiefs doing was administration BS and taking care of personal problems. I went from fearing that I wasn't good enough for the job to fearing that the job was no longer good enough for me.

But the main reason I did not want to make chief and did not study for the SWE, except for those few situations, was fear that the promotion would, in reality, cause a demotion for me. I was having trouble making weight with the regular biannual weigh-ins and in Petaluma did not make all of them. If I made chief, I would have to weigh in before advancing, during Chief's Call To Indoctrination (CCTI), during the Chief Petty Officers Academy (CPOA), and God knows when else. That is at least three more weigh-ins than normal. If I failed any of those, there would be very negative consequences, including being back on the "fat boy" program, not graduating CPOA, losing my anchors, and possibly being discharged from the Coast Guard. I thought the elusive advancement would be my ticket out of the Coast Guard. The longer I was in the Coast Guard and the more health problems I started to have, the less I wanted chief and the less I tried for it. A couple people who knew me well noticed that I wasn't really trying for it. One guy even tried to call me out for it and "mentor" me. I think, for the most part though, I had people fooled. I wanted to fool the command so that my evaluations and potential awards would not be affected by my lack of motivation. I don't know if I really did or not; in the end, it didn't matter.

It's weird what people consider normal. How you are raised is normal to you until you are in a different environment later in life, and things are not the same. The way I was "raised" in the Coast Guard is that everything in my job was affected by how much I weighed. My evaluations included a section for health and well-being. Low evaluations can affect your overall score after the SWE and your place on the list to advance. My award on the *Mellon* was knocked down because I was on the "fat boy" program twice. There were more consequences in Petaluma and it eventually led to my discharge. For ten plus years, I thought this was normal. I did not realize how unhealthy this was for me until I started seeing my therapist. For ten plus years my self-worth, my identity, my happiness, and my physical and mental well-being were all wrapped up in what I weighed. I understand that most people worry about their weight. I understand that most people's health and their weight can go hand in hand. I say can because it doesn't always. For me, my weight meant even more than those things. I did not consider myself to be that fat. My self-image was not that bad ... until the Coast Guard told me it should be. Can you imagine not wanting or not being able to get a promotion at your job because of what you weigh? Can you imagine your pay depending on your weight? I understand most of the reasons the Coast Guard and other branches have weight standards. I'm not saying that it is unfair or that they shouldn't. The guidelines and procedures for weigh ins and especially for calculating BMI need to change, though. And at the end of the day, a healthy weight does not equal healthy, your weight does not determine your self-worth, and I am happy I am no longer in that environment. I have a new normal now and it feels great. At the end of the day, I have no regrets about not making chief.

COAST GUARD 6535

"Coast Guard Sector Mobile this is Coast Guard Helicopter 6535, we are departing ATC Mobile enroute to Mobile Bay to conduct training with the M/V *Solomon*. We have four people onboard and XX hours of fuel. Request you assume our radio guard, over."

It was Feb 28, 2012. I went to bed pretty early, around 7:30 or 8 pm. The phone rang and I was awake enough to hear it but asleep enough to not want to answer it. Then came the voice-mail alert: It was Sector Mobile's Response Chief/SAR Mission Controller. "Hillary, we need you to come to the command center as soon as possible. A Coast Guard helicopter went down in the bay."

I was immediately awake. A Coast Guard helicopter. One of our own. Down in the bay. I threw on a sweatshirt (I did not bother with my uniform) and drove like a bat out of hell to the base. The gate, which is normally shut at night, was manned and the guard waved me right on. I drove back to the command center.

I walked in and most of the watch standers were on the phone. The guy at the SU desk was helping the CU because there was so much radio traffic. I sat down at his desk and used his computer. The OU handed me all his notes. So did the CDO. We had a computer program to keep a timeline of events, as well as scan in all important documents. I immediately started typing their notes into the program and answering phone calls. Bit by bit I was starting to understand what happened and what was going on. It was so surreal.

Sector Mobile assumed the radio guard for CG 6535 and

other helicopters just before sunset. The CU was requesting and receiving operations and position reports from all the helicopters, as per regulations, and everything was going well. CG 6535 eventually called in and reported that they were done with training for the night and were heading back to ATC Mobile. At the next required check in time, the CU could not reach CG 6535 on the radio. The CU began Coast Guard lost communication's procedures. The CDO had a really bad gut feeling and called Station Dauphin Island to launch a small boat. Then the M/V *Solomon* came over the radio and reported, "Coast Guard Sector Mobile this is the M/V Solomon, I see a Coast Guard helicopter tail sticking out of the water in position..."

There were two Aids to Navigation (ANT) team boats in Mobile Bay conducting training that night. Ordinarily, we do not use ANT teams for search and rescue, but the BMs are trained, and they were right there. One of the 26-foot boats found the first flight member. The crew performed CPR all the way back to Sector where the ambulance met them. Unfortunately, the flight member did not make it. There were three other flight members missing.

The CDO briefed the command and asked for additional help on the watch floor. Shortly after SMC called me. I arrived about an hour after the report of the crash. Now I was in the command center doing everything I could to assist the watch and praying that the crew was still alive. The Captain and others in the command came up for briefs and to see the search plans. One of the other CDOs was a former pilot so she came up to lend her expertise. She was extremely helpful. When it was reported that helmets were found, she had to excuse herself and cry in the bathroom. She knew that finding helmets was a bad sign. We all had to excuse ourselves at one point or another. The atmosphere was full of shock. We were like robots. We were doing our jobs with muscle memory. It was the epitome of why we trained as hard as we did. We were putting together search patterns and dispatching units. Several Local Government Agencies (LGAs) volunteered to help. We were using a white board marker to write down who was going where and what their estimated time of arrival (ETA) was. We were a well-oiled machine, pushing our emotions to the side to try to find our shipmates.

Families were calling in to find out if it was their son, daughter, or spouse on the flight. We eventually found out who the four crewmembers were, but we were not allowed to release the information until the families were notified. We were told all those affairs were being handled by the Air Station and to forward those calls over to them. I was thankful that I did not recognize the names. The Command Duty Officer did, though. He knew one of the guys very well. He took a minute to himself and then kept on with his job. There was a possibility his friend was still alive, and he wanted to save him if he could.

Along with the SAR aspect of the crash, investigators wanted to know what happened and why the helicopter crashed. It was very important to them to collect evidence, such as what was left of the helicopter and the black box. They were respectful and patient, but that was one more element that we had to arrange for.

Most of that first night is a blur to me. At some point the next day's watch started to show up. Pass downs and future plans had to be given and made. I started calling all of the OUs and SUs to make new schedules to account for the additional help that would be needed.

It took divers three times to find out if there was anyone in the helicopter's cockpit. At the confluence of five rivers, Mobile Bay's water is never clear. They could not see through the muck the first couple of dives. The investigators wanted the helicopter and the black box to start their investigation into what exactly happened. Once the cockpit was cleared, they hoisted it out of the water and brought it back to Sector. I refused to go look at it. I did not want to see a mangled helicopter. My rule, in general, was to see as few pictures as possible. That was my way of separating things. That was my way of making things less real. Several other watch standers went out to see it.

Eventually the command set up the Incident Command System (ICS). A group of people was put together to strictly deal with almost all things helicopter related. The OU's still had to plan searches for Coast Guard assets and the CU's had to maintain communications on the radio, but we also had other cases coming in that needed our attention. We were not equipped to handle the volume of phone calls and radio traffic for the crash and our other case load. ICS was used to supplement those phone calls and some radio communications for the crash, so we could also respond to other cases in our AOR. One of the things the ICS team came up with was to divide Mobile Bay into a grid and assign LGAs certain sections of the grid to search every day. The small boat stations in Pascagoula, Mississippi, and Pensacola, Florida, sent small boats and boat crew members to the station on Dauphin Island. At least one small boat was on scene, searching at all times. Air Station New Orleans sent aircraft to ATC Mobile. ATC Mobile personnel and assets were not to be used in the search; they were all on a safety stand down. Twice a day Coast Guard personnel and LGAs met in the Incident Command Center (ICC) for debriefs of the day's events and briefs for future searches.

On March 8, 2012, nine days after the initial crash, the fourth flight member was recovered 2.5 miles southwest of the crash site. I was in and out of the command center all nine of those days. Sometimes I was standing watch; others I was assisting the watch. I did my best to gather the information the investigators needed when I was assisting the watch so the watch standers could focus on their job. I put together briefs for the Command and ICC as well as separate briefs for the families of the flight crew. I kept track of how many miles were searched, by whom, where, and when. I did my best to make sure everyone was doing all right and had what they needed. We took several reports of people in the water during our search and after. Some were logs or dead boars; some were actually people. Our hearts dropped into our stomachs every time one of those reports came in. Our jobs lent to having dark senses of humor. There were extremely tough days when no one spoke to each other; we just did our jobs and went home. There were other days when we were making incredibly inappropriate jokes trying to cope with the tragedy of losing our own. I remember at one brief with the entire base, including the support rates, YN and SKs, one of the commanders made a joke. All of the OS's laughed. The rest of the base looked horrified that a commander would ever say something so awful. The captain understood where all of his crew was coming from and did his best to quickly change the subject. All of us called our families and told them we loved them. Some people couldn't drive home without shaking, crying, or making those phone calls.

The investigation was running parallel, as much as it could, to the search. Once the search was over, the investigation went into over-drive. The night of the crash, the CU on duty was standing his first watch since qualifying as CU. He was scared out of his mind that he did not correctly respond to the situation. I kept reassuring him that I had seen all the evidence, listened to his radio calls, read his logs, looked over his paperwork, read the manuals and policies and that he did everything he could. He followed all of the procedures that were in place at that time. After the case, more procedures were put in place that came from lessons learned. Though there were several lessons learned, the CU had done everything correctly, as did all the other watch standers that initial night. Sector was "cleared" in the final investigation report. That didn't offer much relief, though. At the end of the day, four of our own were still not with us anymore. None of us would ever be the same again.

An LT was dispatched from Houston, if I remember correctly, a couple days into the search. She was to provide Critical Incident Stress Management (CISM) for anyone who needed it. I spoke with her a few times on the watch floor, but never in private. She was very kind and well needed during that time. We all appreciated her being there whether we used her services or not. I'm not sure if she went to the other units or if other qualified CISM members did but everyone, as far as I know, was offered whatever they needed to help them cope with what happened.

Funerals were planned. The CDO whose friend was a crew member took leave to attend his funeral. A memorial service was put together at ATC. A lot of Sector personnel attended. I did not.

The Mobile community really wrapped their arms around all of us. The gate at ATC was full of posters, flowers, and cards for the fallen and the Coast Guard members still stationed or training there. I passed a Shell gas station and their sign said "Thanks Coast Guard for all you do. We love and pray for you."

I don't remember how I first saw the gas station or if someone told me about the sign. It was not in a part of Mobile that I normally frequented. However, I made it a point to fill up at that gas station the next few times my tank was near empty. And I took a picture of their sign and put it in my binder with all my newspaper articles.

A local owner of several restaurants, including Ruth's Chris Steak House and Blue Gill Restaurant, offered Coast Guard personnel 50% off their meals at his restaurants for one weekend a couple weeks after the crash. My best friend, one of the SUs, and I went to Ruth's Chris. The staff was extremely kind to us and the meal was phenomenal.

In June 2013, the Thomas Cameron Memorial Foundation put together the first Aviator Memorial Run in Milton, Florida. Thomas was the pilot who passed away in the crash. I participated with the OS1 who had helped run the command center with me. Alex Cameron, Thomas' brother, crossed the finish line first, completing the race in a little over fifteen minutes. I hope to participate in the race next year. I'm sorry I missed it this year.

One of the many lessons I learned during my twelve years

in the Coast Guard was to look for the good after any tragic event. The community in Sabine Pass, Texas, came together after Hurricane Katrina to help all the survivors from New Orleans. After Hurricane Rita hit, more people came in to help the Sabine Pass community, including *Extreme Home Makeover*. The community in Mobile supported the Coast Guard after CG 6535 crashed. I saw it again in California after fires devastated nearby towns. It is always extremely bittersweet to me to see food banks, fundraisers, donations, the "cavalry" from other areas coming into town, and people rebuilding their lives. It always makes me thankful for what I have and makes me look for ways that I can pitch in. It gives me hope in the strength and kindness of humanity.

The crash was hard for me, for obvious reasons, but I did not know the four flight crew members. I thought that I came out of the situation relatively unharmed. One of the lessons in Operations Specialist A-School is Critical Incident Communications. A critical incident (in the Coast Guard) is an incident of national interest. The lesson includes three posters with pictures of incidents for the students to read about and determine if they were critical or not. One of the posters had a picture of a mangled helicopter on it. I was shadowing the lesson one of the first weeks I was an instructor and was not in any way prepared to see that poster. I never looked at the helicopter in Mobile when it was brought back to Sector. I had never intended to look at it. All of a sudden, an incident I had some separation from was now incredibly real to me. I had to leave the classroom immediately and it took me some time to get used to seeing that poster. I wanted to avoid hearing, seeing, or teaching that lesson, as well. Eventually, however, I ended up volunteering to instruct it. I also volunteered to instruct the Lost Communications lesson where the students learn the procedures to follow when they lose communications with a Coast Guard asset on the radio. I brought in my binder with all my newspaper articles and the final mishap report for the crash. I told all the students about the crash. I made sure every student that I ever taught knew the importance of keeping good communications with their assets, as well as keeping good radio etiquette and proper radio logs. At first the lessons were very hard for me to teach. Later it became very therapeutic for me. I told all my students that what I was teaching them on a good day would save a fellow Coast Guardsman's life and on a bad day would save their careers. I was proud that this tragic event could bring perspective and instruction to a new generation of Coasties with hope that they would be enabled to save lives.

Coast Guard pilots attend school in Milton, Florida. Once their training is complete, they are assigned an Air Station and go out into the fleet. Eventually they will have to complete T22 training at Aviation Training Center (ATC) Mobile. They also will have to come to ATC Mobile annually for training such as day and night flying and hoisting the stokes litter and rescue swimmer.

The majority of the training is conducted in Mobile Bay. Occasionally Sector Mobile will divert a helicopter for a real SAR case. The M/V *Solomon* was a "retired" Coast Guard 41- foot boat. The owner of the *Solomon* worked hand in hand with the helicopters, allowing them to conduct hoist training on the stern. It was not uncommon for Sector Mobile to have six to ten radio guards for helicopters training in the Bay. If Sector was unable to reach one of the helicopters on the radio, Sector reached out to the *Solomon* to see if they were working with the helicopter.

LPO AND 1.4

The Senior Chief and I reported into Mobile the same day. Sector Mobile was his "Twilight Tour" meaning it was his last tour in the Coast Guard before retiring in 2013. The chief in charge of the CUs retired in 2011, and the chief who replaced him retired from Mobile, as well. The chief in charge of the SUs also retired from Mobile.

I don't want to say that they did not care about their jobs; they all did. I don't want to say that they were bad chiefs; they were not. However, Mobile was their last tour. They weren't exactly going above and beyond, either.

One of the other OS1s who transferred to Mobile in 2010 really liked communications and jumped into the chief's role in the Comm's room almost right away. He began assisting the CUs with their qualifications, sitting in on their boards, doing their bi-annual evaluations, loading codes when they were due, making sure all the equipment was running properly, and just overseeing everything Comms related, in general.

I had slowly started doing the same thing for the SUs and OUs. As said before, the SU desk was the hardest desk for me to get qualified at due to all of the information being completely new to any OS. Immediately upon passing my board, I made an extensive study guide for future SUs and updated it regularly throughout my time in Mobile. OU was slightly easier (for me) but I also made a study guide for that desk.

Over time, I began volunteering for other roles and duties. I wanted to make chief, so I figured everything I was doing was preparing me for that role in the future. I slowly started tracking all of the required mandated training for everyone in the Command Center. I wrote awards for departing members. I assisted a lot with training. In January of 2012, a memo was drafted, and I officially became the Lead Petty Officer (LPO) of the OU desk. The OS1 in the Comm's room was officially designated the LPO of the CU desk and an OS2 was designated LPO of the SU desk. I assisted all the OUs with their qualifications, sat in on their boards, did their bi-annual evaluations, made the schedule, reviewed cases, put together case studies, etc. I also assisted the OS2 a lot with everything on the SU desk.

Eventually, I stopped standing regular watches and started working 8-4 every day. The OS1 in the Comm's room did the same thing. The OS2 did not. This was part of the reason that I was called in when CG 6535 crashed, and part of the reason I was there for most of the nine days. It also allowed me to work out on a consistent basis with the personal trainer, run all the 5Ks I ran, and volunteer with Make a Wish. These opportunities and more were all good things about the position. There were a few bad things, as well. I wish I had had a little more guidance in the role. I wish I could have written up the departing awards better. Or at the very least, someone would have come in behind me and polished them up. Everyone got the awards that I put in for them; that's the good news. The bad news is that the way they were written could have been better, and those people all deserved better. What I was most excited about, though, was the opportunity to use what I learned to become a CDO and a chief someday...

Toward the end of summer and beginning of fall in 2012, the Coast Guard updated SAROPS with a lot of changes. They soon realized that everyone currently using the program would need to be retrained, but there was not time nor money to send everyone back to SAR School. SAR School Train the Trainer became the solution. Every unit would designate one or two people to go to Yorktown, VA, for two weeks and learn how to use the "new" program. Those people would then return to their unit and train everyone else how to use the "new" program. The same civilian who went to Command Center

School with me and I were chosen to be the representatives for Sector Mobile. We were not put in the same class, though, and I don't remember who went first. After we returned, I put together a schedule with times for all of the OUs and CDOs to train with the civilian and me.

It didn't take too long for the OUs to start complaining about the "new" program and saying that it didn't work. I started noticing the same issues when I stood watch. I started calling the help desk on my watches whenever there was a glitch. I became really good "friends" with one of the guys there: waking him up in the middle of the night on a pretty consistent basis for a good month or so. Then, I sent an email to the instructors at SAR School with a very specific, very detailed list of everything that was wrong with the "new" program. A CDR who had transferred to Headquarters was still on the email list from being previously stationed in Yorktown. She read my email and immediately called our LT demanding answers:

CDR: LT, are you aware of the email your OS1 sent to SAR School?

LT: Yes (She wasn't)

CDR: And you read it and you approve of it?

LT: Yes (At that point Senior told me she was on the phone and I had forwarded her the email. She was scanning it as she was talking to the CDR)

CDR: Why did she send that email to SAR School?

LT: Because she was told in class that if there was a problem to contact them.

CDR: Has she contacted the help desk?

LT: Yes, would you like to see the call log or emails?

CDR: Well, you know that there was training for the "new" program, and if your OS1 is having trouble with it, she should go to the expert at your unit for help.

LT: She is the expert.

CDR: Oh, well . . . next time the email needs to go through you to District and then to SAR School . . .

LT: Ummm, Ok.

Come to find out, there was actually a problem with D8's server. A little while after that email, the problem was found and fixed. The "new" program still had some glitches, but it ran much better after the server was fixed. The civilian and I trained all the OUs and CDOs and Sector Mobile was fully operational.

To Recap Events So Far:

2011-2012: had trouble making weight due to working out with a personal trainer.

Jan 2012: became LPO of the OU desk.

Feb 2012: CG 6535 crashed.

Apr 2012: became Sector Mobile's first and only E6 CDO.

Summer 2012: Day worked, trained new OUs and CDOs, wrote awards for departing personnel

Sept 2012: Was chosen as one of two people to represent Sector Mobile at SAROPS Train the Trainer School

End of 2012: Discovered problem with D8's SAROPS server

Entire 2012: Ran at least one 5K per month, volunteered with Make A Wish (started in 2011), and was taking piano lessons.

CANCER SCARE

In December 2012 into January of 2013, while still on birth control, I started my period and it never stopped. I bled for an entire month! And I was angry. I was extremely angry. During my period, I usually lost sleep and I was depressed. I found it hard to get out of bed the week before and the first few days of. I would cramp and crave chocolate. This time around, I wanted to fight. I was mad at the world, but I didn't have a reason to be.

Towards the end of January, I went to see Coast Guard medical. I don't remember too much about the appointment other than the doctor listening to all my symptoms and everything going on and saying, "Well, it could be a simple hormonal imbalance or change, or it could be as serious as cancer. I doubt it's cancer, but it could be. I don't want to scare you, but I don't know, so I'm going to refer you out to a gynecologist."

It could be cancer. That's all I really heard. What if it was? Would I still be able to stay in the Coast Guard? Would I have to have chemo? Would I have to have a hysterectomy? Would I be able to have kids? I wanted to have kids. Not right that minute, but I always wanted to have kids.

My appointment with the gynecologist was set for three to four weeks after my Coast Guard appointment. I was a "new patient" and they did not have anything available before that. So, I would have to live with the possibility of having cancer for a month. I would still have to go to work, and I would still have to work nights, and I would still have to save other people's lives.

I called Calvin. I told him I didn't want to go into too many details or tell him too much, but I had been bleeding for a long time. I told him I was scared and asked him to pray for me. Calvin was very supportive.

FINALLY, the date came. I went to the gynecologist. This lady was pure evil. She only listened to some of my symptoms. She would ask me a question and then cut me off when I tried to answer her. She focused on my depression and being angry and told me she was going to prescribe Prozac.

I didn't want to be on Prozac. The anger wasn't normal for me. None of my symptoms were normal for me. Clearly something else was going on. What was going on? She agreed to take blood, did a pap smear, and ordered a vaginal ultrasound . . . and then scheduled an appointment in MARCH to discuss the results!!

March!! I would have to wait another month to find out what was wrong with me!?! What the hell?!?

In the meantime, the real world was in the middle of Mardi Gras. One of my friends had invited me to go to the LaShe's Ball with him and his wife. I asked a good friend to go with me, and he agreed. Then a week or so later, he met a girl he was really into and told me that he couldn't go with me anymore. He didn't want the new girl to think he had a girlfriend. Remember how I said I was mad at the entire world?!? Well, he got my FULL wrath.

I called Calvin, who lived in South Carolina at the time. I told him I would pay for everything; a flight or his gas, the tickets to the ball, his tux rental, literally everything, if he would come with me to the ball.

God bless Calvin. I could always count on him. He flew down. He had something going on at that time, too. When he got here, we both cried on each other's shoulders for a minute. Calvin's hair stylist was a drag queen and we had been to her show a couple of times. I remember making a joke about how the two of them could help me find wigs if I had cancer. I thought it was clever. Calvin got pissed and told me not to talk that way. He really took me off guard. He usually made the same kind of jokes.

After we had our moment, we agreed to put our problems on pause. I don't remember whose idea it was, probably his. #problemsonpause really should have been the hashtag for his visit. Calvin met and hung out with some of my friends. We went to a parade and got a ton of beads!! We found him a tux (with tails) and rented it. And on the night of the ball, four of us got a hotel room, hung out for a while, then got dressed, and went to the ball. We had a really good time that night.

I do vaguely remember getting mad at Calvin for something stupid. I have had a bad habit of that, especially if it is a late night. I don't remember what it was, and I don't remember being too mad, but I think I was rude to him. I vaguely remember apologizing to him when we got back to the hotel room and him kind of laughing because he knew how I was. He forgave me. The trip was great! It was fun, in general, and it was really nice to have something to focus on and do, instead of worrying about possibly having cancer. I loved Calvin for coming out and "rescuing" me.

On March 7, 2013, I went back to the gynecologist. She told me that all my test results were normal. There was nothing wrong with me at all. December/January was just a glitch. She then asked if I was still angry and again offered to write a prescription for Prozac. Of course, I was angry but for an entirely new reason now. I turned down the Prozac.

I don't actually know the date of the second visit; my memory is not that good. Ironically, I'm writing this book in March 2019. Today, my Facebook "memories" reminded me that March 7th, 2013, my Facebook status was, "Next time a doctor tells me I might have cancer, I'm going to punch them in the throat!! Actually, next time I'm skipping the doctor altogether . . . I'd rather fucking die."

If that doesn't say how badly I was treated and how scared I was, I don't know what does. I wish that I had been more assertive at the time or had done more research. I didn't see my blood results. I don't even know what she tested for. And whatever she tested for, was I middle normal? Or high normal? Or low normal? And how much effect did birth control have? Did it cover up some of my symptoms? Was I really OK? Or was there something going on that she just didn't have the time of day to look for?

Hindsight is always 20/20. And I'm not a doctor. I just know from everything that has happened since, you really have to advocate for yourself when it comes to doctors, especially military doctors. Unfortunately, I did not advocate for myself. Unfortunately, by the time I started advocating for myself, it was too late . . .

EXTENSION

I was the LPO of the OU desk, eventually becoming the unofficial training petty officer, and day-worked for a little over a year. I still stood two watches at the OU desk and two watches at the CDO desk every month to maintain both qualifications. I also jumped in whenever it was necessary. I assisted several OS1s and a couple of very motivated OS2s in getting qualified as OU. I assisted several chiefs and officers in getting qualified as CDO. The Response Chief / SAR Mission Controller (SMC) and I got along very well. The new LT and I got along very well and, along with the other OS1 in Comms, I was kind of her "right hand man."

I was due to transfer in the summer of 2013. As said before, the senior chief and all the chiefs had or were going to retire. I wanted to go to Virginia and be a SAR School Instructor. I was unsure if there were any E6 billets available there and I wasn't in a position on the SWE list to advance. The LT started asking me if I wanted to extend at Sector Mobile. Originally, I told her no. Later a Coast Guard message went out saying that they were trying to save money and if people wanted to extend or to stay within the same district/area they were currently in, they were encouraged to do so. The billets came out and there was not an E6 position at SAR School. I finally told the LT I would extend, on one condition: I wanted leave to go to Las Vegas for my 30th birthday. It was way too early to make this request; my 30th Birthday wasn't until January of 2014, but I was making it anyway. The LT agreed, not that it would have ever held up if she changed her mind for any reason (Thankfully, she didn't.) and the senior chief sent an email to the detailer stating that I wanted to save the Coast Guard money and extend. It's always good when the needs of the service meet your personal needs, as well.

The senior chief retired in May 2013 I think. The new senior chief wasn't coming until August of 2013. We were going to go through the majority of a transfer season without a senior chief. The LT depended heavily on the other OS1 and me. Together, the three of us got things done.

Then the new senior chief reported. The new senior chief had just made senior chief and was trying to learn his new role as both a senior chief and a senior chief in a Command Center. He also had some Sector experience and had ideas and goals for how to make Mobile better. At first I was excited when he reported. I was excited that I would not have as many responsibilities or if I did, that I would have more guidance in carrying them out. When the new senior chief started taking away these responsibilities, though, I began to change my mind. One of the first things the new senior chief did was get rid of the OS1/OS2 LPOs at each desk and put the new chiefs in charge. I did not mind the new chiefs having oversight, but I thought the OS1/OS2 LPOs knew what was going on, were doing a good job, and needed the leadership experience to make chief themselves. He could have made another OS1 instead of me the OU LPO, and I would have been OK with that. But he put a chief in charge, and I saw that as a slap in the face to all the work we had done over the summer while we didn't have chiefs. I saw these changes as the new senior chief's need to micromanage all of us and I was not happy. The new senior chief worked very hard and very fast to implement all his ideas. I don't know if he was trying to disrespect or micromanage us or not. He may have felt like he was giving us all a much needed break. Or maybe he just wanted to establish a good first impression and some respect for himself. If I had been in his position, maybe I would have done the same thing. But at that time, I felt that every change he made was personal. I had worked very hard to make the Sector what it was.

I implemented a lot of things he was getting rid of. My anxiety told me that he did not think I was a good watch stander or OS1. Of course, at that time, I did not realize it was my anxiety telling me all these things.

There was another female OS1 at Sector Mobile that I did not get along with at all. We had several disagreements and I thought she was poison in the Command Center. Several of my close friends agreed with me. I did not want to see her punished or wish anything bad on her, but I did not want to see her promoted to the OU desk (She started as an SU.) or see her get rewarded for anything, either. The former chiefs and senior chief did not trust her. They never directly told me their feelings towards her, but I had a good idea that they were weary of her. I knew the LT did not want her to break in at the OU desk because the LT did not feel like she was ready for that responsibility. The new senior chief wanted everyone to have a clean slate with him, including her. Eventually the new senior chief let her break in and qualify as an OU.

It came time for bi-annual evaluations and mine were lower than they had been the entire time I was at Sector Mobile. It was the *Mellon*, the "Clams," OS1, and Ramona all over again and I still did not know how to respond or handle life. I started by appealing my marks. I met with the new senior chief (not the captain of the base this time, although that might have been better) to discuss my marks. I am so embarrassed by that entire meeting. I cried. Yes, I cried. And I apologized for crying because I didn't want to cry. Crying was not professional, but even more so, in my mind crying showed that I was weak. I did not want this new senior chief to think that I was weak or to give him more reasons not to like or respect me.

We went back and forth and back and forth over everything. One of the biggest marks we argued over was "loyalty." The new senior chief told me he thought I was loyal to the LT and to the Coast Guard, but not to him. He was right. Technically petty officers are to obey all orders given by the chiefs/

senior chiefs and to support the command. The new senior chief used this as his argument for giving me the lower mark. I responded by saying that if I did not think an order was "the right thing to do" then I shouldn't have to support it. (We were talking about a very, very specific situation when I said that. I cannot write about that situation because of how incredibly personal it is to someone else.) We talked about everything that had happened since he got there. It was a long, emotional conversation that resulted in some of my marks being raised. I thought we left the meeting with an agreement to start over, and I tried to be happy about that. Mostly, though, I was exhausted, physically, mentally, and emotionally.

A few weeks later I found out that the other female OS1 got really high marks. The way that I found out was really questionable. The new senior chief had a new and valid reason to not trust me and I did not trust him. I saw myself making the same mistakes I had made on the *Mellon*. Sometimes mid-conversation I would realize I was wrong, but by that time I was in too deep. Thankfully, like Chief G, the LT liked me, so I never got into any real trouble. I walked a very thin line. I very much regretted extending in Mobile. I had a good reputation up until that point and I saw it slowly disappearing. That wasn't really true. I was still highly respected around the base. I knew that when I was mouthing off and relied on that to stay out of trouble. Later, though, my anxiety would tell me that I was becoming a joke to everyone.

In September billets came up. There was still not a position at SAR School, but there was one at OS A-School. Having been an OU and CDO, I thought I was much more suited (and probably was) to teach SAR School. However, I liked the idea of going to California, even Petaluma, over going to Yorktown. I put OS A-School at the top of my list.

The new senior chief and I stood some watches together. We ran some cases together and he even complimented some of the things I thought of. We didn't fight all the time. There was some mutual respect. The female OS1 and I attempted to be friends several times. She was a good cook and would bring food in for me sometimes. We were both worried about weight and we walked together a couple of times. I did my very best to help her at the OU desk, if for no other reason than because lives depended on her. In ways it was very hostile, and I was making the same mistakes as the *Mellon*, but in some ways I had grown. It is not a period of time I would ever wish to repeat.

In January of 2012 I did go to Las Vegas for my 30th birthday. This was separate from my trip with Calvin a few years earlier. As stated before, what happens in Vegas stays in Vegas. I will not write about that vacation, except to say that I had a very Happy Birthday.

Around March, I found out I had orders to transfer to OS A-School. I was very happy. I was very fortunate my entire Coast Guard career to always get my top pick when I transferred. I wanted to leave Mobile as soon as humanly possible. I filled out all the paperwork to leave Mobile in May. I had no desire to stick around any longer than I had to. Because of my previous "positions" in the command center and my relationship with the LT, it was second nature to go to her any time I needed anything. This was something else the new senior chief did not appreciate, as I was "jumping the chain of command." He was patient at first as he knew it was second nature to me, and I tried hard to come to him for things, but I never really did. I don't remember what the issue was with my paperwork, but there was an issue with my transfer paperwork and the yeoman's email implied to me that it needed to be taken care of ASAP. The new senior chief was not there so I took it to the LT to sign. He found out later on and lost him temper. He was 1) not happy that I was transferring in May and 2) not happy that I jumped the chain of command again. He did not know why I did not respect him.

Later, after he calmed down, I was able to explain to him what had happened, and I showed him the yeoman's email. He apologized to me for losing his temper. I really couldn't blame him. I didn't show him the respect he deserved, and I didn't have a good track record; there wasn't a reason for him to trust me. I gained respect for him for having the leadership skills to apologize to me and admit he was wrong. The paperwork stayed the same and I did transfer in May.

MISCELLANEOUS FAREWELLS TO MOBILE

My three-ring binder is full of newspaper reports about Coast Guard activities: capsized vessels, two teenagers kayaking in a tropical storm, CG 6535, vessel fires, and persons in the water (PIW). The two teenagers kayaking were rescued in the middle of the night. They had a lot of jellyfish stings and lacerations and the early stages of hypothermia, I think, but they both lived. I am proud of the work I did that night, but the helicopter crew deserves a lot of recognition on that case, as well. Search conditions were less than optimal, and they were rock stars. Besides CG 6535, there were three other cases that will haunt me forever. I was in Mobile for five years, so I figure approximately one haunting case and several successful cases per year is a good ratio. I consider myself to be very lucky. God only gives you as much as you can handle. Sometimes I feel like Xena: Warrior Princess talking about all my cases and dealing with all my health issues. Other times, when I think about my ratio of good to bad cases and how much worse my health could be, I don't think God asks me to handle much at all.

In two of the four bad cases, the case itself was bad, but the haunting part was talking to the families. I was in a unique position being an E6 CDO. Usually, E6s don't have to brief families. Chiefs or officers, people with more time and experience in the Coast Guard, are the ones who brief the families. When I was filling the role a chief or officer would fill, I had to take on all the responsibilities of that role. In one case, we had a missing young adult male. We searched the entire area several times and had not found any trace of him, his kayak, or, sadly, his dog. I had to ask his family and close friends if there were any possibility that he wanted to disappear. I asked if he was in debt, mentally ill, if he had just broken up with his girlfriend, or possibly suicidal. I had to ask the questions. I know I did. I had to eliminate all the possibilities of what could have happened. I can only imagine what his family was thinking when I asked those questions. All of them said he was very happy, he had nothing to hide, and he was not suicidal. To be clear, I don't think people in debt, with mental issues, or otherwise going through hard times, deserve less of an effort or deserve to die. Hearing his family and friends talk about what a good guy he was made not finding him that much harder. We never did find him or the dog. We think we found the kayak. We had educated guesses as to what happened, but we never did find out the truth. Talking to his family and friends along with the mystery of this case will keep the case in my head forever.

The second case involved a Coast Guardsman's father-in-law. He and two other men went out and did not come back when scheduled. It was late at night so I launched a Coast Guard helicopter and sent an 87-foot cutter to search. I did not send a small boat, as small boats are not good search assets at night, and I thought I might need them the next morning. The Coast Guardsman's wife didn't understand Coast Guard search policies and procedures so there was absolutely no way to explain them to her. What she did know was that her husband came home and "complained" about getting underway for other "bullshit" missions all day long, but now there was a SAR case, involving real people, involving her father, and I was not sending her husband in his small boat to search. "Why are you not getting the small boat underway? Why are you not sending my husband to search? Why don't you want to find my father?" she was demanding over the phone.

She insisted that I was not doing anything, and I did not care. I understood her point of view. I understood she was scared. I did my best to try to explain what I had done, who I had sent to search, and what my plan was moving forward. I did my best not to use Coast Guard acronyms. I tried very hard to stay calm. She didn't want to hear any of it. In her mind, the small boat was the only boat that mattered, and they were dockside, and that was my fault. I tried to change the subject and ask her questions about the boat, about her father, about the other people onboard, and where they went. She was too upset to answer any of them. On the positive side, we did rescue one of the guys that was with her father. We found her father, too, but unfortunately, not alive. The third guy was never found. The sole survivor was interviewed about what happened. After hearing his story, I still doubt sending the small boat out to search would have changed the outcome. I doubt that the facts of the case will ever matter to his daughter, though. They would never matter to me. I hope that she has somehow found peace with the situation. I hope that this case did not affect her husband's career or their marriage. I will forever hear her begging me to get her husband underway. Maybe I should have, just to ease her mind.

The last haunting case that will stick with me forever wasn't even really our case. I got a call that a boat had hit a bridge. Before I could do anything at all, I was informed that local police were on scene. I confirmed details and ensured everything was taken care of and that was it. The boat was a small speed boat. An adult male and his young daughter were onboard. The male had been drinking, lost control of the boat, and crashed into the bridge. The male had minor scrapes and bruises. His daughter was not as lucky and was rushed to the hospital. I was bummed out but reminded myself it wasn't really my case and went about my night.

I did open an official case for it and kept a timeline in the computer program I talked about in earlier chapters. Local police called the command center and gave us more details about the case the next day. Then they emailed pictures.

The adult male was not just casually drinking while enjoying a day out with his daughter. The pictures that were sent showed the boat literally cut into two pieces. On the back of the boat, local police had gathered all the beer cans and glass liquor bottles and stacked them in one giant pile. This guy had gone through an entire case of beer and a fifth of vodka! While boating with his young daughter! I was irate! But then, to my complete shock and horror, next to all the alcohol stacked up, was a small child's pink lifejacket. I completely lost it. (Hence my later rule of not looking at any pictures / not looking at the mangled helicopter.)

I do not know what ended up happening with the little girl. I sincerely hope that she made a miraculous recovery and is living a phenomenal life with a non-alcoholic parent figure. What really happened was probably not good.

This is a very fortunate or unfortunate part of being in the Coast Guard. OSs, BMs, MKs, aviators, etc all work extremely hard responding to cases and rescuing people but once those people arrive at the hospital, HIPPA laws prohibit doctors and nurses from ever telling us what happened later. There are several cases that I ran that I do not know the outcome of. In the case above, I truly believe I lost a child. Losing a child is never easy for any first responder.

**There are four watches at a Sector / in a Command Center, the CU, SU, OU, and CDO. While I am talking about these cases from my point of view, and what I did, at least three other people were on watch with me, working just as hard as I was, and helping me make those decisions. I've also mentioned the SMC and District 8 in other chapters. Those are other people higher up the food chain that influence cases and decisions, as well. All the assets and people physically searching deserve credit, too. I may put a plan in action, but they are the ones carrying it out. SAR is a team effort. I do not want it to sound like any of my successes were mine alone. I also do not want it to sound like any of my decisions were mine alone, either. I had a huge amount of influence, but there is a system of checks and balances.

...

While in Mobile, I rescued my (first) dog from the Mobile SPCA. Casey is a white, male miniature poodle. He was partially trained when I first got him, knowing how to sit and go outside when he needed to go. Someone, however, in his short life, was really bad to him. They burned his paws. When I first got him, his pads were raw, pink, and not "spongy" at all. If there was a dog version of me, Casey is just that. He is extremely anxious, has a weak stomach, fears change, and hates being alone. He loves to play fetch, will wear out a tennis ball in one day, is friendly with people and patient with kids, but is scared and intimidated easily, especially by men and other dogs. He is a very picky eater and stubborn as hell. Sometimes Casey and I comfort each other and other times we feed off of each other's anxiety so we both get worse. He is the main man in my life and there were a few times when thinking about what would happen to him was the thought that kept me alive.

My best friend had a Belgian shepherd and was actually the one who picked Casey out for me. They had grown up with dogs and had dogs their entire life. They knew a lot about taking care of dogs, training dogs, and matching dogs with people's personalities. I had looked at the website and narrowed it down to three dogs; two poodles and a beagle. My best friend told me to get Casey. They told me that Casey had kind eyes. We had keys to each other's houses and took care of each other's dogs whenever we had watch or went out of town. The two dogs did not get along at first (mainly because of Casey) but became best friends after a short period of time. The dogs became so close that if my friend or I was out of town for a long period of time, the dogs would literally get depressed when my friend or I got back into town and took our respective dog home, separating them. The next day we would have to get back together, just so the dogs would know that the other dog was still alive, and they would still see each other.

My best friend was a couple years older than I and from California. When we got along, we got along very, very well. We were there for each other and complemented each other and I truly believe I am a better person because of some of the lessons they taught me. But when we didn't get along, it was extremely toxic. I have never in my life been spoken to the way they spoke to me and I, in turn, have never spoken to anyone else the way I spoke to them. We bounced from one extreme to the other the entire four years we were stationed together. We built each other up and then ripped each other to shreds. I have never before nor after had a friendship like that. I love them, to this day, but I am glad we do not keep in touch. I hope I never have a friendship like that again. I know some of the issues and demons they were battling. Now I understand better the issues and demons that influenced me. I have gotten help and I sincerely hope they have, too. Maybe someday we will meet up again. Maybe someday we will treat each other with respect. Maybe we won't. I hope they are happy on their own journey. I'm slowly learning how to be happy on mine.

. . .

After volunteering in Petaluma and Seattle, I was excited to be at a permanent land station where I could get even more involved. I participated in the Partners for Education (PIE) program in Mobile for two years; this time actually assisting in classrooms instead of helping out the librarian, but I still wanted to do more. I originally applied for Big Brothers and Big Sisters, but I think my interview didn't go very well. Whether I am right about that or not, it did not work out. One of the other OS1s told me that his wife volunteered for Make a Wish Foundation and suggested that I become involved with that. His wife was able to get me in contact with the right person and was my partner in my first few wishes. Make a Wish provides training, but it isn't until you get hands-on experience that you fully know what you are doing. His wife walked me through the entire process. We were Wish Coordinators. It was our job to meet with the families and interview them to find out what the wish was and narrow down logistical items, such as a good time to travel (if it was a travel wish), health concerns, participants in the wish, etc. His wife let me start off interviewing the kids and then taught me how to interview the adults, walking me through all of the paperwork. They transferred a year or so later, but I continued to volunteer, meeting several great people along the way, both volunteers and families. I continued to volunteer in California, too, until the time I was discharged.

. . .

I had so many going away parties in Mobile it became a joke as to what number I was on. Along with activities outside work discussed above, I took piano lessons while I was stationed in Mobile, too. I wasn't good or bad. I purchased a digital keyboard to practice on and practiced a couple times a week (not every day, like I was supposed to). My teacher was impressed with my ear. She could play songs for me and I could remember how to play them without music. Not complicated songs, by any means, but I could usually figure out how something was supposed to sound rather quickly. My teacher prefers to teach children rather than adults because children are usually easier to mold. Children do as they are told and don't analyze or overly complicate things. Ironically, my strict Baptist upbringing coupled with my military training helped me be more "childlike" in this situation. I didn't analyze or complicate things, either, just strictly did what she told me to do. I played in two recitals while I was stationed in Mobile, my second one being one of my going away parties, in a way. I have no problem at all with public speaking, but a musical performance is a different story. I get bad stage fright, so I was shaking from head to toe during both performances. I was proud of myself for going through with them, though.

I was even prouder and happier that I learned how to play "Faithfully" by Journey as that is one of my all-time favorite songs. I did not play at the speed that Journey does, but you could kind of tell it was "Faithfully." I thought I would continue taking piano lessons in California, but I didn't. I kind of regret that. I sold the digital keyboard to a family with two children. I hope they are enjoying it as much as I did.

Another going away party was a casino night in Biloxi, MS. I don't gamble too often, but I do love playing roulette. I went with a Yeoman (YN), her husband (maybe boyfriend at the time), and one of the OS3s. We had a nice dinner and gambled for a little while. It was fun getting dressed up, as I very rarely did, and going out for an "adult" evening.

Of course, there was the official work going away party. The year I transferred, several other people were transferring, too. The entire Command Center went bowling. I love bowling. I have been on leagues on and off my entire life, which reminds me, I was on a bowling league for one of the years I was in Mobile. I'm not a good or bad bowler. My average is 145. I do not bowl well (or compete in any sport well) under pressure. I was never the last bowler; most of the time I was the first one. I also never paid attention to my score. My mom couldn't understand this. She was the opposite. She gets better under pressure and always bowls last. If I was having a bad night, though, knowing how badly I was doing depressed me. If I was having a good night, I didn't want to jinx myself. I just took it frame by frame. Every time I got up to bowl, it was a new chance to get a strike. Ironically, now, I'm trying to live my life the same way—day by day. Every morning is a new chance to make things better. The previous day and the score do not matter.

The last going away party was the most bittersweet. I had become very good friends with my neighbors. Their son was eleven or twelve at the time and was heavily involved in the Boy Scouts and baseball. My neighbors could not afford all the equipment, uniforms, and other miscellaneous stuff he needed plus the camping trips. He started mowing yards to make extra money, including my yard, and after my best friend with the dog transferred, he became my dog sitter. His younger sister was eight or nine and saw him making money, so she wanted to make money, too. Of course, there wasn't much she could do at her age, so I started letting her wash my car. I swear, she was always soaking wet, and the car was never actually clean!! But she worked hard and loved every minute of it. I would give her $5 for her effort. She liked the dog, too, and would play with him when her brother dog-sat. I think they shared that money. I was one of the first people who had come into their young lives but now was moving away. The little girl was having a hard time dealing with it. Before I left, their mom and I planned a special evening for us. I took the kids to a hibachi restaurant for dinner. They had never been before and loved the show! Then we went to the bowling alley, which also had laser tag and an arcade, and played games for a few hours. We all had a really good time. Before I actually moved, I had already found a house, so I bought the younger sister some stationary, pre-addressed ten envelopes and put stamps on them, and told her if she wrote to me, I would write to her. She sent me letters the first year I was in California. After that, she made friends at school and didn't miss me as much, but I still kept in touch with her mom. When I moved back to Mobile in February, 2019, her mom was my realtor. I saw the sister in a school play and briefly saw their son, who is 19 now, an Eagle Scout, and hopes to become a pastor. They both still remember the hibachi restaurant and bring me up every time they go. They're busy teenagers, but we all hope to go out to eat again soon.

I don't know what award the Senior Chief or LT originally put me in for, but the Response Chief / SMC bumped it up to a Commendation Medal! A Commendation Medal! Two awards higher than an LOC. Three award points for the SWE. Enlisted people do not often get this award! I was so honored. The award is written so well and so thoughtfully, too. It mentions some of the cases that I was involved in and am most proud of. The entire time I was stationed in Mobile, the entire command, not just my immediate command, supported me. The entire command encouraged me to obtain the qualifications that I earned. District Eight Command Center (our "boss") was not happy an E6 was a CDO. The first few cases I briefed them on, they would not take my recommendation, until the SMC personally told them he agreed with me. One JG argued with me about one of my stations and starting a case. She did not realize the station was part of a Navy base and the case wasn't really ours to start. Sometimes they refused to allow us to get a helicopter airborne. It didn't take long for the SMC to have enough and to put them in their place. I also stopped answering the phone as "Petty Officer Herbst" and started just saying "this is the CDO" It was the exact same person answering the phone, but you have no idea how much more respect the second answer earned. I worked very hard and am proud of myself, but I would not have been able to achieve everything that I did if the command had not supported me. As with most people, I work much harder when my work is recognized. The very first LOC my LT wrote for me, the one praising me for getting all three qualifications in less than a year, was the exact same award I left the *Mellon* with after 2.5 years of accomplishments. I felt more appreciated in the first year in Mobile than I ever did on the *Mellon* and to all the Captains, Officers, Chiefs, and OSs who I worked with during my time in Mobile, thank you from the bottom of my heart for all of your support, encouragement, and recognition.

To get orders to be an instructor at OS A-School, your command must write a letter of recommendation. It is a special assignment, and it requires a special breed of person to fill it. (In theory, anyway. I will tell you that during my time in Petaluma some not-so-special people slipped in.) The Captain wrote something for me and so did the new Senior Chief. For all of our differences, he could see the good I was doing and the potential I had. He was not vindictive, nor did he hold a grudge. He, along with the rest of the command, was support-ive of me and my goals. I wish I could remember the exact con-versation, but I shook his hand before I left and apologized. I thanked him for the award because I thought he wrote it. He told me that SMC had written it. He accepted my apology and told me if I ever needed anything, he would be there. We're friends on Facebook now. We don't talk or really comment too often on each other's stuff, but we do have a lot in common, including our political beliefs. Despite all the bullshit and pol-itics, I have a lot of respect for him. Both of us could have han-dled the situation we were in a lot better, but both of us could have handled it a lot worse, too. It was a unique situation that doesn't happen too often, and we were both passionate about our jobs. I'd rather have two people fighting to make the world better than the alternative.

A couple years down the road, the female OS1 hit me up and apologized to me. She had a lot going on while she was down here. In fact, the entire reason she was stationed in Mobile in the first place was because of the unique situation she was in. I knew that at the time and started off very kind and patient to-wards her. The longer her attitude continued, though, the less patience I had. I was only somewhat compassionate, not fully understanding the depth of what she had going on. A couple years later she was in a much better place. I apologized to her, as well. We are friends on FB, too. We don't talk at all, but the pictures of her "baby" boy are adorable, and I hope she is doing well. A mutual friend told me this past weekend that he was talking to her and mentioned he was coming to my house-warming party. Apparently, her response was, "We didn't get along very well. I didn't like her, and she hated me. But the Coast Guard lost one of its best people." If you're reading this, thank you for saying that. I do not hate you.

In May 2014, I departed Mobile, AL, with both a heavy heart and much gratitude. I was sad to be leaving everything and everyone behind, but I was also excited to instruct in Petaluma.

THERAPY WITH THE PASTOR

I struggled with "suicidal" thoughts on and off while I was stationed in Mobile. I put suicidal in quotation marks because I never had a plan like on the *Mellon*. I wasn't reckless, not caring if something happened to me, but at the same time, I just wished I had never existed. Because I knew some people cared about me and would miss me, I didn't want to actually die. My parents had already lost one child (an older sister who I never met), and it would not be fair to them. Parents should never have to bury a child. I didn't want to be alive because I hated myself and my life. I just wished there had been a way to erase me. I felt like I wanted to disappear so anyone who ever knew me would never think of me again; kind of like *Men in Black*. They'd remember the rest of their lives, just not me.

After the cancer scare, I decided I had to do something. Growing up, my mom's best friend was a Pastor. He and his wife were always really nice to my sisters and me, but I hardly liked them. Whenever we would misbehave and my mom wasn't sure which Biblical law we were breaking or how to punish us, she'd call the Pastor. We'd have to sit and listen to this phone conversation and then, after she hung up, she'd get out her Bible, and we'd have to listen to a sermon or lecture on what we did wrong and how to correct it. Those conversations seemed like hours (and sometimes were). After all the talking, we'd usually get spanked. This is what I associated with the Pastor.

Here I was, as an adult in 2013, and I needed help, but

the Coast Guard couldn't find out. I hated my life before my "You're just fine" hormonal issues which made things worse. I was good at my job. I enjoyed it. I did not want to lose my security clearance or be tossed out. My situation would only get worse if I could not provide for myself and became homeless.

My younger sister told me that she had been talking to the Pastor, and he had really been helping her out. I was surprised. I didn't know she had kept in touch with him.

I reached out to him and told him what was going on. We started talking on the phone for about an hour every week or every other week. I started to feel better. To my surprise (and great relief), he did not constantly quote scripture. I had a notebook so I would write things down to remember or think about throughout the week. I remember writing about guilt. Guilt serves only one purpose: to change you. Once you have made a change in your life or to your behavior, guilt is no longer needed and should be let go.

At the time that made me feel a lot better. However, to this day I feel guilty for everything I have ever done. Since I have a good memory, all those things haunt me on a consistent basis.

One of the very first things I brought up was my absolute hatred of being ignored. I could not stand it when someone claimed they cared about me but didn't stay in touch. I am very good at keeping in touch with people. It is one of my highest priorities. I've had every work schedule you can imagine, but I still find time to keep in touch. To me, you find time for what is important to you. If people could not find time to keep in touch with me, I automatically assumed that I was not important to them. If someone ignored me for a long enough time (which, back then, was not that long) I would stop talking to them altogether. I told the Pastor that I was tired of losing friends so we agreed that the next time someone ignored me, we would talk about it before I stopped talking to them.

The Pastor and I talked weekly for about a year. I had a notebook and I would write down some of his advice. Some of it was very good, and I still try to remember it and use it now. Some of it was terrible. The Pastor condoned my chocolate addiction. People joke about being addicted to chocolate; most of the time that means they love it, or they have a piece every day. I was truly an addict. There would be days when my entire diet was mainly chocolate. I would have a piece of chocolate cake for breakfast, a sandwich and two candy bars for lunch, and a piece of pizza and a milkshake for dinner. These days were mostly around my period or when I was really stressed out or depressed. Since I was trying hard to stay within the Coast Guard weight standards, I wanted to stop eating my feelings. The Pastor told me that everyone has a vice, examples including smoking, drinking, drugs, etc. The Pastor said it was especially normal for people with high stress jobs to depend on their vice more than others or to develop more vices than one. The Pastor thought I was being too hard on myself for just liking chocolate. Compared to smoking, drinking, and drugs, chocolate was harmless. For a hot minute, I believed him and almost felt good about my addiction. Thankfully, that didn't last too long since chocolate is essentially sugar and is just as dangerous, if not more so, than all the habits listed above. But I digress.

In June of 2014, it was time for me to move to California and take the instructor position in Petaluma, California. I hate change. Moving is extremely hard on me. (Remember, I was The Band Camp Geek in A-School.) I also hate driving and staying in hotels. I hate living out of a suitcase and being unsettled. I don't really know anyone who enjoys this, but my hatred and anxiety over it is worse than most.

The Pastor wanted to put our therapy sessions on pause, if you will, while I traveled across country; kind of like taking a break if you are in a relationship. We could resume sessions after I was settled in California and had a routine again. In his defense, I think he was trying to relieve me of the burden of a weekly phone call. At that time, I didn't know how to explain that I needed him and our phone calls during my travels and my move more than ever. Shouldn't he know that, anyway? He had been talking to me for over a year and had known me my entire life. Shouldn't he know that this was going to be a hard transition for me?

Traveling across country in 2014 presented even more challenges than I thought it would. I was very excited before I left. A couple of friends had talked me into making a road trip out of my travels instead of doing my normal drive from Point A to Point B as fast as humanly possible. I made plans to stay with some friends and family members along the way. A friend suggested I drive through Moab, Utah, since I had never been. He told me how pretty the mountains were and that I would love them. I thought that was a great plan and so traveled that route.

This was the first time my dog, Casey, was with me going across country. Remember my mentioning his anxiety and issues in previous chapters? He was all right when I stopped to see a friend in Louisiana. We met my friend at an outdoor bar and watched volleyball, so Casey could sit with me. He didn't like all the people and didn't leave my side, but he was all right. He was actually great in Texas. He loved my friends there and only got in one minor little tiff with their small dog. After Texas, however, he was done. By the time we reached my cousin's house in Arizona, I could not be out of his sight for more than 30 seconds, or he would whine and bark loudly the entire time I was gone. When we returned from dinner, my cousin and I found out from a slightly annoyed neighbor that my dog scratched on the door and whined for the entire three hours we were gone. From Arizona to Utah to California, I was out of friends to stay with. I couldn't leave Casey alone in a hotel room or in the car, which resulted in my eating a lot of fast food and being terrified of weighing in when I eventually arrived in Petaluma. His anxiety also had me really on edge because I wanted to make him feel better and had no idea how.

Speaking of Utah, I think my friend was right. I think the mountains were gorgeous. I didn't really get to look at them much because I learned that high altitudes make me very sick. I felt nauseous and had a terrible headache the entire day. There were a couple of times I thought I was going to go right off the side of the windy mountain roads. There were a couple of times I wanted to. I called my mom from the hotel that night, bawling my eyes out because I was so scared about the next day. I don't remember if I tried calling the Pastor or not during my travels. I think I at least texted him. I know we did not actually talk.

I found a house in California before I left Mobile and had already put down a deposit. The house wasn't quite ready when Casey and I arrived, so we stayed with some friends for a week before we moved in. Casey settled down more and more the longer we were with them and immediately freaked out again when we got back in the car to go to our actual home. Once in our home, I immediately texted the Pastor and told him that I was ready to resume our therapy sessions (our relationship). His reply was, "Let me know when you are free." I sent back days and times. He did not reply after that.

A few days later I texted him again saying I needed to talk. His reply was the same. I sent back days and times. He did not schedule a time.

This went on for a couple of months. Sometimes he would even initiate the texts asking me when I wanted to talk. But after I told him when I wanted to, that was it. Casey's anxiety was through the roof. He wasn't listening to me at all. He had accidents in the house a couple of times. If I let him out, he ran away. I was scared to report into work, not only because I was nervous about my new role, but I was also terrified of what I weighed. I needed therapy and The Pastor basically ghosted me. Apparently, our relationship was no longer on pause; apparently we had broken up.

I was beyond furious. How could he, of all people, do that to me? He was the one I trusted. He was the one who actually knew how much that particular act hurt me. He should have known how hard change was for me. He should have known I needed him during the entire move. Where was he? Why was he doing this to me?

I understand people, especially Pastors, are really busy. I understand the world does not revolve around me. I understand more now than I did back in 2014 because I have a real therapist now. If the Pastor had called, texted, or emailed me saying that his church needed him for something or he was having some family issues or anything, I would have understood. If he reassured me that he still loved me, I would have felt even better. But he did not do any of this. He wasn't even really truly ghosting me, to be honest. Instead he was playing a game with me. Texting and asking when I was free, getting my hopes up high that we would resume therapy, and then ignoring me, literally crushing my heart and destroying me.

I deleted his phone number. I unfriended him on Facebook. I was no longer going to be played with. If he didn't care about me that was fine, but he was not going to humiliate me on top of that. What little power I had left, I was keeping.

Luckily, I did not weigh-in when I reported to work. The moving company brought my furniture in a couple weeks after we moved into the house. Casey saw the couch and was suddenly himself again. He stopped having accidents in the house and stopped running away. I survived the *Mellon* and I was determined to survive Petaluma. Fuck the Pastor. I didn't need him.

Months later, I remember my mom telling me that the Pastor had asked about me. My mom never "took his side" *per se*, but she wanted to know why we weren't talking and why I hated him so much. My mom thought I should call him. I was lost as to why he couldn't call me. I guess he noticed I unfriended him on Facebook, but my phone still worked. I was not going to call him. I was done with him. That is how I was back then. Once I was done with someone, I was done. And I was beyond done with the Pastor. Or so I thought ...

In July of 2015 my younger sister was getting married. I have not written much about my family in this book. One reason is that this book is mostly about my military career so it does not involve my family much. Another reason is that some of my family might actually read this and if you don't have anything nice to say…

I did not want to attend my sister's wedding for several reasons, but my dad insisted on my being there and since he never put his foot down, ever, I didn't want to "disobey" him now that he was. My sister asked me to be in her wedding, and I did say no to that.

Lo and behold, my sister had asked The Pastor to be officiate at her wedding. My anxiety was already acting up on the way to the wedding, but I did my best to put on my "happy face." I got to the wedding, said "Hi!" and hugged my mom and stepdad. As various family members arrived, I hugged them and tried hard to be polite and make small talk. I met my future brother-in-law and his family and really liked all of them. My cousin came up from southern Illinois and I was really happy to see her. There were a few other select people I was excited to see, too, until they started in with the, "You never come home," and "Your family misses you," lectures. When those started, I quickly excused myself so I would not actually say "Bull shit!" out loud.

The ceremony began and my dad walked my sister down the aisle. My stepsister was the maid of honor and the groom's brother was the best man. They were the only two in the wedding party. Before the Pastor began, he not-so-subtly asked me if I wanted to stand up, too. Up until that point I was prepared to handle seeing him in one of two ways. Ideally, we would ignore each other. If we actually talked, though, I was ready to accept an apology. I was being friendly and polite with everyone else, why not him, as well. Plus, I was still a mess, so if we could let bygones be bygones, maybe we could resume therapy again. When he asked me if I wanted to stand up, though, I was ready to choke him. My feelings about my sister aside, how dare he draw attention to my sitting?!? This was embarrassing for both of us and completely unnecessary on her day.

He also had more than a clue as to the reason I was sitting. We talked about my sister during our therapy year. We talked, and he actually encouraged me to set more boundaries. What could he possibly be thinking?!?

After the ceremony, there were several family pictures. The photographer was really cool. My stepsister and I photo bombed a picture with my aunt and sister. Later I photo bombed a picture with my stepsister and her boyfriend. The photographer did a couple of the standard poses, but she played along with all of our personalities—including the new in-laws' shenanigans (not photo bombing, but just as goofy), and took a lot of really good "candid" photos. I started to relax a little for the first time during this wedding.

After the pictures, though, the Pastor confronted me, again, not so subtly. And when I say confronted, I mean he confronted me. He was angry. He demanded to know why I unfriended him. He even had the nerve to say, "I thought after you found out I had cancer, you would at least call me to see how I was, but you didn't call then, either."

Exactly who the hell did he think he was?!? I swear if I had not been on my "best behavior," putting on a polite show for the sake of the wedding, he would have gotten an entire ear full. I type that all badass and everything, but he wouldn't have. The truth is, he embarrassed the absolute hell out of me. I'm super spunky and witty when I'm in a good mood, but when taken off guard or extremely pissed off, I go mute. I somehow managed to spit out that I was not the one who stopped calling; he was. To his credit, he reluctantly acknowledged that that might have been the way it happened, but he again angrily asked me why I didn't check in on him when I found out he had cancer. I vaguely remembered my mom mentioning that to me in passing. My mom is really good at mentioning serious life (and death) issues in passing like it really isn't that big of a deal. I had also just finished up five years of Search and Rescue. I'm very numb to bad news and didn't think anything of it until he brought it up. I told him I didn't know he had cancer. He was surprised but accepted the answer.

Suddenly feeling incredibly stupid (I assume) and finally realizing that he was making a scene, he apologized to me and asked if he could call me the next day. Desperately wanting out of that conversation, I agreed to it, and tried to leave ... my stepsister caught me and convinced me to stay. My anxiety was back on high.

The Pastor actually called me the next day. He said something about wanting to take me out to lunch since he had egg on his face. I don't remember what all else he said. He didn't continue to piss me off, but he didn't say anything I wanted to hear either. I did not want to have lunch with him. I was just over all of it. I was still mad over him ignoring me when I moved and I was absolutely horrified by his behavior at the wedding. I wanted to give him an earful. I wanted to tell him that I already had a mom and not one, but two dads, and at 31 years old, I didn't allow any of them to lecture me, so who the hell did he think he was. I wanted to ask him what the hell he was thinking, embarrassing me when he should have already known I was uncomfortable. But it just wasn't worth it. He wasn't worth it. I told him I had plans and could not have lunch with him. I agreed to keep in touch, so the conversation would end, and immediately upon hanging up, I blocked his number and blocked him on Facebook, so he could never reach me again. Fool me once, shame on you. Fool me twice, shame on me.

Unfortunately, that attitude prevented me from wanting help ... and I was rather rude at my first therapy visit when I was finally pushed into it later ...

On the positive side, after the wedding, my younger sister and I put a lot of effort into our relationship, and we get along fairly well now. I don't think this would have happened if I had not attended her wedding, so I am very happy that I went.

I was diagnosed with an anxiety disorder at the end of 2016 and started seeing a real therapist. (More on all of that later.)

What I have learned since then is what anxiety does to you. Among many other things, anxiety tells you that people do not love you; in fact, you are not worthy of love. Anxiety tells you that people are only friends with you because of something external that you have to offer, such as money, or because it is required of them. For example, a therapist would be required to like his or her patient because they are being paid to. Anxiety tells you that once people don't need you anymore, they will discard you. This is part of the reason why being ignored hurt (and still hurts) me so much. Being ignored validates my anxiety. Being ignored tells me since you no longer need me, I am no longer a priority to you. It also tells me that you were never really my friend in the first place; you were just using me. I have tried very hard to overcome this feeling. My friends get more of a benefit of the doubt now than they have ever been given in the past. However, if you tell me you are going to do something and you don't do it, I see that as a lie. If you lie to me more than once without a valid reason, I'm done with you, even if that lie was a simple, "I'll call you tomorrow." And after six months to a year of my trying and not receiving any return, I'm most likely going to delete your number or unfriend you from Facebook. This does not necessarily mean that I won't answer a phone call out of the blue later in life, but I will never reach out again, either. There are exceptions to this rule, but overall this is the rule. Maybe it is reasonable or "normal;" maybe it's not. Everyone has boundaries, though, and this is mine for better or worse.

LAST NEW ROLE

My first chief in Petaluma was a great guy, and we got along well throughout the rest of my service. When I reported, I could have asked for the usual ten days for house hunting, but I told him I already had a house. He gave me five to get settled in. I think I had my household goods delivered and unpacked during that time. Casey became a new dog! As soon as he could jump up on "his" couch, all his anxiety was gone. I breathed a heavy sigh of relief.

There are approximately thirty OS1/OS2 OS A-School instructors. When I first reported, there were also eight civilian instructors. (Later, it was cut to four.) The instructors were divided into three pods. Each pod would meet a class the first day of school and see that same class through to graduation. Two of the OS instructors in that pod would be the Class Advisors and all of the instructors in that pod would divide up and teach all the lessons. School was 15 weeks long (Later it was cut to 13 weeks.) with a two- or three-week gap between classes. I was assigned to Pod Three. The previous class had just graduated, so they were on break. I started shadowing other classes and learning how to use the simulated R21 system we had. I even gave a few students some fake cases on the radio.

Another OS1, Arnold, reported the same day as I. He had fourteen years in the Coast Guard, I believe, and had just come from South Carolina. We had a few mutual friends and got along well. We spent the first week learning the base, checking in together, and figuring life out. He was my cubicle-mate in the office, too. I thought I made my first friend in Petaluma, but then...

Arnold is married with three kids. His oldest son joined the Air Force. I don't remember why Arnold had to take leave, but he took leave shortly after reporting. In order to become qualified as an instructor in the Coast Guard, you are required to attend Instructor Development Course (IDC). Since it was transfer season and there are eight A-Schools in Petaluma, there was a long waiting list for this course. Arnold had been assigned to a class but since he was on leave, I took his spot. Shortly after that, he decided to move into the other office with the other instructors. His move had little to do with me, but I still called him a traitor and Benedict Arnold. From that point forward, we were frenemies.

Remember my A-School story about singing the "Bill's class is always late" cadence? Well, that Bill was also an OS1 and he and I were assigned as the Class Advisors for the next class. I was excited at first. We hadn't kept in touch since A-School, but he was a familiar, friendly face. We talked about a lot of things before class started, and I thought we were on the same page and had the same goals. I looked forward to teaching and advising and learning my new role.

My first A-School class was awesome!! I cannot say enough good things about all of them. They were eager to learn, there was very little drama, they had good personalities, and they were everything a new instructor/advisor would want and more. We did have one student who really struggled and one of the men's barrack's rooms always failed inspection, but those were really minor things compared to other horror stories I had heard—and would later experience.

It didn't take long for Bill and me to start fighting, though. I was his break-in, and he did not let me forget it. I had some say in how things were done, but the final decision was always his. We had very, very different leadership styles. I hated the way he did room and uniform inspections. It wasn't a great experience so we wound up in the Chief's Mess a few times because I would not "submit" to his will. I didn't care if I was breaking in or not, I was an OS1 just like he was, we had been in for the same amount of time, both had served on a cutter and at a sector, I had more qualifications at both of those units than he did, and I was not going to let him treat me like he was better than I.

Despite all of that, by the end of the 15 weeks, I was instructor- and advisor-qualified, and all sixteen students graduated. All sixteen students graduated! I was so proud. It was rare for the same number of students who started in a class to finish. The CDR that was SMC in Mobile had transferred to TRACEN Petaluma and was now the Training Officer. I requested that he be our Command Representative at graduation. Luckily, Bill did not have anyone he wanted to be the guest speaker, so I asked the Officer (former OSC) that I had stayed with prior to moving into my house. The class went out to dinner before graduation. They gave Bill a large lint roller as a gag gift because of how strict he was on uniform inspections. I got a box of chocolates and one of the girls drew me a picture on canvas and the entire class signed the back of it. Graduation was awesome. Everyone had a bet that I would cry. I almost did, but I'm proud to say that I didn't. I still keep in touch with a few of them. Two of them are officers now. They were a phenomenal first impression in the instructing world. They also spoiled me rotten which didn't prepare me for the future . . . as my second class would prove challenging, to say the least.

THE NIGHTMARE BEGINS

California, like most places, has a lot of good and some bad things about it. One of the good things I was most excited about is the amount of healthy food and how much healthy living is promoted. Shortly after I moved to Petaluma, one of the girls at work had a Saladmaster Party. Saladmaster promotes healthy eating and living by making cookware and other kitchen utensils of 316 stainless steel that is stabilized with titanium which is non-reactive to the acids and enzymes in your food. You don't ingest metal or toxins when you eat, and you get more nutrients out of your vegetables and other food. Everything is super expensive, but it comes with a lifetime warranty. As an added bonus, Tammy, the sales representative for this party, offered cooking classes twice a month, for free, if you purchased any products. She is a breast cancer survivor, having beaten it by changing her diet and lifestyle and not undergoing chemotherapy. Her story is inspiring, so I wanted to learn from her. I'm not a good cook, either, so I needed lessons. I purchased the Saladmaster itself, an electric pan, and a regular frying pan and began taking lessons and cooking healthier meals. The portions were so large I even started sharing food with people at work.

A couple of the girls at work loved running and knew all about all the 5Ks in the area. I ran with them on the trails around base after work, and we often ran weekend 5Ks. Despite that, I was still having trouble with my weight.

It was October 2014 and time for bi-annual weigh ins. Unlike Mobile, Tracen Petaluma had specific days for everyone to weigh in. One of the other female instructors was over and waited until the end of the month. She told me to do the same thing but for some reason I was stubborn and didn't. I thought she was breaking the rules, and I didn't want to be known for that. I let my pride get in the way of my sense. I weighed in two pounds over the required amount. Two weeks later, still in the month of October, I weighed in under the required amount. I had to sign paperwork that said I was on the weight program, but I wasn't really on the program since I lost it so fast. That was strike one.

Also, towards the end of 2014, my plantar fasciitis started acting up very badly. When I had first reported to Mobile, I found a massage therapist who also knew how to do myofascial release and saw her every month or so until her mom got ill, and she stopped doing massage. I then saw another therapist, but less frequently until I moved. As you know, I also ran a lot in Mobile. Running with plantar fasciitis is kind of tricky. The less you weigh and the more fit you are, the better your feet feel. Of course, running is literally pounding pavement and hard on your feet and knees so it can potentially cause or worsen plantar fasciitis. I found my "sweet spot" was running two to three miles at a time for a total of about ten miles per week. I also had to stretch well before and after I ran and use ice and Epsom salt at night. In Mobile, I never really had any issues with my feet. Here I was in Petaluma and some nights I could barely walk. I was also in a lot of pain in the mornings when I first got out of bed. I hadn't found a massage therapist in Petaluma yet. Being an instructor, I was on my feet a lot more than when I was doing SAR. I was also wearing my dress uniform with its awful dress shoes more than I had in my entire career. I was scared to death I was going to be discharged after all the hoops I had had to jump through to join, but I knew I had to say something. I made an appointment with medical.

Luckily, it was no longer an issue for someone to have plantar fasciitis in the Coast Guard. The medical LT was extremely helpful and referred me to a podiatrist to be fitted for new orthotics, and to physical therapy. I really enjoyed physical therapy and by December 2014, I was released from care, and my paperwork said my condition had improved by 70%. The podiatrist fitted me for three pairs of orthotics, as well. I got a dress pair for my work dress shoes, a "normal" pair for every day, and a pair for running. I had no idea that there were different kinds of orthotics. The dress shoe orthotics made the dress uniform shoes more bearable so I could continue running! At this point, I was really happy with Petaluma medical, especially the LT.

I believe it was at the end of the CloCal 5K (Clover Milk is a popular brand in California and Clo the Cow is their mascot.) that I met my chiropractor. I had broken my collar bone when I was younger and have seen chiropractors on and off my entire life. I wasn't really looking for a chiropractor in Petaluma, but she was at the end of the race and was offering a huge discount on the first visit, including x-rays, thermography scans, and an adjustment. I figured I didn't have a lot to lose so I scheduled an appointment. I saw her for four years. When The Roommate moved in with me, he started seeing her, too.

At some point towards the end of 2014 or beginning of 2015, my hormonal symptoms returned. I was still on birth control, but my periods started getting heavier again, I was moody, I wasn't sleeping, and I had bad cramps. Cotati Physical Therapy shares the building with an acupuncturist. One day before my physical therapy appointment, I had a very bad headache; it was probably a migraine. I was in so much pain in the waiting room I could hardly sit still, and I wasn't sure how I was going to get through my appointment. I also wasn't sure if I could drive home. The acupuncturist happened to walk by, and I told her I would pay her any amount of money if she could make my pain go away. She grabbed my hand, pushed on a pressure point for a few minutes, and no lie, my pain went away. I was freaked out and grateful at the same time. I was shocked she was able to cure my headache so quickly but also incredibly relieved it was gone. I went through physical therapy, and then asked the acupuncturist if she could help me with all my hormonal issues. She said she could so I set up an appointment.

My symptoms started getting a little bit better with the acupuncture. I decided to stop taking birth control since it was obviously not helping me anymore. The LT in medical knew all of this. I don't know how often, when, or why I saw her, but I do know that she was aware that I was seeing an acupuncturist and that I stopped taking birth control. The chiropractor was also listed on my paperwork at every visit as an outside doctor who I was seeing. Coast Guard medical was aware of my every move. The LT did not have any problems with these things, in the beginning.

Most females lose weight when they stop taking birth control. Not me. I gained a significant amount when I stopped taking it. In April of 2015, I weighed in nine pounds over the required weight! (Strike Two) The LT was out of the office so when I went up to medical for my required assessment, I saw a CDR instead. I tried telling the CDR about all issues I was having and told him I thought something else might be wrong with me. The CDR—the medical "doctor"—told me, "Well, even if you do have a thyroid problem, on thyroid medication you will only lose four to five pounds. You are nine pounds over, so even if your thyroid is a problem, it's not worth really checking out."

That is not a typo. You read that right. A "doctor" told me that it didn't really matter if I had a thyroid (real health) problem, medication for that problem would not help me get back within Coast Guard weight standards. In his defense, I imagine there are many people who go to their medical assessments with all sorts of excuses as to why they are over the weight limits. He probably thought that since I went along with what he said, I was making all my symptoms up. It's really hard to defend him, though, when most of my issues were documented in my medical record. I also did not just go along with what he said ...

My chiropractor and acupuncturist were both fairly certain I had thyroid or some other problem causing symptoms on and off birth control. My acupuncturist gave me a coupon to go see her dad, who happened to be an endocrinologist. That was the first time I had ever heard of that type of doctor. Even with the coupon, I paid around $200 for my first office visit with him. I paid even more to have an extensive blood panel done. It was worth the money, though. The endocrinologist did not just test my TSH levels (the only levels the Coast Guard tested up to that point) but also my T3 and T4 levels, which are what matter when you have a thyroid problem. He also tested a bunch of my hormone levels. I don't remember all of the results or the exact numbers, but the things that stuck out were: my Vitamin D level was 17 (normal is around 50, if you have a thyroid problem you need to be closer to 80), my testosterone levels were three times higher than a female should have, my progesterone levels were low, my cortisol levels were on the high end of normal, and my thyroid was off. I was diagnosed with hypothyroidism, given a prescription for levothyroxine and some other hormonal supplements and medications.

PARALLEL WORLDS

After my first class graduated in 2014, I was qualified as an instructor and class advisor. Along with instructor responsibilities, every petty officer had to stand duty. I was Duty Master at Arms (DMAA) my entire four years in Petaluma which put me in charge of the barracks and students after the workday. There was also movie watch, gym watch, pool watch, and a few others. The down side to DMAA was that you had to spend the night on base. The upside to it was that you stood less duty days per month than the other watches. It didn't take me long to get qualified in that position. After those three qualifications, I was considered fully qualified at TRACEN Petaluma. I did not have to do anything besides instruct and stand duty for the rest of the time I was there. But, we all know that's not the way I operate.

Toward the end of every year, the base does a Master Training Specialist (MTS) kickoff. MTS is designed to be a six-month program that trains instructors in how to better assist struggling students, the background and logistics of training and training commands in the Coast Guard, and how to develop and write curriculum. Only 250 active duty Coast Guard members hold this qualification. It is ACE accredited and worth thirteen college credits. Prior to the 2014 kickoff, it was also worth an LOC.

My Chief wanted me to obtain this qualification. The Royal One (civilian instructor) was still a civilian instructor when I returned to Petaluma in 2014. I'd be lying if I said I was all in immediately when MTS was presented to me. It was a lot of work, and I didn't need it. He remembered me, and neither of us had changed much. I don't remember when or why I was talking to him about MTS, but he made it very clear to me that he thought I should do it. In fact, he very bluntly told me I'd be an idiot if I did not. (He was right.) I told my Chief that if he really wanted me to obtain it, I would not be a Class Advisor for the next class. I told him that I couldn't do both. My Chief agreed, and I started the program during the 2014 "season."

MTS has changed quite a lot, but in 2014, in order to become qualified, you had to be instructor qualified, approved by your command, attend the Student Academic Values Element (SAVE) workshop, attend Course Developer Course (CDC), put on a workshop, write an essay, put together a binder, and complete a set of approximately thirty tasks. It is recommended that you start with CDC. CDC provides an overview for the entire program and step by step training for developing curriculum and putting together Student and Instructor Guides. Unfortunately, that class fills up fast, and I was not able to attend in the beginning of my program. The head of the MTS program, a really bad-ass female Machinery Technician Chief (MKC), debated whether or not to even allow someone to go through the program without having CDC first, but she didn't want to turn away proactive people who really wanted the qualification. I'm thankful she allowed me to go through, but I 150% understand why CDC is recommended in the beginning of the program. I was lost, completely lost, for at least four months. I kept checking off tasks, but I really couldn't see the big picture. I was completing things but had no idea what I was actually doing. My Student and Instructor Guides for the workshop I had to present were terrible. The content was good, but it wasn't easy to teach in a classroom setting. The formatting was atrocious. Later I became a coach and I was embarrassed to show my candidates my Student and Instructor Guides. Mine were more examples of what not to do instead of what to do. Regardless of that hiccup and several more, I completed the program in July 2015. It took me 7.5 months to complete instead of six months. I was one of two people who completed it during the 2014 "season." (Approximately thirty people started; this is normal. Most people do not complete it.) I had been in Petaluma for just over one year, and I was fully qualified plus extra.

Following training, I began to help struggling students by conducting SAVE interviews. Student Academic Value Element (SAVE) is between a qualified SAVE instructor and a struggling student to evaluate why the student is struggling and give them tips to succeed in class. The first part of the interview is an in-depth assessment of how the student learns. There is also an assessment of the broader learning styles of visual, audio, or kinesthetic. After those two assessments, there is a questionnaire to evaluate the student's personal life and mental health. In some cases, students were struggling in class because they were so worried over a financial situation or family emergency that they simply weren't capable of concentrating on the material in class. These are assessments and questionnaires. I will admit that in my first couple of SAVEs, I was very robotic, and they were probably awkward for the student. As I got more comfortable in the role, I started making the SAVE more of a conversation. I filled out the required paperwork, but I was more human and less robotic. I allowed the student to just tell me in their own words what they thought was going on versus "interrogating" them. I learned a lot after that. There were several resources on base to assist a student with financial or personal problems and I would point the students with those issues in those directions. I had my MTS and instructor background, but I also started really researching how people learn. I started giving very specific advice to struggling students on how to form better study habits, retain information, and prioritize their schedule. By the time I left, one of the ET Chiefs was requesting me, personally, to do all the ET SAVEs because of how much success his struggling students had after my interviews versus other people's interviews. When I became a coach or if SAVE instructors asked me to help them, I very specifically told them not to be robots and helped them form more conversations, too. One OS1, a Texan Cubicle Mate, was very successful, too. Of course, he was a natural "human" versus robot on his own, so he didn't need too much advice from me.

The new Training Officer, the CDR SMC I was stationed with in Mobile, decided that MTS should not be worth an LOC. He argued that there wasn't any other qualification that was earned in the Coast Guard that was worth an LOC, so MTS shouldn't be either. Another point he made was that most people who did obtain the qualification didn't do any-thing with it afterward. They didn't go on to conduct SAVEs or coach. He felt if someone did something with the quali-fication, they could argue then that they deserved an award. He also jokingly told me that he had already written me up for a Commendation Medal, what more did I want from him? I admit he had very, very good points. I was disappointed, though, at the amount of work I had done and the fact that only two of us made it, but it was still the first year that an LOC wasn't given.

The summer of 2015 was also transfer season. Peter, an OS1, with whom I was stationed in Mobile, was headed toward Petaluma so we were paired to be Class Advisors for the next class. In Mobile, Peter and I were acquaintances. We were both runners, but he ran far more than I did. He also biked and swam and competed in Triathlons and Iron Mans. We were both OUs and some of my favorite watches were when I was CDO, he was OU, and another guy, a fellow author, was SU. The two of them made fun of me the entire watch, but it was hard to get mad because they were so funny. And if we were busy, the two of them were on top of things. They were one of my A-teams and we all worked well together. I didn't hang out with him too much after work. He is a huge fan of keeping work and home life separate. I respect that.

Since I was one of the only people he knew when he first moved to Petaluma, we became more friends than acquaint-ances. He had a large dog, so we watched each other's dogs when we had duty or went out of town. We also ran a couple

5Ks together. The longer he was there, he met more people with things in common and eventually met his fiancé, so we didn't hang out quite as much. I know he would help me out if I ever needed it, and I would have done the same for him.

I was excited to be paired with him as a Class Advisor, and I was determined to treat him with more respect than I received from Bill. It was fairly easy to do, as we agreed on most everything, anyway. We only got into one fight the entire time the class was onboard, but the timing of that fight was extremely detrimental for our "credit" as instructors.

I had learned a lot from my first class, and I was so excited to implement some new "programs" and help these students succeed even more than my first class. Peter didn't really care one way or the other, so I implemented them. One of the "programs" was the Challenge of the Week. It was one or two questions every week outside of the curriculum. The questions were designed to give the students more of a background or bigger picture of whatever we were learning and to give them basic Coast Guard or OS knowledge. If 13 of the 15 students answered the question every week, even if the answer was wrong, the entire class would get a prize. The majority of this class was completely uninterested in doing this. They were completely uninterested in most of our ideas.

I was baffled. My first class was so awesome, and I regretted that they did not get my best as an instructor. This class was getting the best of me and didn't want it. Peter and I also made a couple of mistakes early on. Three students had a birthday in the same week, one of the first weeks of school, so I brought in a cake to celebrate. Since I brought in a cake for them, it quickly became expected that I bring in a cake for all birthdays . . . and wouldn't you know, almost the entire class had a birthday while they were in school. My personal money (Peter helped a couple times, I think) paid for all those cakes. Peter and I allowed our class to play a lot of volleyball and other sports during mandatory class workouts versus making them run, lift weights, or circuit training. This seriously backfired

WEIGHT OUT

the one day we told them they were going to run. I've never heard a group of adults complain so much about a mile and a half run. I was pissed.

As was customary for all classes, our Chief was meeting with the class every Thursday morning. He would ask how they were doing and every Thursday morning, crickets. Then one Thursday, our Chief was out of town, so another Chief filled in for him. All of a sudden, our class had a list of complaints about us as Class Advisors and about the rest of the instructors. One of the complaints was that Peter and I fought every morning during Class Advisor time and that made the class extremely uncomfortable. Unfortunately, the fill-in Chief had witnessed our one fight so that validated the class's complaint. Peter and I were furious, to say the least. We were both sarcastic and poked fun at each other, but we were friends. We only got in one actual fight. Did these students not understand friendly banter?!? All the other instructors were upset, as well. The class's complaints were asinine. The actual Chief, upon returning, was pretty upset, too. Not only did he know most of the complaints were asinine (He knew Peter and I were friends enough to care for each other's dog.) but he was also upset that he had crickets every Thursday, but the fill-in Chief got an earful. The damage had already been done, though. The fill-in Chief made most of the instructors apologize for shit we never did and took away all remaining credit we might have had with the class. There are so many more stories and examples, but out of respect for everyone involved I will end it here. We were all happy when they graduated. I've never been more disappointed in my entire life.

I actually received my first and only negative page 7 (official reprimand) in the Coast Guard as a result of all the drama. Admittedly, venting on Facebook is not professional and was stupid. However, my privacy settings are pretty private, so a "friend" of mine betrayed me. I over-reacted to that, as well. I deleted half my friend's list, mostly former students, since I wasn't sure who actually betrayed me. I shouldn't have posted

267

what I posted, and I shouldn't have over-reacted. I did think the negative page 7 was funny, though, and since it was my first one and the class did suck, I joked around about framing it and hanging it on my wall. I still have it, but I never did frame it. I know I should have learned a valuable lesson, but I still think it is funny. My second class was the extreme opposite of my first class, so I had no idea what to expect of future classes.

Outside of work, all the doctors' appointments, 5K runs, and workouts, the summer of 2015 was insane. My younger sister got married in the very beginning of July, so I went home for the wedding. (As mentioned in the chapter about the pastor) My stepsister and her family came to visit mid-July. Immediately after they left, I had two Japanese Foreign Exchange students for three weeks, and then mid-August The Roommate moved in. I am used to living alone and doing what I want when I want. I was excited to see my stepsister and to host the Japanese Exchange students, but quickly became overwhelmed in both situations. I was rude to my stepsister for a day or two, and they almost flew out early. Luckily, we were able to talk it out and they stayed. After the Japanese students left, I went into complete isolation before The Roommate moved in and even for the first couple weeks that he lived with me. This cost me another friendship for almost a year. We made up later and are still good friends to this day.

The Roommate: During the transfer season, the Chiefs switched up the Instructor Pods. I went from being in Pod 3 to being in Pod 2. I joined Pod 2 in the middle of a class that was in session, at the beginning of their radio / SAR section of class. This class was right before my actual class, the one I talked about above that sucked, and this class was phenomenal, especially my four students in my district. (My first class, this class, and one other are my favorite three classes in all the time that I taught.) Like my A-School experience, when it was time to learn radio etiquette and how to respond to distress cases, the students were each assigned a Sector, four to a district (instead of six or seven), and two instructors oversaw them. One of my students, Evan, overheard me tell another instructor I had a spare bedroom, so he inquired about it. His best friend in the entire world and former college roommate had been accepted into the Park Ranger Academy at the local college but wasn't going to be able to attend if he could not find a place to stay for the four months of the class. Evan swore he was a good guy and would be a good roommate. I cleared it with the Chiefs and The Roommate moved in mid-August.

The Roommate is one of the best people I have ever met. I will always be incredibly thankful that he was in my life, even though he is not currently. Without him and Elad (my therapist), I would not be here today. He's from Denver, Colorado, is 6'6, and one of the most patient and positive people I have ever met, despite a rough life of his own. He was there for me through most of the hard times in Petaluma, and I will forever love him no matter what happens in either of our lives or if we never talk again.

The Park Ranger Academy is incredibly similar to Coast Guard boot camp. The Roommate shined boots like nobody's business but wasn't that great at ironing, so I often ironed his uniforms. The Academy was Tuesday through Saturday, from early in the morning to late at night. You could say it was better than boot camp because future rangers could come "home" every night, but they came "home" with homework, tests to study for, and uniform maintenance.

The Roommate never went to bed before midnight and had to get up at 0700 the next morning. Sundays became "roommate" days. We would go see a movie or play miniature golf or whatever. Mondays were The Roommate's day to himself. The Roommate is an only child and very independent. Unlike me, who is very social and requires a lot of interaction with people, The Roommate almost prefers to be alone. Mondays he was able to go hiking or fishing or take care of his academy obligations. It worked out very well.

The Roommate often held study sessions at my house, so I got to know a lot of the people in his class. Most of them were from different areas and were staying at hotels or renting rooms. The Roommate was one of the few people who "had a house."

One of the funniest things that happened was when his class was learning how to breach houses, looking for people with outstanding warrants or what not. I drove into the driveway, hit the garage button, and nearly drove into my den!! One of the guys in his class was sitting in the loft of the garage with a fake gun. He was the "bad guy" hiding from the Rangers inside, searching the house. When I recovered from my heart attack, I gave him a beer to drink until he was found. Later that night, I let some of the people "arrest" and cuff me. There weren't very many girls in the class, so they appreciated my volunteering. I also didn't know the rules they had to follow, so they could really practice giving their instructions the proper way.

In a later training exercise, The Roommate had to be pepper sprayed like I was in my Coast Guard training. I did my best to prepare him for it, although it is hard to describe that pain unless you have actually done it. Unfortunately, The Roommate had an extremely bad reaction to pepper spray. I tried my best to help guide him through the after care, as well. While I was helping him through the academy, I was struggling with my weight and everything I mentioned in the previous chapter.

The Roommate really didn't like running, preferring to either lift weights or swim, but he had to run for the Academy, so we ran together a couple of times. He was a great cook and tried his best to cook for me and get me to eat vegetables. Most of all, he just listened to me when I had a hard day which is really what got me through everything. In October 2015, I made Coast Guard weigh-ins. I had to starve myself and sit in the sauna for a while beforehand, but I weighed in at exactly 160.

To give his class a much-needed break and to celebrate my victory, we threw a huge Halloween Party. That was one of the best parties "I" have ever thrown. Of course, the next day was extremely painful. The Roommate told me he would help me clean up everything, if I could just throw out the jungle juice. That was mostly what he was drinking, and the smell was killing him. I agreed, if he would throw out the remaining Jello shots!

In December, I convinced The Roommate to run a 5K with me. The Great Santa Run was at Crissy Field in San Francisco. I had run a couple other 5Ks on the same course and thought it would be a great first 5K for him. The trail goes along the bay and you get several great views of the Golden Gate Bridge. The trail is also flat. Unfortunately, the day of the race, a monsoon hit San Francisco!! Seriously, it wasn't just sprinkling, it rained so hard that in the middle of the race a group of us just stopped and huddled together for a few minutes until the rain let up a little, and we continued. My headphones also completely shit the bed since they were so soaked. Luckily, I had a waterproof case for my phone. The Roommate and I had a lot of good laughs after that day, but I doubt he will ever run another 5K.

Shortly after the 5K, he graduated from the academy and went home for Christmas. He wasn't supposed to stay with me much longer than that, but life is "funny" sometimes and due to a lot of crazy circumstances, he ended up living with me for two years.

WRONG DIAGNOSIS

I'm not sure of the exact date, but sometime after I had failed two weigh-ins, I tried another personal trainer. She was a Coast Guard wife, as well, and we worked out in her shed. She was nothing like Lisa. She had a very specific format for her workouts and couldn't or wouldn't modify or adjust them in any way. There are certain exercises, such as deadlifts, that I cannot do. Don't ask me why, my body just doesn't work that way. I can't keep my back straight or keep good form. Lisa would just give me a different exercise to build up those same muscles. I loved kettle bell swings. Lisa said my form with those was better than any client she had ever had. Everyone is different. Our bodies are different. Our capabilities are different. Lisa knew this. My new trainer did not. She just kept insisting I do deadlifts and the other exercises I struggled with. Thankfully they were transferring, so I did not have to "fire" her.

A year or so later, I tried one more. She was a friend of a friend and her husband had hypothyroid or something similar to what I had so she thought she could help me. She was the personal trainer who was absolutely appalled at how the Coast Guard determined BMI. According to the machine she had, I was 10% less than the Coast Guard's measure. She asked what method the Coast Guard used and named off several. When I told her what the Coast Guard does, she said she'd have to look that up as she had never heard of it. I don't remember if the other branches do the same thing, but the military or Coast Guard is the only one who uses their asinine method.

Anyway, working out with her was fun at first. She listened

to what I said and modified things as needed. A mutual friend worked out with us from time to time, and I enjoyed that. But three things happened that caused me to "fire" her. Sometimes we worked out at her house or ran just the two of us, but most of the time we worked out at a martial arts gym where she taught other classes. She knew everyone at this gym and halfway through our workouts, she'd start talking to others and quit paying attention to me. The entire purpose for a personal trainer is to make sure your form is good to prevent injury. When she wasn't watching me, I stopped working. The second reason I "fired" her was because I wasn't losing weight nor seeing many results in general. I also "fired" her was because I could not afford her anymore.

I told the medical LT that I had seen the outside endocrinologist, and he had diagnosed me with hypothyroidism. I gave her copies of the doctor's notes, prescriptions, and bloodwork. She scolded me about how I shouldn't have to pay to see an outside provider but was otherwise OK with everything. Lies! She wasn't OK with some of the hormone supplements he prescribed and told me not to take those. I didn't understand the policy at the time and still don't but agreed to stop taking them. I couldn't really afford to keep paying for them, anyway. The LT even went so far as to try to help me get Tricare to pay for more visits with the outside provider (It never worked, but she did try.), and she did bloodwork for me prior to my visits with him so, at least, I would not have to pay for that anymore.

I hate it when doctors ask me if I'm feeling better. I can rarely say that I actually feel better. Some symptoms are better, but others are often worse. Sometimes I have new symptoms altogether. They bounce all around. At that time, I felt better for the most part. I went from having "controlled" periods on birth control to heavy periods with painful cramps, to acupuncture and no birth control pills, to somewhat normal periods, to having no periods whatsoever for a year or so, to having a period every other month to, finally, having "normal" periods again. However, even now, sometimes I will have a very painful month or skip a month altogether. It's rare, but it still happens. My hair was getting thicker and my nails were longer. I thought I wasn't as cold as usual but wasn't sure since it was summertime. One symptom that never got better (to this day) was my sleep. I don't sleep. The biggest thing I noticed that improved was depression. I noticed I had more energy and wasn't as sad as often.

Around April 2016, the next weigh-in, I started asking about a weight abeyance (waiver). I ended up making April's weigh-in, so the waiver became a nonissue (until later). Suddenly, seeing the outside provider became a huge deal. The LT did some bloodwork for me and noticed my TSH was less than one. I've been told by several doctors and reliable sources that 1) TSH is not the number you need to concern yourself with: T3 and T4 are more important; and 2) TSH bounces around a lot, especially in the beginning when you are still trying to figure out effective doses. Nonetheless, the LT freaked out, saying the outside provider was a quack. He obviously misdiagnosed me and now was trying to kill me. I could have serious heart problems with a TSH that low. There was no way I could have a weight abeyance based on anything he said, and I should quit seeing him altogether.

The next couple months, I became a medical lab rat. Since I still insisted something was wrong with me, the LT started "guessing" at what it could be and ordered all sorts of MRIs and CAT scans and blood work. Of course, everything kept coming up normal. Then the LT started lecturing me about how I ate and that maybe, instead of going to the gym once a day, I should go twice a day. She was always very passive-aggressive about it. She was overweight, too, so some visits she would say she understood the system was broken and unfair and that she hated it. The next appointment she'd do a 180 and blame me for being overweight. Finally, after several months and several "normal" tests, she decided to send me to an Air Force endocrinologist.

The Air Force endocrinologist was a complete asshole. He barely spoke any English, which I complained about on numerous occasions. If I wanted to be referred to another endocrinologist, the LT would make that referral, but none of them spoke very good English. The LT said that she wasn't sure why, but it seemed like endocrinologists were always of a different ethnicity. She suggested that I have a nurse come in the room with me so she could translate for me. The nurse was always busy so that never happened. The last suggestion was to take a notebook and write down exactly what he said. Then the LT would look at his notes, and we could compare the two. I took my medications wrong several times due to the differences between my notes and his orders and the pharmacy instructions. But I'm getting ahead of myself...

Backing up to my first visit, the Air Force endocrinologist said he was almost positive I had polycystic ovarian syndrome (PCOS) and asked if I had seen a gynecologist. I said no and he immediately ordered ultrasounds. Then he told me that he wanted more blood work, but it had to be "clean," so I was to quit taking all my thyroid medication. When I tried to explain to him that the thyroid medication was making me feel better and that I wasn't as depressed anymore, he insisted that I see a psychologist right away because I was obviously clinically depressed. It did not matter what I told him; his mind was made up. The orders were in. I was to stop taking my medication and see a psychologist right away.

I went back to Coast Guard medical for a follow up with the LT. This appointment she was mean. I told her I didn't want to stop taking my medication, admitting that I might do something stupid if I did. She told me I could quit taking it and follow the "real" doctor's orders, or I could be discharged for being overweight. She completely ignored my comment of maybe doing something stupid. She had done everything she could to help me and as far as she was concerned, everything wrong with me was in my head. I should feel lucky that she was letting me see an endocrinologist at all. She didn't say all of that. But that is how I felt. Every appointment with her she was either hot or cold. I never knew what mood she would be in and if she would actually help me out.

I stopped taking the medication and saw the Coast Guard psychologist, after a lot of encouragement from my first Chief in Petaluma and The Roommate. I was scared to see the Coast Guard psychologist and debated lying to him. After everything I had been through, I didn't want to find out what was medically wrong with me (potentially PCOS) just to be told I was also clinically depressed, lose my security clearance, and be discharged anyway. When I was in the guy's office, though, I decided to just go for broke and be honest. After all the "normal" tests, I was starting to feel like maybe I was just fat and lazy and looking for an excuse. Maybe nothing was wrong with me. Maybe I was a hypochondriac. I wanted help, and I figured the only way to get it was to be honest about my symptoms.

First of all, the psychologist told me that I was wrong about losing my security clearance if I was clinically depressed. He said that it can happen, but it takes more than just the diagnosis by itself. People are diagnosed with depression for several reasons. If you are diagnosed, put on medication, and get better, then you don't lose your clearance. It's only when you are put on medication and do not get better or have to be prescribed certain medications that it escalates to possible discharge. Let me type this again, "say" it loud and clear for everyone in the back of the room, A DIAGNOSIS OF DEPRESSION BY ITSELF DOES NOT EQUAL DISCHARGE.

Then the psychologist told me he had good news and potentially bad news. He said it wasn't really bad news, but he wasn't sure how I would take it. The good news was that I was not clinically depressed. I had some symptoms of it, but I was not on the actual spectrum. The potentially bad news was that I had a borderline anxiety disorder. He said he was not sure if the anxiety was caused by all the medical stuff and weigh-ins or if it was rooted in other things or if it was hormones or a combination of all those things. The psychologist told me that he could prescribe medication, but a possible side effect of the medication was weight gain. He said it was very little gain, if any, but in my situation, knowing a weight gain could cause more anxiety and render the medicine ineffective, he suggested I start seeing a therapist, instead. He said if I started getting better just by talking to someone and getting my hormones in normal ranges, then I would never have to see him again. He said if I didn't get better after talking and hormone adjustments, then we could talk about medications. I was thrilled to have a doctor who actually listened to me, diagnosed me, and gave me a reasonable solution. It turned out that therapy was the best thing that the Coast Guard ever did for me.

I had the ultrasounds. I literally asked everyone I knew to pray for me to have cysts. It's not that I actually wanted to have cysts, *per se*, it's that I wanted an answer. I wanted a diagnosis. I knew something was wrong with me, but the LT was making me question that and feel insane. If I didn't have cysts, I wasn't sure there would be any remaining options for me. Several people had a hard time praying for cysts, but they all knew what I was actually hoping for. A few weeks later, I found out I had multiple cysts on not just one, but both ovaries. The Roommate and I celebrated. I was beyond elated at this "good" news.

When the endocrinologist got his "clean" bloodwork, he determined that he was right, I did have PCOS, but the outside provider, my acupuncturist's dad, the "quack," was also right: I had hypothyroidism. The endocrinologist let me start taking the medication again, only a much lower dose. He also insisted that I take birth control. I outright refused. I had been on birth control for seven years. Birth control had not made me any better. If anything, birth control masked my symptoms and made me worse. I was not taking that again, and he could not force me to. He put me on Metformin and Aldactone instead. My bloodwork improved as I continued to see him and as said, my symptoms changed all the time. Even so, every single time I saw him, he asked me to take birth control. He also asked about my depression when the "clean" bloodwork came back. I told him that I was not clinically depressed, but I had an anxiety disorder. He continued to insist I was clinically depressed every time I saw him, too. He never listened to me. I hated him the entire time, but the answers I was given stood, so I didn't feel as if I had much of a choice.

In October 2016, I was twelve pounds overweight. I again asked for a weight abeyance. The medical LT wrote a very nice, long essay requesting the abeyance, citing all I had been through and the fact that I was paying out of pocket for outside care, such as the endocrinologist, chiropractor, personal trainer, nutritionist, and others. I was impressed with what she wrote and happy that she was taking her happy pills when she wrote it . . . but she didn't submit it until November. It wasn't approved until November 29th. So, even though I had not one, but two legitimate medical diagnoses and was granted a weight abeyance (I was no longer on the weight program so if I had to weigh in, it would not count.) because the abeyance was written and approved in November, the Coast Guard still gave me strike 3 for having been on the weight program in October through the beginning of November. After all the bullshit I had been through and after proving something was wrong with me, I was still penalized. This solidified my idea that the medical exam after you are put on the weight program is a complete waste of time. You are not given an abeyance if you cannot work out. You are just told you cannot work out. So, in some cases, an option to help you lose weight is now removed. If you actually stand up for yourself and insist on more than the exam (bloodwork, a referral to a different doctor, etc) and if it is determined you have a legitimate health issue, you better hope all the paperwork is in and approved before the end of April or October or you are still given a strike. So, someone please tell me why this is a required step?!?

Strikes: Three strikes in a row, just like baseball, you are out (discharged). Four strikes in one enlistment period, you are required to get a waiver to reenlist, should you want to. (Which is what I was now concerned about.) I thought strikes could occur any time you weighed in but am now (still) confused on this policy. Along with the bi-annual weigh-ins, you are required to weigh in when you transfer, accept orders to any schools or any other temporary duty, advance, during CCTI, etc. If you fail the weigh-in before you transfer or accept orders, the orders to transfer or to that school can be denied. If you fail during promotion, you must wait to be promoted. I do not know if it is an actual strike or not, though, if you fail a weigh-in that is not a bi-annual weigh-in.

After I got the weight abeyance, I thought I could finally relax, eat healthier, and start running again, while adjusting to the medications which would, hopefully, cause weight loss. I "fired" the personal trainer. I didn't like her, and I couldn't afford her. I put fired in quotation marks because it seems like a strange thing to say. She kept working; just not with me. Does that mean I fired her? It just seems odd to me.

Speaking of eating healthier, I met a nutritionist through my chiropractor who also did neurolingual testing. Since I was having all of these health problems, I wanted to learn if there was more, I could do to help myself. Beyond the advice I was given during the weight loss camp, I wanted to know if there were specific foods that were good or bad for my specific medical conditions. I also wanted to learn more about my medications and supplements. Neurolingual testing determines if certain medications or supplements will benefit you. The way it worked was I laid down on a massage table and the nutritionist pressed different pressure points. I would give her a baseline number for the pain I felt, if any. When a couple of points were pressed, I nearly jumped off the table. After she had the baseline numbers, I would put the medication or supplement on my tongue. I had to taste the actual medication or supplement, so capsules had to be broken open. Then she would press on the point again. If the pain was less, the supplement or medication was thought beneficial for me. If it got worse, then it was likely not beneficial to me. If it stayed the same, a different supplement or medication might work better. It sounded kind of silly to me, but my mom was an herbalist when I was growing up, so I had heard of similar things and wanted to keep an open mind. I had her test everything: everything she suggested, every prescription (including hormones) I had from the "quack" doctor, and all of my current prescriptions. Remember I said there was a point where I nearly jumped off the table? When I had the supplement in my mouth, I wasn't in any pain whatsoever. The nutritionist kept adjusting and pushing in the same area, but at slightly different angles. I was confused and finally asked what she was doing. (She had tested so many points, I had forgotten.) She said that she wanted to make sure she was pressing in the same spot that caused such extreme pain before. Even with all her experience, she had seen numbers improve, but she had never seen anyone go from a 10+ to a zero. She said that that supplement needed to be my highest priority. Metformin also tested beneficial to me, which made me feel a lot better and kept me stubborn about not taking birth control again. I took the medications I was prescribed along with holy basil, fish oil, vitamin D3, and probiotics. I feel like I'm forgetting something, but it doesn't matter. The point is I was doing everything I could to heal.

The nutritionist and chiropractor both explained to me how acid reflux really works. I quit taking that medication and started adding lemons to my water and drinking apple cider vinegar at night. The Roommate and I would actually take "shots" of apple cider vinegar. We would also compete to drink the most water. In the beginning, The Roommate and I pushed each other to be healthier and work out more. He had a membership at 24-Hour Fitness and swam a lot. I went with him a couple times and ran on the treadmill. Our water competition was one of the best competitions I have ever been in.

Win or lose, we were both still winning. Toward the end of his stay, though, when both of our situations became most stressful, we became bad influences on each other, both of us eating our feelings.

I finally had some answers and some solutions. I hoped I would begin to feel better and that I could save my Coast Guard career. Little did I know what more was in store . . .

REAL THERAPY,
REAL HELP

As per the psychologist's recommendation, I began therapy. I was referred to a local guy in Petaluma named Elad. I went willingly. I drove myself there despite my many reservations about therapy. I really didn't want to go. We introduced ourselves and began the session. Elad asked me why I was there. I was very proud of myself because I had perfected my "elevator speech" in explanation of the past year or so. I concluded saying "So, I don't know if my anxiety is hormones or something else, but I figured I might as well give you a chance."

Elad then asked what I hoped to get out of the session. At that time, I really didn't know what I wanted, but I did know what I didn't want so I very bluntly told him, "I do not want to come in here and cry about my childhood or anything else. I am not a victim. What has happened to me has happened. It is what it is. I'm 32 years old and responsible for my own behavior. What I do is what I do and it's on me. Who cares why I do it, let's just make sure I stop doing it."

I thought for sure I was killing my first impression. I thought I was being outright rude, and he might not want to work with me. I don't know if he chose to ignore that, decided I needed more help than I thought, or appreciated my honesty, but the next question he asked me was, "Have you been in therapy before?"

I very angrily told him about the Pastor. I probably started shaking then, too. He replied, "Ok, well let's make a deal. If I ever do anything that upsets you, please tell me. I will try to correct the wrong." I was surprised and impressed by his response, and I agreed to tell him if he ever upset me. I'm trying to think now if he ever has. I don't think so.

Then he asked me, "Is there anything specific that you want to work on?"

I answered that I wanted to treat The Roommate with more respect. I said that I wanted to be a better friend to people, in general. I told him that I had very high standards and it was impossible for anyone to live up to them, and I was tired of losing people because of this. I also very desperately wanted to be happy, but I don't remember if I told him that. At the time, I didn't think my happiness was ever possible, so I think I just stuck to a more attainable goal. Elad scheduled an appointment for me the next week.

So far, I've tried my best to write this book in chronological order because a book has to have some sort of order. But therapy is different. There isn't really a chronological order of events for therapy. I didn't go in every week, explain what was going on in my life, receive feedback, and just immediately apply it and immediately feel better. Therapy is not like math class. I didn't learn 1 + 1 = 2 and then the next day have that memorized and move on to 2 + 2 = 4. Therapy is more like going to the gym. When you first start going, you try all the machines. You find a couple that you like. You start off with lower weights and learn the proper form. As you continue to go, you continue to add things to your routine. But routines are hard to keep. If you injure yourself, you have to adjust for that. If your hours at work change, you may have to adjust your hours at the gym. If something happens, you may not go to the gym at all for a while. When you come back to the gym, you may have to "start over again" or "back track" for a little while until you regain your strength.

That is therapy, or at least how it is for me. I would see Elad every week, discuss what was happening in my life, receive feedback, try to apply it. Sometimes, I completely understood what he meant, and it was "easy" to apply. Other times, I came back the next week and asked for clarification or more guidelines. I would start to feel better and think my life was back on track, then something would happen. Most of the time, the Coast Guard threw another curveball at me, but sometimes it was my personal life. It's easy to talk to people when things are going well. As soon as I got mad, I would re- vert to old habits. Some topics were hard to digest and Elad had to "push pause" on them for a few weeks and circle back. For a long time, it felt like I was taking two steps forward and one step back every week. Then, one week, I walked into ther- apy completely terrified. Nothing had happened that week. I didn't have anything to talk about. But I knew I wasn't healed yet. I knew I needed to keep seeing Elad. He kindly laughed at my terror; not in a condescending way at all. Elad said that when people are in "crisis mode," therapy is spent dealing with the crisis and putting out fires. That was the mode I had been in for several weeks. Elad continued, saying that once people are out of "crisis mode," the true healing can begin. That is when they are a bit more open-minded, and they can learn techniques to avoid or better handle "crisis mode" in the future. I was so relieved that I could continue seeing him.

Support during therapy is an interesting thing. It can be extremely helpful, but sometimes it can also kind of make things worse. Sometimes you must be careful about what you wish for.

The first lesson I had to learn was about "future wrecking." I always anticipate the worst- case scenario in every situation. That isn't bad, in and of itself. Sometimes, it is very helpful for planning purposes. It helped out a lot when I was doing SAR. Unfortunately, or fortunately, I guess, real life is not always SAR or "crisis mode." While anticipating the worst-case scen- ario helped at work and is helpful with some future planning, my pendulum swung too far to one side, and it was not helping me out at all in two different ways. The first had to do with how I interacted with the people in my life. Something would happen or I would do something and then I would anticipate how someone would react to what happened or whatever I did. If they did not react at all, I would anticipate what they were thinking or why they did not react. Instead of talking to that person and trying to find out what they were actually thinking, I would automatically turn my fears and anxiety into facts. I did not need to talk to them; I knew exactly what was going on. I would then act out towards that person based on whatever I anticipated happening. In other words, I would be mad at someone for something I thought they were going to do. I didn't trust people even though they hadn't betrayed me. I just somehow knew that everyone would eventually hurt me or betray me, so I "sped" things along.

The second way future wrecking really hurt me (and still does sometimes) was in planning for my future. Let's use this book for example. I wanted to write a book. I wanted to tell my story to try to help others who might be going through some of the same things I did. But what if I'm unable to write what happened in a clear and accurate way? What if my book doesn't flow well? What if I can't figure out how to publish it? What if it doesn't sell? What if someone gets offended by it? What if, what if, what if?

Remember how I said I had several ideas for books in the past? That Hillary was too scared so writing a book was just a silly idea which she mentioned to friends in passing. That Hillary never once thought she would be an author and never really tried to become one. Do you know what happens when you don't try to do something? My fears became a self-fulfilling prophecy and when that happened often enough, at least in my case, I just saw myself as a complete failure, incapable of doing anything. But look at me now! You are reading my book! I am an author!

Another thing Elad and I discussed was my relationship with food. We discussed all the weigh ins, all my bad habits, the foods I did and didn't like, the fact that I was addicted to chocolate, etc. We made a "rule" that moods don't lead to food; meaning that I couldn't just start binge eating whenever

I was sad or depressed. (I follow that sometimes; sometimes I don't. It's easier said than done.) Elad was also able to elaborate on something my nutritionist had said and, all of a sudden, my light bulb went off. My nutritionist had given me a form to fill out. I had to write down what I ate, how I felt immediately after, and then several hours later. Now this seems very straight-forward, but I didn't understand what she wanted me to do. I would write down what I ate and then write down that I felt "fine" after. Or sometimes I would write that I felt "full" or "still hungry." Writing down how I physically felt was good and was partially what my nutritionist wanted. I did very quickly learn what foods aggravated my acid reflux and started avoiding those. But Elad wanted me to focus more on how I felt emotionally. Sometimes, I would come into therapy and say I was sad or depressed. Elad would ask me what had happened, but nothing had happened. He would ask why I was sad, and I had no idea why I was sad. I was frustrated because I did not want to be sad, but I did not know how to be happy. Elad asked what I ate for breakfast or lunch. Elad asked what I ate the night before. Suddenly, the form my nutritionist gave me made more sense: how do I feel immediately and several hours later? Sugar is bad for you. Everyone knows this. But anyone who has ever craved sugar knows that while you are eating it and for a while after, you feel better. That is why I ate chocolate when I was depressed. What I did not realize was how I felt several hours after. After that immediate "rush," I would begin to feel tired, sluggish, fat, useless . . . depressed and sad. Holy crap! Sugar really is bad for me! Twice in 2017, I successfully gave up sugar for a month at a time. I never made it past a month and haven't tried since. I noticed considerable differences when I gave it up. I didn't completely give up all sugar. You'd be surprised, if you started reading labels, how many foods have sugar in them. I started by giving up cakes, cookies, candy, chocolate, and other desserts. My goal was to eventually cut back on other sugars, but I didn't get there. I hope that someday I will. Sugar was not the only food that caused me to be depressed, either. It's the easiest one to write about because I feel like everyone can relate to that. Some people prefer salty foods over sweets, though. How do you feel immediately after you eat potato chips? How do you feel several hours later? I began modifying my diet less by "society's rules" of healthy eating and more by listening to my body and how it responded to my diet. The changes were very dramatic and very good. I have since fallen out of this habit but hope to get back into it soon. It would probably improve my acid reflux!

Elad and I discussed several little "rules" or mantras to help me stay on track. I loved talking to him and always felt better after a session. I slowly began to trust him. Then, one day, he asked me if I liked the Coast Guard. I answered yes. Then he asked what I liked about it. Everything I named off was in the past. I mentioned hardly anything that was current. He asked me if I had thought about getting out of the Coast Guard. I answered, "Of course not! Why would I do that? I have eleven (I think at that time) years in. I have two more units. I will get a pension. Why would I get out?" He left that topic alone for a while and then eventually circled back to it.

Along with a very good friend and mentor at work and a few other people, The Roommate was very supportive while I was in therapy. I don't want to leave the other people out of this book, but since The Roommate lived with me, he was around more and had to put up with more than the others, so he will get more of a spotlight. Just know, though, while it takes a village to raise a child, it takes another village to keep Hillary sane. In some ways, I think I treated The Roommate a lot better after I started therapy, and in some ways, I think I treated him worse. I felt guilty over it all the time (sometimes I still do), but Elad told me not to and The Roommate didn't seem to mind too much, at the time.

The Roommate knew the term "future wrecking" and that I was working on it in therapy. The Roommate was used to me "spinning out" but prior to therapy, he didn't really know what to do. He tried really hard. He would consistently tell me to "think positive." But I had no idea what that meant. I had no idea how to. What if, what if, what if? Eventually he'd give up and just let me rant a bit. God bless him for doing that, but it wasn't doing either of us any favors. After I began therapy, I would start spinning out, and The Roommate would just look at me and calmly ask, "Are you future wrecking?"

I'd stop dead in my tracks. I was "future wrecking"! I'd take a deep breath and then ask what he thought. He'd tell me his interpretation of the situation. This was helpful in a couple of ways. One, it stopped me from "spinning out." Anyone who has ever had a panic attack knows how incredibly valuable it is when someone is capable of stopping that! The second way it helped was enabling me to start putting myself in other people's shoes. It enabled me to think differently and give people the benefit of the doubt. It often enabled me to try things I would not ordinarily try. I would not have my own business right now if not for The Roommate. I will write more about that later. I will give myself credit that I have done the majority of the work to make it happen. But if The Roommate had not stopped me from "spinning out" and doing something stupid, my business would not exist.

So, what did I mean earlier when I said that sometimes support can make things worse? What did I mean about being careful about what you wish for? Since The Roommate was so good about calling me out on "future wrecking" and since I wanted to treat him better, I asked him to call me out on all the harmful things I was doing. I was very serious about want-ing to be a better person and wanting to feel better. I knew I could not accomplish those things on my own. I knew I did things without realizing that I was doing them. It made sense to ask The Roommate to point them out to me, right? The Roommate started calling me out, but after a while I forgot I asked him, and I just didn't realize the extent of the things I was doing wrong. After a month or so, I thought The Room-mate was mad at me all the time, and I was convinced he hated my guts. I had no idea why he was friends with me. I felt so guilty for always letting him down. One night we had been "fighting" (I guess) and just talking in circles for hours. Literally, this started at like 6 or 7 pm and went until midnight or 1 in the morning. I don't even remember what I did or what he said, but he called me out on something. and I hard core spun out. Why was he living with me? Why did he go places with me and do things with me? Why did he let me treat him so poorly? Why, why, why? I kept asking him why he was friends with me, and he really couldn't answer. He wanted to stop talking, but I wouldn't let it go. Finally, after several hours, he asked me, "What are you hoping to get out of this conversation? What is your end game?"

I stopped dead in my tracks. What was I hoping to get out of the conversation? What answer did I want? Why wouldn't I let this go? I was just as exhausted as he was talking in circles. It wasn't making me feel better. I thought about it for a long time, and I finally said, "Everyone has good qualities and bad, right?" He agreed. "If you're friends with someone, then the good outweighs the bad." He agreed again. "Well, I just don't see how my good outweighs my bad when you are always telling me how bad I am."

He then, very calmly said, "Isn't that what you asked me to do? Didn't you want me to call you out on your shit?"

I was stunned. Yes, it was what I asked him to do. I was mad at him for what I asked him to do. I literally couldn't talk for a few seconds as I just sat there amazed at what had just happened. I weakly asked, "So you're not actually mad at me, you're just trying to help me?"

He answered, "Most of the time."

I was really taken aback. I thought about it a little more. I finally "recovered" and said, "Well, you can stop now. That's my end game. Stop calling me out on things."

He simply replied, "Ok. Can I go to bed now?"

As funny as that story might be now, at the time it was brutal. I actually learned a very valuable lesson, though. Anytime

I'm upset about anything, and I'm thinking about confronting someone about it, I try to think about my "end game." I try to ask myself, "What am I hoping to get out of this?" I encourage all of my readers to do the same thing. It helps me calm down and think a little more rationally. Sometimes, there is no end game. Sometimes, I know I can't get anything out of it. That leads to me to make another decision. Other times it helps me be more direct and prevents talking in circles for hours and hours. It's a great strategy, but it is also easier said than done so I'm still a work in progress.

The Roommate also helped me realize just how passive aggressive I really was. Past experience told me that if I was upset over something, I would confront someone; they would tell me how incredibly irrational I was being; I would apologize to them; I'd feel better for a half-minute; then I would realize I apologized to them, but I was still upset. If I tried to confront said person a second time, I was then re-hashing an old fight and would be accused of not letting things go so I would apologize again. Several people in my life were extremely manipulative and I learned very quickly that I was just incapable of getting respect or "winning fights." Since I was tired of apologizing to everyone for things I didn't do, I became very passive aggressive. The Roommate actually thought this was kind of funny most of the time. I would do incredibly stupid things, like turn off all the lights when I went to bed, so he would have trouble seeing when he got home. He had a flashlight on his phone, though, and in the beginning didn't even realize I was mad, but just thought I forgot to leave them on. Then I'd get even madder that he didn't notice I was mad, and then I'd take it up a notch. The Roommate was not a mind reader, and he started getting annoyed that I expected him to be one. He started to take more notice of the stupid things, like the lights being off, and he started "making me" talk to him. Sometimes he had to swear over and over and over again that he would not be mad before I even said a word. But he was true to his word. And the majority of the time, after we talked, I felt silly for being upset in the first place. I tried really hard to stop being passive aggressive and to just start talking to him.

As hard as I tried to talk to him, though, I had never talked to anyone before, so I didn't really know how. Life was great when The Roommate noticed I was mad at him and "made me" talk to him. It was fantastic when he just listened to me and reassured me. But what happened when he got mad at me? What happened when he told me I had done something to upset him? Or what happened when we were both mad? I still apologized whenever I thought I couldn't win an argument. I still apologized for things I didn't think I was doing wrong. If I could not articulate how I felt, I didn't bother trying. After I had been in therapy for a while, if I couldn't articulate how I felt about something, Elad would help me work through it. Elad and I would discuss things that happened between The Roommate and me and suddenly I knew how to "defend myself." I was very rarely upset with The Roommate. I didn't want him to apologize for anything. I wasn't even really upset that I had apologized to him. I was wrong sometimes. When I say I knew how to "defend myself," it wasn't that I didn't do something wrong; it was more about the intention behind what I did. In my mind, The Roommate thought I was more immature, childish, vindictive, etc, than I really was. In my mind The Roommate was upset because he thought I intentionally disrespected him and most of the time it was not intentional. I wanted him to understand me better. I wanted him to know where I was coming from. I wanted him to realize all my destructive patterns, and I wanted him to give me grace and help me work through them. I didn't want blind forgiveness, and I didn't want him to let me walk all over him. Similar to a toddler learning to walk, I wanted him to let me fall sometimes in order to finally get it right. It took me too long to realize that, though. For a while, every Tuesday night I'd go to therapy, and then I'd come home to re-hash some "fight" The Roommate and I had had in the past. The Roommate was very patient and had most of these conversations with me, but we talked in circles a lot. I have no doubt that at some point he went from happy and supportive about my therapy to dreading my coming home on Tuesday nights. I was emotionally drained, too. Eventually I figured out my end game. And eventually I was able to tell The Roommate what I wanted. My plan for how to do that failed hard core, and I really upset him. God bless him, when I explained how I had come up with my plan, he immediately acknowledged what I had meant to do and that I had not meant to hurt him. Unfortunately, though, I had hurt him. I'm not sure if he ever really gave me grace after that or not. As said, he had a lot going on, too, and he was only so capable of giving me so much. We did, however, stop talking in circles every Tuesday night, and that was a blessing.

I put fights in quotation marks because The Roommate and I rarely fought. We had little disagreements here and there. We were both always stressed out for various reasons and took it out on each other, even when we didn't mean to. We both had a lot going on at that time, and we both had demons from out pasts. (Hell, we both still have a lot going on.) I know The Roommate shared some characteristics that some of my manipulative "friends" had, and I know that sometimes, when he said things, he triggered things in me. I am fairly certain I remind him of someone, and that pushes his buttons, too. We never discussed that, though. Despite all that, we really didn't actually fight. We were rarely genuinely pissed at each other. Irritated and annoyed, yes; pissed off, no. That is probably the one thing I love the most about The Roommate. He only raised his voice to me twice the entire time I knew him. He never called me names and he never, ever made me feel like shit just because I made him feel like shit. He was not vindictive. He was calm, rational, patient, willing to listen to me, but also assertive about what he had to say. In this regard, he was everything I was striving to be. He also made me realize that I never wanted to have another friend who I couldn't talk to. The Roommate single-handedly changed my perspective on friendships and potential future relationships.

We did get in one really big fight, though. I was very close to telling The Roommate to get the hell out and he was very close to packing his shit up and getting out on his own. You could cut the tension in the air with a knife and The Roommate and I were both avoiding the house because of it—well, and because of the demon dog that I had volunteered to watch--again. A mutual friend was actually the one who pointed it out one day. I was on base and he asked why I was still there. I said I didn't want to go home. My friend kind of chuckled and said The Roommate took an extra shift a couple nights ago for the same reason. I went home that night and insisted that we talk. The Roommate was hesitant at first as tensions were very high, but we talked. We were both calm. Neither one of us raised our voices, called names, or swore at each other. We both allowed the other to have their say. I apologized profusely to him for not listening to him and for taking him for granted. I was guilty of and was/am sorry for that...however, I didn't listen to him for a reason...and the fight continued to bother me for a long time after it was over.

A few therapy sessions later I told Elad that I was happy we worked things out. I told Elad that I was glad The Roommate didn't move out and that we were still friends. I told Elad I did not want to re-hash the fight at all. I told him I was very happy it was over and wanted it to remain over. But I also told Elad that a part of me was kind of upset that I apologized. I recognized I could have handled the situation better and was sorry for that. But I was not actually sorry for what I did—which was volunteering to watch the demon dog--again. I didn't want anything to change between The Roommate and me, but I wanted to know why I couldn't get past the fight, either.

Elad gave me homework. He told me to think about how my needs were met as a child. He told me very specifically to think about my needs and not my wants. He told me we would discuss it the next week.

I over analyze everything. He wanted needs; I was going

to give him needs. I had learned about Maslow's Hierarchy of Needs during my MTS training. I drew that triangle and started filling it out. We discussed it at the next session. Elad told me that I was neglected as a child. I tried to argue with him. I pointed out several things. Elad finally looked at me and asked, "Do you remember what you said to me your very first session?"

"What part?"

"You told me that you didn't want to be treated like a victim. Have I ever treated you like a victim?"

"No."

"I'm not treating you like one now, either. You were neglected as a child. Your needs were not met. If you look up "neglect" in the dictionary, you will see that you meet the definition of it. This is a fact. It is what it is."

From there we discussed how I needed one thing (to help out a friend) and The Roommate needed something else (a quiet house without a demon dog to take care of while I was at work). I watched the dog, which essentially took care of my need, but The Roommate resented me for it, since he needed something else, and I resented him for resenting me. Neither of us had done anything wrong, *per se*. Elad said that it was impressive that we got past it: a testament to our friendship. He said that most marriages fail when needs are not met. The reason I was having a hard time getting past it, though, was because my needs hadn't been met for a long time so I apologized to The Roommate for essentially meeting my needs, which rubbed salt in an open wound. Had The Roommate apologized to me, though, he would have felt the same way. It seemed to be a no-win situation, except that we both survived it. Elad then asked if we could finally start talking about my childhood. From that point forward, everything in my life was fair game. Not only had my friendship with The Roommate survived, but therapy had just "become real."

Elad eventually circled back to the question of why I liked the Coast Guard and if I wanted to stay in. I finally started thinking about my health and if I should really stick it out eight or nine more years. The more things happened with medical and admin, the harder it was to justify a career in the Coast Guard. Elad started helping me come up with a new plan for my future.

THE END OF
MY CAREER

My weight abeyance (waiver) was signed and went into effect the end of November 2016. The weight abeyance was approved because I was diagnosed with PCOS and hypothyroidism. Its terms were for six months. That is also when I started therapy with Elad. I was going every Tuesday. I finally thought I could breathe again. I finally thought that having a career was possible again.

I wanted to come up with a "total package" health plan that was sustainable for the rest of my life. The first place I needed to start was my diet. Everyone I knew kept telling me how great the Keto diet was, especially for someone with PCOS. The Keto diet may be great for some people, but I knew that it was way too restrictive for me. I knew that I was disciplined enough to stick with it for six months to a year, but I knew that after that I would fall back into old habits of binging again. I also knew that for that entire time period I would be miserable, and I would make everyone around me miserable, as well. I no longer wanted to live that way. I decided to track everything I ate and eat the foods that made me feel better; both immediately after I ate and 24 hours later. I thought that listening to my body along with the medications I was on would be all I needed to do.

The next thing I needed to address was my workout routine. My personal trainer was not helping me, and I did not want to spend more money, so I fired her. My chiropractor, after learning that I did, in fact, have hypothyroidism, was concerned about my adrenal glands. She told me that running too much would stress my adrenal glands and slow down my metabolism, making me gain weight rather than losing it. This made sense to me since I had never fully recovered after any workout and I kept gaining weight in California despite running all those 5Ks. A number of different people suggested various workouts and some even worked out with me. Each time I sought out advice from a new person, they told me what I was previously doing was wrong. Maybe I didn't stick with anything long enough for it to work, but nothing ever worked as far as losing weight was concerned. The workout I probably enjoyed the most was yoga. I have never been that flexible and I always had a really hard time "recovering" after workouts, so I figured that would solve both problems. The specific instructor I found was inexpensive and taught all levels. Sometimes I would spend the entire class in child's pose. We became good friends and I probably did that for eight months to a year. But then she lost the place she taught, and we had a falling out, so I quit yoga. At the end of the day, I decided that if absolutely nothing was right for me and nothing was going to aid in losing weight, then I just wasn't going to do anything at all.

I can't remember how often I saw the Air Force Endocrinologist at first. As said in previous chapters, he was a complete asshole and I had a very hard time understanding him. Appointments were consistent though: He insisted that I was depressed and must take birth control. I consistently refused. He finally prescribed aldectone and metformin instead. He didn't tell me what either of these medications were for. I later learned that metformin regulates insulin and is often given to diabetics. Women with PCOS are very susceptible to diabetes and I showed symptoms, so it made sense to me. That is all metformin is advertised for; however, it also aids in regulating periods and fertility in some women. I have never tried to have kids, so I don't know about that part, but my period is mostly regular now. I was also on levothyroxine for my thyroid.

I went back to the nutritionist to have all of my medications tested. Metformin tested strong for my body which validated my refusing birth control. I also continued to see the chiropractor.

In January 2017, I had my annual Physical Health Assessment (PHA) at medical. This is one of the biggest wastes of time and resources in the entire Coast Guard. You are given a questionnaire that makes almost everyone lie. It asks about how you eat, if you smoke, if you drink, how much sleep you get, your sex life, etc. It is supposed to evaluate how healthy you are and bring any issues you may have to medical's attention, since most people avoid medical like the plague. The problem is, if you are honest on the questionnaire, you will likely be red flagged. Most people in the Coast Guard, if they are honest on this bullshit questionnaire, would appear to be clinically depressed, an alcoholic, a sex addict, extremely obese, extremely unhealthy, or a combination of any or all of those things. If you are red flagged, you have to make a second medical appointment to talk to the actual medical officers instead of just the "peon" Health Service Technicians (HS). No one wanted to be lectured about how much they ate, smoked, or drank, so they all lied.

When I went for my PHA, my blood pressure was too high. My blood pressure was something like 145/100. There was no possible way that was accurate, but that is what the HS wrote down. If you have high blood pressure during an appointment, you are required to go back up to medical twice a day for three days for them to re-check it. Every HS that took my blood pressure did it differently. Some used the machine cuff, some read it themselves. Some talked to me; some did not. Some told me to elevate my arm; some did not. My blood pressure was high, but the numbers varied dramatically from day to day. I was told I needed to make an appointment with the LT to discuss this new problem. I didn't want to make another appointment, especially with her. I was already on enough medication and seeing enough doctors. I never made an appointment with the LT.

I hate it when doctors ask me if I'm feeling better. I have no idea what that means. My symptoms continually change. Toward the end of 2016 and the beginning of 2017, I started having periods again but not every month. When I did have a period, some were painful; some were not. My nails and hair were growing back thicker. I didn't sleep at all. I still don't sleep much. My moods varied. The more I learned in therapy and the more I tried to apply it, the better and worse I became. I gained weight while I was off all medication for the "clean blood" test. After that I lost some, but overall, my weight didn't change much at all.

During all this, in the beginning of December 2016 through March 2017, I was Class Advisor again. There was a female Chief who had transferred in over the summer who wanted to "get qualified" so she could have an idea of what her people were doing when she was in charge of them, so she was one of my break-ins. The other break-in was an OS1 who had transferred in over that summer, too. The female Chief and I got along well, so I'm kind of disappointed we haven't kept in touch. I know that is just as much my fault as it is hers. Or rather, I know that is life. But I kind of thought we would both make more of an effort. The OS1 is a hard guy to explain. He had a very bold personality, so he rubbed a lot of people the wrong way. I didn't necessarily like him, but when advising with him, I got to see a different side of him. I think he has great intentions, but his execution is absolutely horrible. I know this is ironic coming from me, but he really needed to be more tactful. Despite all of that, the three of us got along very well advising together. I feel like our strengths and weaknesses balanced out well so the combination of us was better than each of us individually.

This class's achievement and behavior was somewhere between my first class and second class. Some of them were interested in the Challenge of the Week and some were not.

We had to kick one guy out for sexual harassment and stalking so that had some residual effects on the class. Otherwise, they were relatively low drama. Their personalities weren't bad, but none of them really stuck out, either. I enjoyed them for the most part. I keep in touch with a couple of them. I hope they are all doing well.

Toward the end of the six-month weight abeyance, May 2017, I requested an extension of it, stating all the medications I was on, the fact that the doses had been changed a lot, mentioning the symptoms that had gotten better, and saying that I had gained some weight initially but was very slowly starting to lose some and needed a little more time to get it all off. At first, the medical LT told me that there was no such thing as an extension on a weight abeyance. Luckily, the Admin Officer was on the same email, so he corrected her. All she had to do was file a memo.

The medical LT was mad. She wrote me an email stating that she couldn't possibly write a memo for me because she hadn't seen me during the six months of my abeyance. I sucked up and apologized, trying to get back on her good side. I made an appointment with her to discuss the last six months and my health—or rather, my weight.

During the appointment, she accused me of taking the abeyance for granted. She said that I had quit trying to lose weight because I no longer had to try. I wasn't working out with a personal trainer anymore, so clearly, I was not working out at all. Toward the end of the six months, I was not working out, but at the beginning, I had tried several things. I tried telling the LT about all the contradictory advice I was given. She blew off my explanations as if they were all pathetic excuses. I had no proof that I had gained or lost any weight. The numbers she had from my previous medical weigh-in and that day actually showed a weight gain. To her, I was obviously lying to get an extension. She lectured me because I was told to see her after my PHA showed high blood pressure, but never did. She lectured me about not following up with her after my seeing the

Air Force Asshole. She was clearly hot that day. I did my best to defend myself and remain respectful.

I suppose I had some of that coming. I was given advice to track my weight and didn't. I didn't realize that seeing her after my PHA was a "direct order" if you will, but I guess I should have seen her just to keep the peace. I had no idea I was supposed to follow up with her after every appointment with the Air Force Asshole. I know that it is policy after you are referred out to "local" doctors, but I thought since the Air Force was also military the two networks talked. She never told me to follow up with her or checked in to see why I hadn't. But that was her way. She never had a problem with me seeing the other endocrinologist, either, until I asked her to write the original abeyance. She didn't care about me unless I wanted something from her. Then, suddenly, things that had never been problems before were problems, and she couldn't possibly be bothered to help me.

I tried asking for advice on what workouts she would recommend. That was a huge mistake. She was not a personal trainer; she was a doctor. As a doctor, though, she knew I gained weight when I stopped taking birth control, so what would she recommend? She would recommend, if I really wanted to lose weight, that I start taking birth control again! I was seeing red!! I'm very rarely that level of mad and it took everything in me to remain respectful. I probably would not have remained respectful had I not needed her to write a memo for my extension. She was totally OK with my decision to quit taking birth control—fully understanding my reasons for doing so—when I originally stopped taking it. But now that I wanted an extension, how dare I refuse to take it? And that's right, ladies, don't take birth control because it is good medication that will help you become healthier; take birth control to lose weight.

I finally gave up and did a lot of the standard nodding of the head and replying "Aye, aye" to everything she said. She prescribed a low dose of blood pressure medication. Hydrochlorothiazide is actually a water pill. She prescribed it to further help me lose weight. It is for high blood pressure, too, and that is how she sold it. She put me on a very low dose because I did not want to be on more medication and that was part of her sales pitch, too. I, of course, didn't know it was a water pill or how dangerous it is until later. (Also, a quick Google search reveals it is one of the top four worst blood pressure medications.) Even if I had known, though, at that point I was willing to agree with everything she said. By the end of the appointment, she agreed to write a memo to extend my weight abeyance. I was happy until I read what she wrote. She outright said that there was no proof that I was working out, eating right, losing weight, or doing anything to help myself, but there was some improvement in some of my symptoms and I was on medication, so maybe more time would help. She practically called me a liar but requested the extension, anyway.

I was granted an extension, but it was written differently than "normal" extensions are written. There is a way to get "indefinite" extensions. Extensions are good for six months at a time and at the end of six months, a person would just need to renew it, like a magazine subscription. Medical would have to continually articulate what they were doing to become thinner or healthier or whatever. In other words, they would need a medical officer who was willing to advocate for them. That was something I did not have. My extension specifically said that I would never be granted another extension unless I got a new diagnosis of a different disease or issue. My Senior Chief called the Personnel Service Center (PSC) and spoke with a Master Chief to get this reversed. The Master Chief said it couldn't be reversed. The extension was not a "standard form" that just required filling in the blank. My extension had been worded the way it was for a reason. It could not be changed just like the original abeyance couldn't be amended or re-written for October instead of November. My Senior Chief fought hard for me, but the Master Chief stood his ground.

I would like to point out that all of these irreversible decisions were just memos. They are literally a piece of paper. A human typed them. They can be easily deleted from a computer file or shredded. That would make too much sense, though. They absolutely cannot be changed. Why would anyone question that? My fate had been sealed.

At some point, I finally "gave in" with Elad and allowed him to discuss the possibility of my getting out of the Coast Guard. I have never wanted a college degree. I didn't enjoy high school. I didn't enjoy online classes. I didn't want to take a bunch of bullshit basic classes in order to finally take a few classes that pertain to the actual job I want to do. A part of me knew I had a strong resume' and wouldn't need a degree, but, of course, that is a very unpopular opinion. It made my anxiety worse. Elad assured me that I had a very strong resume' and that I would not need a degree. I wasn't sure what I wanted to do or be. I had no idea what actual jobs were out there. Our discussions were more than I can write in this book, but they helped me decide that I wanted a job in the training field. Since I still didn't know much about it, though, Elad suggested I start doing informational interviews. I needed to find a job I was interested in, find someone doing that job, and ask them about the job. Elad knew a couple people in the training field and set the first few interviews up for me. Everyone I interviewed with was very pleasant and happy to help me out. I'm thankful for all of their time and learned a lot; it was an invaluable experience.

One interview really stood out above the rest, and I will always remember his advice. I had already met him because I took his Emotional IQ class on the Coast Guard base. He started out with generic advice for the training field. He was a former Coast Guard Commander so he then gave me advice about transitioning out of the Coast Guard. Then he pulled up the Emotional IQ test I had taken during his class and gave me very specific, very personal advice based on those test results. Everything he said played out exactly how he said it would.

I took his advice and am extremely happy I did. I can never thank him enough.

More research. More Coast Guard bullshit. More informational interviews. Less time on the abeyance. I was ready to get out of the Coast Guard. Have you ever noticed that after months of struggling on the path to making the right decision, everything just kind of starts falling into place? That is what was starting to happen for me. After that, Elad pretty much had me convinced it was time to get out. However, I didn't want my DD 214 to read "failed to meet weight requirements." I wanted to figure out a way to stay in until it was time to re-enlist or find a different, still "legal" way of getting discharged.

Some of the advice I was given (NOT from Elad) was to tell the Chiefs that I was too stressed out to stand duty or to instruct. I was actually given that advice before I got the first weight abeyance and then again after all the bullshit. The goal was to prove I was not capable of doing my job. I really wanted a medical board, but was told by numerous Coast Guard doctors that I did not qualify for one because I was still capable of doing my job. If I started claiming that I was in too much pain or under too much stress, then I wasn't capable of doing my job, right? I could potentially get a medical board. I actually discussed that with the Senior Chief at one point. I told him it was hard for me to be a shit bag like that, and I didn't want to take advantage of the system. At the same time, I told him I thought the system was really taking advantage of me. Senior Chief had known me from before TRACEN and said he knew I was not a shit bag. He said he appreciated my honesty and my situation. He didn't directly say it, but he intimated that I could take that route if I chose to, and he would support me. But ultimately, he wanted to (and did) look for other solutions. Some of those solutions included talking to the Command Master Chief about everything that had happened so he could potentially advocate for me, talking to the detailer about getting early orders to transfer, so I could turn down the orders and be discharged for that reason instead of my weight;

checking with Medical Officers he knew to ensure I did not qualify for a Medical Board (I did not), and calling the Master Chief to see if the memo could be re-written. I will always appreciate our conversations. He tried so hard to help me out but kept hitting the same brick walls as I. He never once made me feel guilty for my weight nor gave me dieting advice. He was a great guy, trying his best to look out for an OS1 he considered to be a great asset to the school and the Coast Guard, who was, unfortunately, not in the right position to enable a change.

I am curious what would have happened had I played certain "cards." What if I had started "calling in sick" *per se*? What if I had said I was suicidal? What if I had hired a lawyer, or even called a Coast Guard legal representative? What if I had written to Congressmen? All of these ideas were given to me by numerous people. All of these ideas were discussed with Elad. In the end, we both decided that I would not be able to live with myself if I was a shit bag and that my mental health would suffer greatly if I continued to fight the system. Elad told me at the point in which I was getting out I was only somewhat bitter about it. I was still proud of all my accomplishments, and I did not regret joining. He said if I did anything shady or if I continued to fight, he wasn't sure if I'd remain in that territory. He thought that more than likely, I'd leave extremely bitter with no pride at all. I do get curious every once in a while. I think everyone plays the "what if" game at times. If I had been given a Medical Board, could I have potentially received a severance pay of some sort? Or could I have been medically retired and kept some of my benefits? Or would I have been dragged through the mud and discharged for my weight, anyway? In the end, I'm glad I did what I did. I agree with Elad. It has been a year since my discharge, and I do still have a lot of pride and am not extremely bitter. I think that is the way it should be.

The Master Chief in charge of OS A-School became the OS Rating Force Master Chief (RFMC) and the previous RFMC took charge of OS A-School during the summer of 2017. The new

Master Chief came in with guns blazing. He wanted to and did change a lot of policies and procedures for OS A-School. I was only onboard with half of what he wanted to do. I was happy I didn't have to advise under him. After he had been at OS A-School for a month or so, he pulled all the instructors into one of the classrooms and told us that "instructor" was a special assignment. He reminded us that we had to get a command endorsement to be there. He felt like some of the instructors weren't following the rules nor being the examples he expected them to be. He informed us that if we did not meet the requirements, including being under the weight requirements, of filling a special assignment position, he would have us transferred. Towards the end of his speech, he said he also wanted to meet with all of us one on one.

When I met with him, he told me that he remembered me. He was part of the ATG when I was on the *Mellon* and in charge of EW. (I remembered him, too.) He pointed at all his awards on the wall and told me that most of those awards were because of people like me. He remembered my training program and he had a lot of respect for me. He said a lot of nice things about my accomplishments in the Coast Guard and what an asset I was. Then he said he knew a little bit about my situation and sympathized with me, however, he had informed the instructors of his standards. Once my abeyance was up, I would have to meet the weight requirement, or he would have to have me transferred. He didn't want to, but he couldn't have favorites. I just looked Master Chief in the eye and said, "Don't worry about it, Master Chief, I'm probably getting out of the Coast Guard anyway."

Master Chief was surprised about my exclamation but after a few seconds of thought said he understood. Apparently, his wife was a big-time lawyer making six figures and started to have health problems, too. She gave up her career and had never felt better. He said that they both missed the paychecks, but neither of them regretted her career change. He told me that it was a shame that the Coast Guard was losing me. He was especially mad the Coast Guard was losing someone like me, and another shit bag was going to be able to retire. (This was when I was offered the opportunity to rat on the guy I wrote about in my "half a clam" chapter. As I said, I did not rat on him.)

I don't know if it was this conversation or a different one, but at some point, I told Master Chief that I wanted the civilian instructor job. Master Chief was thrilled to hear that! If the Coast Guard couldn't keep me as a Coastie, then at least they would keep me as an instructor. He played a large role in my eventually getting that job. It's a shame he couldn't have played a role in getting me a medical board or anything else that would have allowed me to stay in, but that is neither here nor there, right?

After my conversation with Master Chief and all the informational interviews, my mind was made up: I was leaving the Coast Guard. I looked up, found, read reviews, inquired about her services, and hired a professional resume' writer. Yes, you do learn how to write a resume' in the transitional class (TAPS) taken before you depart the military. Yes, there are some advantages to writing your resume in that class; mainly that it is free. However, I do not regret hiring a professional. I would do it again in a heartbeat and recommend it to everyone else, too. A professional is up to date on all the current trends. A TAPS instructor may or may not be. I will give my TAPS instructor credit that she was very knowledgeable. I've heard horror stories from friends about others that were not. You also spend some time in TAPS learning how to translate your skills in the military to skills in the civilian world. I found it much more valuable to try to explain everything to the professional resume writer. In doing this, not only did I learn how to translate my skills, but I was also practicing how to interview, elevate my speech, and answer questions. My resume' got me three jobs which I accepted and several more offers and interviews. Some of those I turned down; some turned me down. Such is life. I do not regret hiring her. And

I repeat, I recommend all military members do the same, unless of course, you joined later in life and already have experience doing it yourself.

I paid for professional portraits and set up a LinkedIn account. I also had other job seeking/hiring sites saved as favorites. The Roommate was a hiring manager at his job and although I didn't want that job, he practiced interview questions with me. He gave me tips and advice. I don't mean to sound arrogant, but I did not learn anything in TAPS that I had not previously learned or practiced, except a little about VA claims. I'm not putting the class down. I understand the reason it exists. The majority of my instructors happened to be good, as well. As said, I have just as many friends who will tell you that their instructors were complete tool bags. If you know you are getting out of the military and have time to prepare, do more to prepare than just attending TAPS. Set yourself up for success in as many ways as possible.

The extension on my abeyance ended and I was ready, mentally and emotionally, to get out of the Coast Guard. The civilian instructor job was open at OS A-School and I really wanted to take that job. Essentially, if I got it, I would be doing the exact same thing I was doing in uniform, just in different clothes. The pay and benefits would be a lot different, but I knew I was qualified for and enjoyed the job. I wanted to get out of the Coast Guard while that job was still open so I could have a job lined up. Ironically, I spent the majority of my career scared to death of not making weight and getting discharged and now that I actually wanted to get discharged, I couldn't!! I failed my weigh in when the abeyance ended, but that did not count as a strike as it was not an official weigh in. So, I was not on strike four, I was just back on the weight program. The first month I lost five pounds. I didn't really try. I think the decision to get out relieved some of my stress and probably lowered my cortisol levels a little. The next two months I did not lose any weight at all. In order to be discharged, you have to show a lack of progress. Admin wanted me to go one more month. I kept preparing for every weigh-in to be the last one and the last one wasn't until February of 2018. Then they had to put my discharge paperwork in and that had to be approved, which took another month! I had spent at least four months in after the abeyance expired. Why had I worried so much in all the years before this? I had to actually "work" to be kicked out.

I never did claim that I was in too much pain or too stressed out to work. I was supposed to be a Class Advisor again towards the end of 2017. Since we had no idea when I was going to be discharged and we were concerned I would start the class and not finish it, another instructor advised instead. I still instructed and tried my best to make all my medical appointments after the workday. That was suggested, too. If I had wanted to, I could have missed work for every single therapy appointment I had with Elad because it was medical and Tricare was paying for it; essentially two hours out of a workday, once a week for over a year. I never missed work to see Elad at all, instead seeing him at 5 pm every Tuesday. I was an MTS Coach for two seasons, including 2016-17 when all the medical stuff was happening, but did not volunteer for 2017/18 again because I did not know if I would be able to finish the season. Schedules were written and edited several times to account for whether or not I would actually be there, but if I could be there, I was.

I mentioned before that I was one of the ETC's favorite SAVE instructors. I conducted a lot of SAVES for struggling students across multiple A-schools and one C-school. One of my last SAVEs was for an ET student who was really smart and doing pretty well in class but was getting in trouble often. During her SAVE, I saw that she could benefit from having a strong mentor. Since there were very few female ET instructors, I volunteered and was given the opportunity to mentor her. We met every Wednesday from 0730-0800. She reminded me of myself in several ways. Most of the advice I gave her was advice that Elad had given me. Strangely, helping her helped me in a lot of ways. "Teaching" her reinforced lessons Elad was teaching me and helped me understand what he was trying to teach me. I also had to be an example for her which helped keep my attitude more positive through a lot of this. She was wrongly accused of something right before graduation and almost did not graduate. One of the most rewarding things in my entire career happened on February 23, 2018, when she was found to be innocent and graduated! I was able to be there, meet her parents, and watch her graduate. I have rarely been filled with that amount of pride. I will always be proud of both her and myself. I am proud of her for all the work she did. I'm proud she took most of my advice; I'm proud she held her head high through her investigation; and I'm proud she graduated! She is "rough around the edges" but I'm also proud of what a strong, beautiful, independent woman she is. I'm proud of myself for taking on the challenge, when I had several other challenges I was facing, for being able to hold my head high and be an example for her, and for having this as one of the last things on my Coast Guard resume'. She's in Hawaii now and we keep in touch every once in a while. I love seeing her free diving pictures on Instagram. I hope she does great things in her life. I hope I do great things in mine. I have faith in both of us.

There were two final "Fuck you!" s before I was discharged; really one and a half. A major computer crashed in the beginning of 2018. My discharge paperwork had already been submitted. Normally, the process took about thirty days, but everyone was unsure of what the computer crash would mean for it. I got an email on March 11, 2018, stating that there was a backlog of discharge paperwork and it would take another eight weeks for my paperwork to be reviewed. Two months! Up until that point, the instructors had been planning for my departure and possible transition to civilian instructor. Good thing I did not purchase an expensive airline ticket and the instructors did not change the schedule. Literally a day later, on March 12, 2018, I got an email saying that my discharge paperwork had gone through and my official discharge date was April 10, 2018. The email said I could calculate my terminal leave (the amount of vacation time I had) to determine my final working day in the Coast Guard. Upon calculation, I had somewhere around 20 days and the Coast Guard added some days, too, for relocation or something. Regardless, when all days were backed up from April 10, the day of the email, March 12 was my last working day in the Coast Guard. No one had any idea: not one single person in the admin building, not one single person in the actual command (the Captain of the base, XO, Command Master Chief), no one in my immediate command, and not me. I left without an award, without a goodbye party, without much of anything in general. I went to work that morning thinking I'd be in the Coast Guard another two months and left before the workday was over, completely done with the Coast Guard.

I did get the civilian instructor job and that is where the half "Fuck you!" comes into play. I did get an award for my time at TRACEN Petaluma. On May 17, I received an Achievement Medal, which is in between an LOC and a Commendation Medal. I received that award five weeks after my discharge and nine weeks after my terminal leave began. I believe that if I had not still been instructing there, I would not have received it. It is also not mentioned on my DD-214 because that was typed up before the award was. On the other hand, it was an appropriate award for the work I had done in Petaluma. Now I had two LOCs, an Achievement Medal, and a Commendation Medal.

SAND DOLLARS

During my four years in Petaluma, OS A-School was 13-15 weeks long. Instructors usually got a two- to three-week break between classes so most of us took leave (vacation). The Roommate and I kind of had a routine. A class would graduate on a Friday and either that weekend or the next weekend we would go on a road trip. We went all over the place while he lived with me. We went to Oregon, Crater Lake, Lassen Volcano National Park, Avenue of Giants, Trees of Mystery, The Chandelier Tree, Big Sur, Klamath, Alamere Falls, Point Reyes Lighthouse, Lake Tahoe, San Diego, Las Vegas, and more. Most of these trips were complete disasters while incredibly fun.

While I am good at planning for SAR cases: you can bet your bottom dollar, I will find you if you are lost at sea, I cannot plan a vacation to save my life. Do you want to know how we ended up in Oregon? We had planned on going to the Avenue of Giants and never really officially found it. We drove around for hours and didn't see what we had intended to see. Cell phone service was bad. The Roommate tried to Google things to do in the area and we did find The Chandelier Tree, which was awesome. We drove through another redwood, too, but I don't remember the name of it. Neither of those things took up the entire day, so The Roommate just began driving up the coast because of all the amazing views. Suddenly, there was a sign for Oregon in a couple miles and we decided "Why not?" We went to a couple beaches up there and took some pictures. It was a good day, but not at all what we planned for. We spent almost all day in the car. The Roommate did all the driving, so he was exhausted. For a hot minute I was in a really bad mood. I was very disappointed that we did not get to see what we wanted to see. I felt guilty about The Roommate having to drive so much. (He took his car and I couldn't drive his car. While I was taught to drive a manual car when I was in Seattle, I hadn't continued to practice and I'm not that great at it. The Roommate's car was a bit older, and he was concerned about his clutch.) At one point, he told me that our situation was not going to change; the fact that I was mad was only going to make things worse. He asked me to cheer up so we could try to salvage the day. I did and that is how we ended up in Oregon. And he was right, the day did end up being fun, albeit incredibly exhausting.

I have no idea why The Roommate continued to let me plan our trips. If he had planned any of them, I'm sure they all would have been better. The first time we went up to the Trees of Mystery, they were closed when we got there. Google had summer hours listed and we were there in the winter. We planned Lassen Volcano Park and Crater Lake for the same weekend. I found a hotel that was 20 minutes from Crater Lake. I didn't realize it was 20 minutes from the North side entrance (closed for winter) so we needed the South side entrance, which turned into an hour drive to and from the hotel and park—after all the rest of the driving that weekend. Crater Lake was actually a place on The Roommate's bucket list. While we did see quite a bit and did enjoy it, between cramming too much into the weekend, all the driving, and being sick, I'm not sure it was the dream trip he had imagined. I have always felt guilty for that. I know he went along with my plan, but it was my plan. All the trips were my plan and my fears, anxieties, and insecurities tell me that all of the "disasters" were my fault. The more guilty I felt, the more of a pain in the ass I was on the trip. I would just get extremely quiet and even though I was trying to have fun and be positive, The Roommate could read me and he knew I wasn't having fun. That would upset him, which would make me feel even guiltier, which would make me even more quiet, which would upset him. It was an endless cycle that neither of us knew how to end.

One of the Chiefs knew that The Roommate and I had been traveling and told me that we must plan a trip to Pismo Beach. Chief and The Roommate both loved Hawaii. It was easily their favorite place; I have never been. Chief told me that Pismo Beach was the closest place to Hawaii he had ever been. He said that in some places it looked just like Hawaii and it had the Hawaiian vibe. He said we had to stay at The Sea Crest Ocean Front Hotel and we had to go to The Splash Café for the best clam chowder outside of New England. I don't like clam chowder, but The Roommate did. I told The Roommate everything the Chief said and planned a trip for us.

In March 2017, right after my last class graduated, The Roommate and I headed south to Pismo Beach. We took my car down so I could help with the driving. On the way, I randomly told The Roommate that I wanted to find a sand dollar on the beach. I had never really been big into collecting seashells when I went to the beach, but I had never seen a real sand dollar. I thought they were very pretty and wanted to find one. The Roommate was a certified diver and was like, "Fun fact, sand dollars are purple and fuzzy when they are alive."

I had no idea sand dollars were once alive. I would feel incredibly stupid if I didn't think most people, including you, don't know that, either. Most seashells serve as a shell for an animal, so it makes sense. But sand dollars don't really open up and I had never heard of an animal crawling out of them. I just thought they were pretty things that washed up on the beach. I didn't realize the shell was the actual animal itself, just dead. The Roommate told me all about how they look when they are alive. We had an entire conversation about sand dollars on the way to Pismo Beach . . . having no idea whatsoever that Pismo Beach is actually renowned for sand dollars!

We arrived and checked into the hotel, which was as amazing as Chief had said it was! Our first room didn't really have a view of the ocean, so we upgraded to a room that had an excellent one. I don't know if we made our way down to the beach that night or the next morning, but we found several sand dollars! The Roommate was significantly better at finding them than I. None were perfect as the front was often smashed, but I was like a kid at Christmas: I was so happy. One laugh we shared is that sand dollars are flat, round, and white. You know what else is flat, round, and white? Bird poop. Just saying. Be careful what you reach for!

The Roommate and I loved mini golf and often on our road trips, we looked for a course. Mr. Putters Putt-Putt is in Atascadero, just north of Pismo Beach. It is an 18-hole course that doesn't look too challenging at first, but on every third or fourth hole there is a challenge wheel. Each player has to spin the wheel and play the hole according to the challenge. The Roommate and I both had a lot of fun and a lot of good laughs. I think we might have even paid to play one more round, just so we could try out different challenges to beat the top score, listed on a board outside the pay station. We also went to Boomers in Santa Maria. Boomers is attached to an arcade and I think we played air hockey and a few games there, too.

We checked out Pismo and San Luis Obispo. We went to Splash Café and The Roommate agreed the clam chowder was amazing. Don't get it in the bread bowl, though; ask for the bread on the side. You get more bread. I got a tuna fish sandwich with waffle fries and loved it, too. Every night we would go down to the hot tub and chill for a while. Some of the other guests at the hotel would give us ideas of where to eat or what to do the next day. We were having a great time, until it started raining and The Roommate got sick.

I love, love, love sunsets! They are my favorite things on earth next to waterfalls and rainbows. (Well, I guess now the beach and sand dollars, too.) I had this vision of seeing the most beautiful sunset over the ocean, but the rain was killing that dream. It was a minor detail that should not matter when you are having as much fun as The Roommate and I were, but it was too much for me to handle. I expected to see a beautiful sunset and when I didn't, I was really disappointed.

It was the last full day we had planned to be there. The Roommate didn't feel like going out or doing anything since he was sick. That broke my heart for him and for me. I absolutely hated doing anything by myself. Nothing is fun if I don't have someone to share the experience. I don't know if The Roommate saw my tears (I hope he didn't.), but I was lying on the couch in the hotel room actually crying. I told The Roommate we should just go home early. He looked at me like I was crazy (Let's be honest. I was.). He had no intentions of going home early. I argued that he was sick and should go home and rest and get better. The Roommate argued that if he had to be laid up in bed, he'd rather see and hear the ocean than be at home in bed. He also said if he could just get a nap, he'd probably feel better and we could do something later on. He told me to go down to the beach to look for more sand dollars since I enjoyed doing that so much. He had to work to convince me to do this, but realizing that he really didn't want to leave and knowing that combing the beach for sand dollars was fun, I finally put on my swim suit and went down.

I was down there for less than five minutes before I had found three of the most beautiful sand dollars in the world! On the bigger side and not broken at all, they were like finding a gold nugget or precious gem! I placed them carefully on a log and took a picture and sent it to The Roommate, thanking him for telling me to go down to the beach. I kept walking and found more broken ones and splashed around in the water a little bit. And wouldn't you know it, the sky cleared up, and that night there was a beautiful sunset that I took pictures of from the beach. At that point I was crying again, but happy tears!

The Roommate did feel a little better and later we did have dinner and went down to the hot tub for a little while. The next morning, as we were packing to leave, I told The Roommate that I was going to put all the sand dollars back on the beach. He again looked at me like I was crazy. "Why?"

I told him that we had enough stuff at home collecting dust, we didn't need any more. They were fun to find, I had a great time, I had pictures of them, but it was time to put them back. I am, by nature, a pack rat. My grandparents are hoarders, truly. They have two homes, multiple barns on my grandfather's farm, several storage sheds on all their properties and every structure is full, from wall to wall, floor to ceiling. Everything, literally everything, has sentimental value to me. I also love knick-knacks. I was actually kind of proud of myself for wanting to put the sand dollars back on the beach. For once I didn't think I was being crazy. For once I thought I was being practical. But The Roommate insisted that I keep them. "You love making things. Marie is watching the dog; make a thank you gift for her. Chief told us to come here; make him something. Make yourself something. Come on, keep them."

I thought he was crazy, but I did really love the sand dollars, so I kept them. We packed everything up, had one last brunch, and headed home.

Upon arriving home, I Googled something like "things to do with sand dollars." I think it was on Pinterest (isn't everything?) but it might have been on a different sight where I saw a sand dollar clock. It was really pretty, but the sand dollars were painted on, they weren't real. I "studied" it and thought "that's simple enough, I can make that."

When The Roommate said I liked to make things, I'm really not sure exactly what he was referring to. I never considered myself an artist. In fact, I considered myself to be whatever the exact opposite of an artist was. I did make scrapbooks from time to time, but they were really simple. The page layouts were a picture with a couple stickers or quotes. I write "poems" sometimes. Otherwise, I'm not sure, at that point, what The Roommate thought I made. I had enjoyed giving people gifts, but not ones I made.

Regardless, the clock I saw was a simple wooden clock with blue stripes and painted sand dollars for the hours. I thought it was simple enough that I could make one like it. I found a business on Etsy, ReclaimdDesigns, which sold "distressed" wood. He basically took apart pallets and then put them back together to form a solid 14x14 piece of wood. I thought it really had a weathered, beachy look to it, so I ordered a board. Peter, the OS1 from Mobile I advised with, had a cool clock in his living room that he had made of old bike parts. He told me that he just purchased a cheap clock and took it apart. I purchased a cheap clock and took it apart. Later I found out you can actually purchase clock mechanisms. I decided I was going to make the clock for The Roommate since he was the one who convinced me to go back to the beach and to keep the sand dollars. Since it was for The Roommate, I wanted to make sure it was well done. I purchased tape so I could get nice straight lines for the stripes on the clock. I was really impressed with how seriously I was taking this and after the clock was made, with how well it actually turned out. It was a very simple design that I had thought I could make, but I didn't expect it to be what it was. I really didn't consider myself an artist.

I framed one of the larger, albeit slightly broken, sand dollars for Marie for watching the dog, I framed one of the three perfect sand dollars I found for myself, made something for the Chief who told us to go, and made a smaller desk clock for my mom for Mother's Day. Those were my very first creations and were the only creations I had planned on making. I was out of perfect or near perfect sand dollars and I thought I was done . . .

I posted pictures of the clocks and framed sand dollars on Facebook. I did not post them with any intent of selling them. I just posted them as a follow-up to our trip. And I was proud of what I had done. Looking back, my mom's clock hands are too long. I didn't know at the time you could find clock mechanisms of all different sizes. But that is very minor. I was still proud of what I had created. And I absolutely loved The Roommate for all of his encouragement.

I did not expect the responses I got to that post. Several people said they loved The Roommate's clock and would buy it if they saw it in a store. A couple people asked if I could make them one. I thought people were just being nice, so I posted something else that said something to the effect of, "If you want a clock, put your money where your mouth is."

I had to take that post down the same day because I immediately had orders! I couldn't believe it! What just happened?!? People wanted to buy clocks from me?!? Now I had to put *my* money where my mouth was. How was I going to fill these orders?

I ordered more wood. I found more sand dollars from various places. And I sold a few clocks to some friends at cost. Then I started looking at all the broken sand dollars. Some of them were completely smashed on the front and just the backs, but others were just chipped here or there or had a small hole in them. I thought they were really pretty and tried to think about what I could do with them. At some point, I'm not sure when or how, but the phrase "broken but beautiful" popped into my head. All the sand dollars were broken, but I did not want to get rid of them because they were still so beautiful. Remember we went to Pismo Beach in March of 2017. I made the first round of clocks in April and I gave my mom her clock in May, for Mother's Day. This was the same time I was adjusting to all of my medications, getting more dieting and workout advice than I could handle, paying large amounts of money for supplements and outside doctors, and I had been in therapy for six or seven months. "Broken but beautiful" really resonated with me. I was definitely broken. There was no arguing that. I had plantar fasciitis, hypertension, hypothyroidism, PCOS, and an anxiety disorder. I was also (according to the Coast Guard) morbidly obese. Was I beautiful, though? My personality was all right. I was making strides in therapy to become a better person. I had a lot of friends. I was good at my job. If it weren't for the Coast Guard weight standards, was I really "obese"? I don't like my face. I really don't. But I have a mole on my left cheek and while I don't look like Cindy Crawford in any other way, people had called my mole a beauty mark and compared me to her. I wanted to be beautiful. I wanted to look at myself like those sand dollars. I was broken but beautiful.

I Googled how to make paint look like it is cracked. It is surprisingly very simple. I decided to make myself a "broken" clock. I was going to paint my clock with blue stripes, like The Roommate's clock, but I was going to crack the paint. I was going to use the broken sand dollars for the hours. And I was going to write "BroKen But BeauTifuL" on the clock in a "broken" font.

Making that clock changed my life. I have goosebumps and am near tears typing this right now. It's a clock. I get that. But it was my clock. That clock was a direct representation of my life. That is how I felt. There it was, staring me in the face. I was Broken. But I was also Beautiful. I showed it to Elad the next therapy session and I think he got goosebumps, too. He thought it was a great metaphor for my life, as well. He told me to look at that clock, with those sand dollars, every day. And I do. It doesn't match any of my Michael Godard artwork in my bedroom at all. My bedroom colors in Cali were white walls (I rented), black furniture, and green bedding. I have several Michael Godard framed posters and my lamps are his vodka bottles made into lamps. His books are on my dresser. And if you are reading this now, Mr. Godard, or someone who knows him is, you are, hands down, my favorite artist and the only artist with artwork in my house that I do not personally know. I only have one of your original paintings because I am broke, but if I ever hit the lotto Elvitini and Batini will be my first purchases. (Or if you feel like sending me Elvitini just for the sake of it, I would love it!) Now that I own my own house, the walls are red and black, and the bedding is a darker green. A blue, beachy clock does not belong next to Michael's big martini glasses, but that is exactly where it is. It is also right next to my "rules" board with all the mantras Elad and I had come up with, which are as follows:

An invitation is not an expectation.

Be comfortable in silence.
Moods don't lead to food.
Listen until "done."
You can never have enough of what you don't need.
Growth is slow, be patient and forgive.
Love myself.
NO expectations on/of vacations.
Feelings are NOT facts.
Aim for compassion.
Mini Goals Help Gain Control.
That board is a 14x14 chalk board with white writing on it. It matches the room a little better. Those are my "rules" for my life. I don't live by all of them every single day, but they are what I aim to live by. And when I'm not in therapy, talking to Elad, they remind me of what he would tell me.

Broken but beautiful has become my life mantra. I have shirts and jewelry with that phrase on them. I'm looking to have a front license plate that says that. It has also become my signature clock and best seller next to my nautical nursery clocks. The Roommate's gentle push towards me walking on the beach by myself and urging me to keep the sand dollars we found literally changed my life forever. How do you thank someone for that? There just aren't words. He didn't intend to change my life; he just wanted a nap. He didn't intend for me to create a business; he just wanted me to keep the sand dollars. (I still to this day don't know why he actually wanted me to keep them) But he changed my life and I created a business. But I'm getting ahead of myself.

. . .

After I sold the original clocks for cost to a few friends, other people started showing interest in my "BroKen But BeauTifuL" clock so I decided that I would start a business. Originally The Roommate and I were going to be business partners. I was the artist and he had a business degree. I thought I could make all the clocks, and he could run the actual business. I told The Roommate upfront, though, that if at any point he got upset with me, and he thought the business was going to ruin our friendship, he needed to back out immediately. I told him that his friendship meant more to me than any business ever would. It didn't take long for him to back out. He didn't want to just run the business. I don't know what else he wanted to do; I actually thought he would enjoy the business aspect of things since he was a manager at his job and he had the degree. I guess I was wrong. I was not upset he backed out at all. It is what I told him to do and he did it. And he still helped me out and gave me a lot of advice for a long time, so I kind of had a partner anyway.

As much as I said I wanted to start a business, I really had a hobby that made me some money every once in a while. Don't confuse that with my business being profitable; it wasn't. I considered myself lucky to just make a little of my money back from time to time. I did not want to deal with the IRS at all, so I found a couple of local consignment shops and sold my clocks there. I even worked at one of them once a week for about eight months. I didn't get paid for my time; I just got a higher commission on my clocks if they sold. Financially wise, it wasn't worth it at all. Networking wise, having something to do, meeting other artists and later, healers, that was all worth it. It wasn't hard work, either. If we were slow, it was incredibly boring, but it wasn't hard. Actually, I enjoy sales.

Most of the store was healing crystals (rose quartz, obsidian, amethyst, etc). The owner of that business is a paleontologist. He hates it when people assign healing powers to his rocks, gems, and minerals, because he just sees them as carbon, water, or other elements. His girlfriend is a phenomenal wire wrapper and jewelry maker. They are quite the dynamic duo and we became pretty good friends. They have live shows on Instagram all the time. If you want affordable, quality healing crystals, jewelry, or fossils, check out #redstoneminerals.

I hated not being able to answer customer questions so I started learning about the crystals and their healing powers. I actually got into it myself. I love blue agate and malachite.

They are each supposed to be good for endocrine problems and anxiety. I figure they are beautiful and look good on me. If they heal me, too, that is a cherry on top. When I first started working at the store, I might have been able to tell a customer if we had a certain crystal. By the time I quit working there, I could tell you what we had, where it was, and the use for some of them. The bigger the crystal, the more power it has. I loved it when a customer planned on buying a $2 item, and I sold them a $10 item instead. I also got to know some of the other artists and tried hard to promote their stuff. In some ways I promoted everyone else's stuff more than mine. I know for a fact that I had more Redstone Minerals business cards in my purse than mine for a little while. In the Coast Guard I was this Alpha Female Badass. In the consignment shops I was still kind of alpha because I was a killer salesman, but mostly I was a laid-back artist who just enjoyed the world for all the beauty in it. It provided a nice balance for my life and at that time, I needed that balance.

The original name for the business was "Dollars in the Rough." In November of 2017, one of the OS Chiefs, my friend, my "mentor," my non-blood brother, was going out of town with his family and needed someone to look after the goats and chickens. I babysat and farm sat for them often. I'm friends with his wife, Mindy, and I love their children. Kevin has a degree in computer science and actually built or re-designed several businesses' websites. I agreed to watch the goats and chickens, if he built me a website. He agreed.

After they got back from vacation, Kevin started working on the website. He thought "Dollars in the Rough" was too long for a website name. After going back and forth with him and Mindy, we finally agreed that the website would be www.hjhdesigns.com. Without me realizing it, he had actually changed my business name. The original website design just had all my products listed as single products. At first, I was kind of upset about the name change. I was incredibly happy with the website, but I liked "Dollars in the Rough" and my business cards had that written on them. That was how I was known in the consignment shops—not that I was really well known. Later on, The Roommate and one of his best friends (a mutual friend for a short time) came up with the idea of my having product lines. As I got to know more artists and my hobby/business developed, I began to use more mediums, such as wine corks since I was in Northern California and healing crystals because of the consignment shop. I also had the framed sand dollars and started making some signs instead of clocks. The Roommate and his friend thought "Dollars in the Rough" could represent the sand dollar art. I loved the idea and that is how the website is now designed. "A Cork in Time" and "Look, No Hands!" are the other two product lines for now.

When Kevin designed the website, he asked if I wanted him to run the entire thing for me or if I wanted to learn how to run it myself. Of course, he was hoping for the second one, but I appreciated him offering the first one. I hate computers. I know some programs, such as SAROPS, inside out because I used them every single day for my job so I had to know them. I had a love/hate relationship with those programs because even though they were computer programs, they were directly related to something I loved and helped me do my job. Do not ask me anything else about a computer. I'm not "your person" for fixing bugs or installing things or coding or anything else. I looked at the website Kevin made for me as another program I would have a love/hate relationship with since it would directly relate to my business. It also did not escape me that I was getting "free lessons" on things he went to college for and earned a degree in. I still am incredibly thankful for that.

After the website was designed, Kevin and I met at Starbucks with his computer where he showed me how to put my products on the site, change the shipping options, update apps and jetpacks, blog, and many other things. Have I mentioned in this book yet that I have bad anxiety? Usually a two-hour session involving anything I hate would result in a panic attack. Kevin is the Hillary Whisperer, though, I swear. I don't know if he is really good at reading me or if it is just his normal personality or some strange combination of the two, but he knows exactly where the line is for what I can and cannot handle in almost every situation we have encountered. He designed the entire website and his "curriculum" with me in mind. Just as I was about to pull the plug on our lesson, it was over. He had shown me everything I needed to know. We had uploaded one product and walked through how to purchase the product and ship it. He told me to go home and upload the rest of my products and play around with everything else and try to "break" the website and let him know if I had any other questions. I waited a couple days (I had to recover) and then uploaded everything. Surprisingly, I did not have too many questions. The site is pretty Hillary-friendly.

The next year Kevin and I both worked on the site. He changed the design around when The Roommate and his friend came up with the product line ideas. After about a year, Kevin turned the entire website over to me. He is still admin on it and I recently asked him to update a couple of things, but otherwise, I run 98% of it on my own. I have not actually sold anything through the website yet. This was kind of on purpose in California as I kept my sales in the consignment shop. Now that I'm in Alabama, though, I hope that changes.

I'm skipping ahead on my timeline a little bit, but I moved to Alabama in February of 2019. I did a decent job of keeping the website up to date while I was in California, but as you will see in the next couple of chapters, I was pretty damn busy, and this really was a hobby and not a business. I sold a clock or two here and there to friends or at the stores in California. I did not turn a profit or even come close to it. I was still pretty impressed with the amount of business I was doing considering the amount of effort or lack of effort I was putting in. One of my goals in moving was to turn HJH Designs into a legitimate business instead of a hobby. I wanted to sell at craft fairs and art shows and maybe eventually open up my own art studio or consignment store for veterans. After I purchased my house, I got in touch with an accountant, and HJH Designs is now a sole proprietorship! That is why I asked Kevin for help on updating the website. I was at the Mobile Flea Market a couple weeks ago and I will be at another craft show the first weekend in June. Now I hope the website generates a lot of business. I also opened an Etsy shop. There is another HJH Designs in Virginia. A lady named Hannah sells jewelry. So my Etsy shop is HJH Design (no "S" on the end). I realize that Etsy is a well-known website and people may not trust my website. I hope my website blows up, but I like Etsy, too. I also have a Facebook business page and am on Instagram. If you want to check out the "BroKen But BeauTifuL" clock or any of my other art, please visit any one of these pages or websites. I look forward to hearing from you! I would love to make a custom piece of art for you or a loved one!

The Roommate moved out in October 2017, due to some family matters. We went back to Pismo Beach a week before he moved and found many more sand dollars! We invited his friend from Las Vegas to join us and that is the friend who helped come up with the product line ideas and created the logos for Dollars in the Rough and A Cork in Time. We also went back to Mr. Putters Putt-Putt and the Splash Café. While we were in Pismo, fires broke out in Santa Rosa, just north of where we lived. Since everyone was evacuating, we extended our vacation for another day. When we got back home, the air was so thick with smoke and ashes, we could hardly breathe. It was very bittersweet. I was thankful we did not personally lose anything, but I knew people who lost everything. The Roommate didn't have a big going away party or anything. He just packed his bags, said goodbye to a few people, and moved back to Denver.

The Roommate and I kept in touch until January 2019, when we unfortunately had a falling out. A lot of things happened in 2018 that led to our falling out. There is his side of the story, my side, and in the middle is the truth. Both of us had a lot of things going on in our lives. Both of us also have a lot of baggage. In my opinion, we were both so caught up in what we had going on, we were not capable of seeing or realizing what the other person wanted or needed. We were also so stressed out, neither of us had the capacity to be patient with each other. I know I betrayed The Roommate's trust. I assume that I hurt him. I am incredibly sorry for both of these things. I know The Roommate has trust issues in general and I never, ever wanted to be the cause of more. Unfortunately, The Roommate betrayed my trust, as well. Finally, after years of being passive aggressive, I tried to be honest and look for some reassurance, only to be told that it was not his job to reassure me. In some ways I regret being honest, even though I know it was the right thing to do. The Roommate really hurt me. I do not blame him for what happened. I am not mad at him. I doubt he ever intended or wanted to do anything that would make me regret opening up to him. The entire time we knew each other we either helped each other out tremendously or drove each other completely insane. We handle stress so differently and have very different needs. In 2018 and at the time of our falling out, both of us were just trying to keep our heads above water. It really sucks that we drown each other in order to save ourselves, but that's what happens when you are trying to survive. I hope that one day, when we are both in better places in our lives, we will reconnect. He is truly one of the most beautiful people I have ever met. He showed me what patience, kindness, and compassion looks like. He encouraged me to get help, to step out of my comfort zone, to take risks, and to be a better person. I am a better person for having known him. I will always be thankful for that even if we never reconnect.

LIFE AFTER THE COAST GUARD

My terminal leave started on March 12, 2018. I left work that day in complete shock. I had fought incredibly hard to keep my career and then, when I realized that was not going to be possible, I fought incredibly hard to expedite my discharge. Now that it was finally happening, I was filled with dread and regret. What was I going to do? How was I going to make it? Quick, what could I do to reverse my discharge?!? Could I lose 20+ pounds in two days?!? Convinced that I was going to be homeless by December, I worried about what would happen to my dog, Casey. Who would take him in?

Normally, when I start spinning out, I text Elad and ask him for his next available appointment. Elad was my official therapist referred by the Coast Guard, so Tricare paid for it until September 2017. A month or so earlier, Elad had told me that he was going to retire. I had been in therapy for about a year and made a lot of improvements, but I was still in the Coast Guard fighting to stay and then fighting to get out. I did not want to lose my therapist in the middle of one of the biggest changes in my life. I asked if he had any recommendations for another therapist. His wife is also a therapist and we discussed transferring my care to her. In September, Elad told me that he and his wife had decided he was going to keep about ten clients and continue to work about three days a week. The ten clients he was going to keep were clients that he felt didn't need to talk to him once a week anymore but could still benefit from some therapy. He planned to travel a lot, and the clients would have to be able to handle that. The ten clients would also have to pay him out of pocket since he was no longer going to accept insurance. He asked if I wanted to be one of them. Full of relief and gratitude (and being used to paying for my health care, anyway) I immediately said yes. After that I started seeing Elad every other week and then eventually once a month. Here we were in March, and I was now jobless. A part of me wanted to talk to Elad and a part of me wanted to save every penny I had. I didn't know what would be better.

I called my mom. Sometimes, she is extremely helpful and other times she makes my spin worse. Thankfully, this time she helped. During our phone call, I had mentioned that I wanted to get a tattoo. The artist who did my first tattoo was still in California when I moved back so in 2016, he did a piece on my left forearm. I was guessing the tattoo I wanted now was going to cost about $800. I wanted a phoenix on my left leg. I wanted to show that I had survived hell and that I was going to rise from the ashes. (Even though I wasn't completely convinced of that in that moment, somewhere deep down, I knew I would be OK.) I wanted the tattoo on my left shin because when you march, the first step out is with your left foot. That was Ken's idea and I loved it. I started laughing when I was talking to my mom. "I can't spend $X on a therapy session, but I can spend $800 on a tattoo. What is wrong with me?"

My mom shocked me! I mean my jaw hit the floor. Remember I was raised in the Baptist church. My mom holds a strong belief that your body is a temple, so tattoos are wrong. I'm an adult so I make my own choices. I don't believe that tattoos destroy your temple so long as you go to a reputable artist in a reputable shop. My mom knew I had other tattoos and didn't lecture me for them by any means, but she didn't gush over them either. But here I was debating getting an $800 tattoo after I just lost my job, and my mom asked me, "What would make you feel better right now, therapy or a tattoo?"

I answered, "I think a tattoo."

My mom did not share my belief that I was going to be homeless by the end of the year so she wasn't as concerned about money as I was. She went on to say, "It's hard to compare the longevity of a tattoo to the effects of therapy, but that $800 would be for something that will last you the rest of your life. If that makes you feel better, I think you should get one."

What did she just say?!? Could she repeat that? Did she just say I should get a tattoo? My Baptist mom who thought tattoos destroyed your temple just told me to spend $800 on a tattoo instead of calling my therapist. Holy cow! This was a very strange day . . .

With my mom's encouragement, I called the artist and booked an appointment. That's right, ladies and gentlemen, the first thing I did when I lost my job was make an appointment to get an $800 tattoo. I recommend it for anyone who thinks they might be homeless. It's a totally sane, logical, responsible thing to do.

The second thing I did was apply for the civilian instructor job. Master Chief and I had already been talking to the company, so they already knew who I was. I sent my resume' and they set up a phone interview with me. I got the job. On March 19, 2018, I went back to work as an OS A-School Instructor, but instead of being in a Coast Guard uniform, I was now in business casual clothes. I was jobless for one week in total. And since I was on terminal leave, I didn't miss a paycheck.

In the prior year, my tattoo artist had donated a gift certificate to a silent auction that The Roommate held for Make-a-Wish and my Texas' Cubicle Mate had won it. He had never used it. He kept mentioning ideas for tattoos that he wanted, but he had two kids, and my tattoo artist was down in Berkley. Before my appointment, he gave me a wrapped gift for departing the Coast Guard. Inside was the gift certificate. In April 2018, I got my phoenix tattoo on my left shin. The tattoo goes from just below my knee down to my ankle. My first tattoo is on my left ankle just above the ankle bone. I also have a green

M&M on the inside left ankle above the other ankle bone. The phoenix's tail feathers curve to the right, toward the M&M, and the tattoo fits perfectly in between the two others that are already there. After we subtracted the gift certificate, I paid only $400 out of pocket. I will always be thankful for my Texas' Cubicle Mate and to the tattoo artist for what they did for me. If you are in Northern California and want a tattoo, I highly recommend Ben Cheese. Look him up on Instagram.

Kevin's (Chief, friend, "mentor," "brother," and website designer) best friend from high school is a manager at a local restaurant. We would eat lunch there from time to time. I'm very outgoing, swear too much, and have a dirty mind. Kevin is more strait-laced, especially when he is in uniform. I never went out of my way to embarrass him, but I almost always did. One day towards the end of 2017, we were eating lunch at the bar in the restaurant and I said the f-word a little too loudly. Kevin immediately put his head down in shame, as there was another lady sitting at the bar. I was laughing at how embarrassed he was, but since it is a pretty vulgar word and I was in uniform, I began to apologize to the lady. Then, I noticed she was also laughing. It was clear that she was laughing at our conversation and Kevin's reaction.

I later found out how old Kearsten really is, but she only looks to be a few years older than I. She always wears cute punk or rock-ish clothes, her hair is fierce, and she is full of tattoos. I found out sitting at the bar that she is a hairstylist and photographer. Her daughter is a make-up artist. I immediately got a great vibe from her and hired her for a photo shoot. She insisted on my looking at her portfolio first, so I did, but I already knew I would love her. The first photo shoot we did was head shots for my LinkedIn profile, as I was preparing to get out of the Coast Guard.

I told everyone that one of the first things I was going to do after getting discharged was smash my scale to pieces. I never ever again wanted to care about how much I weighed. I was telling Kearsten about it as she was dying my hair, and she loved the idea. I asked if she wanted to do another photo shoot and capture my epic moment. She was onboard!

The day of the shoot, I also had another idea. Smashing the scale would not require too many pictures or too much time. A lot of military people have trouble transitioning from the military to civilian life, especially if they joined the military at a young age or served for a long time. I was fortunate that I had a while to prepare for my transition, and I had an easier time than some, but I still felt like I was eighteen again, fresh out of high school, and had no idea how the real world worked. I thought it would be fun to do a photo shoot capturing some of the struggles in a funny way. Kearsten's creative gears started turning and that photo shoot was epic!!

Kearsten revealed the photos to me in a comic strip format. There is a picture of me in nice dress pants with my uniform dress shirt on, holding two pairs of shoes, looking super confused on what I was supposed to wear. The second picture I have curlers in my hair and a brush and straight iron in my hands, again with a confused look of "How do I do this?"

The third picture is a bit on the serious side. I'm in a nicer shirt, and I'm looking down at a lot of sand dollars in my hands. The fourth picture I'm holding my scale in one hand and giving it the middle finger with the other. The fifth picture, I'm smashing the scale!! Kearsten took a series of pictures of me, first throwing the scale and then jumping on it. She Photoshopped them together to show the scale flying through the air and smashing to pieces on the ground! I absolutely love that picture! It is so incredibly empowering—as was smashing the scale! I was so happy that I had decided to capture that moment on film instead of just planning to smash it at home. Inevitably, I would have just thrown it away. The very last picture is me in the nice shirt again, holding my BroKen But BeauTifuL clock, smiling, knowing that I was going to be OK.

I posted those pictures everywhere I could and shared them with as many people as I could. That photo shoot perfectly captured my transition and empowered me to keep moving forward. I wanted other military people to see that comic strip and either get a good laugh out of it, too, or feel empowered themselves.

I told Kearsten that at some point in the future I really wanted to do a boudoir photo shoot. I always thought something like that would be a lot of fun, but just didn't love my body enough to do it. I told her that once I decided I was OK with my body, I would let her know. She told me she looked forward to it . . .

The Civilian Instructor job paid well, but I lived in California and it was just me. I wasn't married so had just one income. I interviewed with a place in San Francisco on the advice of a Make-a-Wish family that I had kept in touch with. The job was supposed to be full-time, but I wanted part-time for several reasons. After speaking with the guy on the phone, he was really excited I offered to work part-time, nights and weekends. That was just as good as full-time because those were the shifts most people did not want. I'm not sure what his position was. HR makes sense, but I can't confirm that. At any rate he told me he had to check with the COO to see if I could be part-time instead of full-time. A day later he said I could be and asked if I could come in for an interview. That interview was a bit shaky. It was my first real one out of the Coast Guard, and they asked a few questions I was not prepared for. I really wanted that job. I am equally thankful that I did not get it.

After that interview, I applied for a job at a restaurant and was offered a job. After I read their dress code, though, I turned it down. I just got out of the military; I didn't want to be back in it!! I then applied for a job at Sprouts and was hired as a part-time cashier. There were a couple bumps the first month or so there. I hated sharing a register. A couple times I "got in trouble" (slap on the wrist, but still) for my register being off, but I wasn't the only one on it. Whenever I was counted, I was always dead on. It annoyed me. But after that issue was resolved, I worked there for eight months, and it was one of my favorite jobs I have ever had. I started off part-time but went to full-time right before I moved to Alabama. I'm getting ahead of myself again, though.

I enjoyed being a civilian instructor. Along with the tattoo and before the photo shoot, I dyed my hair, got fake nails (That was a mistake. I don't know how to function with those!) and got another piercing in my ear. I loved being able to wear whatever I wanted to wear. Due to California employment laws, I was not allowed to work overtime. I had the same job that I had before with fewer responsibilities and less bullshit. Besides the pay, what was there to hate?

But the pay . . . Instructor jobs in Petaluma are not General Schedule (GS) jobs. Instead they are contract jobs and that contract goes up for bid on a regular basis. Of course, the lowest bidder always wins. Therefore, you could hold that job for over ten years and never accumulate anything as far as benefits and you could potentially get a pay cut instead of a pay raise. The other civilian instructors were retired and had other means of income. They weren't doing the job as a career to pay their bills; they were doing it because they enjoyed it and wanted to. I was 34, though. I needed a second career. I needed a job where I could move up in the company. I knew I couldn't stay at that job forever; I knew it was just a place holder.

I didn't intend to move as fast as I did. I hated change and I had just been through quite a bit. I was so happy when I got out of the Coast Guard, I was literally glowing. I even had people ask me if I was pregnant. I also dropped 10 pounds the first month I was out. Nothing in my lifestyle or routine changed, I just wasn't stressed out anymore. I really had no idea how badly I had been doing until I started doing well. The difference was like night and day. I was blown away and all the compliments on how good I looked confirmed that getting out of the Coast Guard was the right decision. I was content to keep working as a civilian instructor and cashier for a while and just adjust to my new life.

Remember, I said I was given very specific advice during one of my informational interviews based on my Emotional IQ test? Part of that specific advice was to not take the first job I was offered when I got out of the Coast Guard. The concern was that I would be so afraid of not being able to pay my bills that I would jump on the first opportunity that came along whether it was right for me or not. Then I would be so comforted by the stability that I would stay in that job forever. The fear was that I would end up being just as miserable in five to ten years with my new job as I was in the Coast Guard. I believed all of that. All of that sounded like past-Hillary. I had taken the first job that was offered to me because I did have bills to pay but I was not going to stay there forever, especially with the pay concerns mentioned above, so I posted my resume' on Indeed Jobs.

I sent out a couple emails to a couple of places that were hiring, too, but overall, I was not pro-active in my job search. I wanted to take the advice I was given, but I also wanted to chill out for a little while, too. I wanted to put feelers out, but I did not necessarily want another job right away. The very next day I got a call from the HR manager for a transportation broker wanting to know if I was interested in being a transportation trainer.

The phone interview went well except I had asked for a higher wage on Indeed than what they could pay. The HR manager asked me if there was some wiggle room. I told her what my limitations were, and she asked if I could come in for an interview with the local manager. I think our phone call was on a Thursday or Friday. I remember that the local manager was going out of town, so the HR manager said that I would have to come in Monday or Tuesday, or I would have to wait two more weeks. I had already taken Monday morning off work for a medical appointment, so I just took the entire day off instead to go to the interview after. I went online and looked at the entire company web page. I looked at all of the company biographies and noticed everyone had been there for over ten years. I called my mom and she looked over everything. I wasn't exactly sure what a broker was, so my mom explained that to me. I wrote down a list of questions I had for the local manager.

It is so much easier to interview for a job when you already have a job. Don't get me wrong, I had practiced several interviews before I got out of the Coast Guard and had learned from all the real interviews I had done after, but the knowledge that I already had a job and didn't need this one gave me a lot more confidence. I think the comparison could be similar to how having a few drinks helps some people talk to new acquaintances. I went in and talked to the local manager. I answered all of her questions and asked her mine. The interview went really well until we talked about pay. I needed more than they were offering. It wasn't that I had a huge ego or thought that I brought a lot more to the table than I did (Although I did bring a lot to the table); I literally needed more than they were offering in order to pay my bills. After that interview, the local manager asked if I could come back in and talk to the regional manager. The interview with the regional manager was actually a presentation I had to put together to show her. Of course, the local manager was still going out of town, so she asked if I could come back the next day for the interview/ presentation. I told her it depended on what the presentation was. I said if I had to prepare posters and set up a "classroom" of sorts then there was no way I could prepare for that in one day with another job. She told me it was less of a presentation and more just answering three questions. She told me I would not have to put together any posters. I agreed to come back the next night.

The job was advertised as a "transportation trainer." The actual title of the job when I took the job was a Quality Assurance Specialist (QAS). Apparently, they advertised the job as QAS and they kept getting IT people applying and that wasn't really what they were looking for so they advertised it as a trainer instead. The job was partly training drivers and that was the part of the job I ended up loving. If that had been the entire job, I'd still be there today. But it also included site visits, audits, route audits, investigations, and more. The presentation I had to do was basically to show that I could manage my time properly and handle all the responsibilities of the job. I also had to answer "what if" questions based on commonly occurring issues.

My strongest qualities are that I'm pro-active and organized. If I consider myself to be a subject matter expert in something, I'm also extremely confident, decisive, and assertive. I'm not confident, decisive, or assertive if I'm learning something or don't know anything at all. Time management has never been an issue for me. My presentation was solid. I even color coordinated the chart I put together for how I would schedule myself for a month, and I had charts outlining two different options because I was unsure of how long an audit or route audit usually took. Both options hit the required numbers I would have to achieve in any given month. Both the local and regional manager were impressed. Truthfully, so was I. I was less impressed with my skills and more impressed that they were useful in the real world. I knew I was a rock star in the Coast Guard, but I wasn't sure how much would transfer to civilian life. Turns out, a lot transferred over into the real world. I had a solid resume' and solid skills.

I was offered the job and we worked out a compromise for how much I would be paid. The local manager went out of town, I gave my two weeks' notice with OS A-School, and I planned a trip to go back out to Boston. Jack, from when I was in A-School, was married now with a daughter. I needed to go meet his daughter. I had a great time and saw some other friends, too. When I got back, I started my new job as a QAS.

The first three months I was on probation as I trained and worked with the local manager. I loved her. She was awesome. Her husband was a Marine veteran, so she knew a lot of the "struggles" I was going through as I transitioned. Since she was a female, she also understood my female issues. We had

a lot in common and she was a good trainer. I enjoyed working with her, and I enjoyed the job. I was once again glowing.
People were once again asking me if I was pregnant. I wish I
could describe the amount of confidence I had knowing that
my resume', my interview, and my skills landed me a job that
I was excited about just over a month after getting discharged
from the Coast Guard. I had just proven to myself how capable
I really am. I was not going to be homeless by the end of the
year. Elad was right. I had what it took to make it in the real
world.

Speaking of Elad, in July I "graduated" from therapy. Elad had
continuously told me that I would know when I was done,
and I would have control over when we stopped therapy. In
June, I told him how excited I was about landing the new job,
and that everything he predicted would happen after I got out
of the military, did happen. In July, it was obvious that I was
done with therapy, but I was scared. I had all the tools Elad had
given me: I had survived getting out of the Coast Guard, I had a
job, but what if something unexpected happened in the future
that I couldn't handle? Elad told me that he wasn't going anywhere. If I needed to ask him a question, I could always text
him. If I needed an emergency session, we could always have
one. He told me that he cared about me and hoped I would
keep in touch, anyway. I told him it was time. I told him I was
done with therapy. I was so proud of myself.

After my probation period had ended, I was officially
offered the job. I was also put in for a raise as per the agreement
we had during the interview. That is when the job started
going to hell. I can't give too many details as I signed a non-disclosure agreement upon leaving. During the probation period
there were certain things that did not happen. The local manager told me that and tried to prepare me for it, but there was
no way to prepare me for it. It was very similar to SAR. I can
tell you all day long that someone will die on your watch. You
can think that you are capable of handling that death especially if you do everything right. But until someone actually

dies on your watch, you really have no idea what it feels like or if you can actually handle it.

August was all right. I felt like I was keeping my head above water. I was rough around the edges, but I was still excited for the job. September 2018 was one of the worst months of my life. Everything that could go wrong did. It wasn't like one person died on my watch; it was as if I had a boat full of children that sank offshore, and all the children died. The local manager got hand, foot, and mouth disease and was actually quarantined. I handled a couple of situations that I had never been in completely on my own. I did not handle them wrong; I was rough around the edges. I sent one email that I should not have sent but even that is misleading. I was supposed to keep this person informed of the situation and everything I told her was the truth of what happened. Unfortunately, I gave too many details and it upset her. I specifically quoted some-one else and yet she read the email and thought that was how I felt. That situation escalated so quickly, I had to call the local manager while she was quarantined, and the other lady beeped in in the middle of my conversation. The ripple effect of that one email went on for miles.

I was also certain one of the companies we oversaw was corrupt from the top down. After having several serious in-cidents in a short time, I was recommending that we get rid of our contract with them completely. The local manager did not agree with me, but rather tried to give them not just the benefit of the doubt, but whatever goes above and beyond that. I was angry that she was ignoring my opinion, and I was angry that she did not have my back in the email situation. I still hadn't gotten my raise, either. It got so bad that I called Elad for an emergency session.

In September or October of 2018 I went back to therapy for three weeks. I told Elad everything that had happened. At that time, I was unsure of how much responsibility I should be taking for what had happened. I was still new to the com-pany and maybe my ego was too big. Maybe that email really was a bigger deal than I realized. Maybe the company we oversaw wasn't corrupt. Maybe I was making all the mistakes that I was accused of making. Maybe I needed to be humbler. But there were a lot of other orange flags. The more I learned how to do the job and the more paperwork I looked over from the past, the more I saw how disorganized this company really was and how many other people were making mistakes, too. My gut instinct was telling me that something really bad was going to happen and I didn't want any part of it. Elad listened to and sorted through everything I said. I did need to take responsibility for some of it, but Elad said my orange flags were actually huge red flags. Elad agreed the company was not what it seemed to be, and that I should probably not be working there.

Deciding not to work there brought up more questions. It was expensive to live in California. I needed a job. Should I go back to be a civilian instructor? Should I apply somewhere else? Should I use my GI Bill and go to college? I really didn't want to do any of those things. Elad reminded me that I could go anywhere and do anything. He asked me why I felt I had to stay in California. What was in California for me? Of course, there were people I cared about, but overall the only thing California offered was it was in my comfort zone. Elad began asking me where I wanted to go and what I wanted to do. I felt like Will in *Good Will Hunting*. "I want to be a shepherd. I want to get a flock of sheep and I want to tend to them." I wasn't a smartass, but still, I had no idea what I wanted to do.

I think I had three therapy sessions in total. I finally decided I wanted to move back to Alabama and turn my hobby, HJH Designs, into a business. My VA claim had been processed and I had received my rating and back pay in August. That money would go a lot further in Alabama than it would in California. I would not need two jobs in Alabama; I would need a part-time job or I would need HJH Designs to be really successful. I also had a large network in the South of people who were from the South or retired, so they would not be moving in a couple of years when their tour was up. I also decided that it was time for me to love my body . . .

I told Kearsten that I was finally ready to do a boudoir photo shoot with her in August or September of 2018. Kearsten told me that she would love to make that happen for me, but she was moving to North Carolina and didn't think she would have the time. She recommended a female photographer and Jason Guy instead.

I initially emailed the female photographer, but after I did not hear from her for a week, I emailed Jason:

"Good afternoon. I've done a couple photo shoots with Kearsten Leder and have finally worked up the courage to ask her for a nude/bedroom shoot and she's moving. She suggested I contact you.

"A little background, I did twelve years in the Coast Guard, getting out in April because I failed to meet weight standards. I have hypothyroidism and PCOS and have always battled with my weight. It has taken me a long time to like my body and myself. My journey is far from over, but I'm hoping a nude shoot will help me see my body in a new way and help me grow even more.

"If you are interested in working with me, please let me know your availability and rates. Thank you so much!"

Jason replied the same day and I immediately knew I wanted to work with him when I read, "I would absolutely love to give you this experience and help you change the way you see yourself!"

Jason and I met at a winery for my initial consultation. Jason has a boudoir guide and it literally answers every question you would ever have. My favorite part of the guide, however, were the before and after pictures of some of Jason's subjects. I was extremely nervous about how to pose. I don't consider myself to be sultry or seductive. I was afraid that instead of looking sexy and beautiful in my photos, I would look like a little girl playing dress up with her mom's clothes (or lack thereof). Jason assured me over and over that he would pose me, and I would look great—and I trusted him—but seeing the before and after pictures really proved his point.

There are several options for doing a boudoir shoot with Jason Guy. I was going for a blend of classy, sexy, fun, and affordable. I also really wanted to be me. The entire goal was for me to love myself and my body. I have never been tanning. My hairstyle has always been very simple. I don't wear make-up. Some of the "prep" work suggested in Jason's boudoir guide may be very appropriate for other women, but it just didn't seem right for me.

I purchased some lingerie and groomed myself as I would if I were about to go out on a date. I looked at some B&B's and options for a beach photo shoot, but I couldn't find anything affordable in Northern California. It was also late in the year and the weather was not conducive for an outdoor shoot. We did the photo shoot at my house in front of a crackling fire in my fireplace.

I have a lot of respect for models!! Posing is not easy or comfortable!! And shooting all day is exhausting! But Jason was very true to his word. Jason taught me how to "smize" (smile with my eyes) and how to get the pouty, seductive lip look. In every photo Jason twisted my entire body exactly the way he wanted it. There were a few photos of me looking out the window where I was looking directly into the sun. But after some of the pictures, Jason would show me his camera, and I looked phenomenal!

While the poses were uncomfortable, I was incredibly surprised by how comfortable I felt. I rarely walk around the house naked when I'm home alone. Here I was naked with a "strange" guy, but I was carrying on full conversations like he was a long-lost friend visiting for a few days. Even after the shoot, as Jason was packing up his gear, I was not in a hurry to get dressed. I cleaned up some of the props we used first and scheduled a date for the reveal.

Oh. My. Gawd!!! My picture reveal was a-may-zing!! I definitely do not look like a little girl!! I have never felt so beautiful in my life. I loved my body. The pictures were so classy. There was one picture he just zoomed in on my face. It wasn't really what I expected from a boudoir shoot, but the way I look, relaxed in the chair, with my hand in my hair, and the light hitting my face with some cool shadows on my shoulder . . . my face is stunning! The picture is truly breath-taking! I never thought, in a million years, that I could look that good.

My photo shoot quickly went from affordable to insanely pricey! I had originally intended to purchase ten pictures, at the most, and maybe have one enlarged. I purchased twenty pictures and had one enlarged!! And it was the best money I have ever spent!! I would love to do another shoot with him on a beach in the future!

I highly, highly, highly recommend #jgboudoir (info@jasonguyphotography.com). Words cannot describe the amount of confidence I gained during and after my photo-shoot with him. Ladies, you do not need to be young or a size two to be beautiful!! Our bodies are unique, just like us, and Jason fulfilled his promise to make me see myself as other people see me. I also highly recommend, for hair and photos, #kearstenlederphotography. My comic strip photos with her were the steppingstone to my boudoir shoot with Jason. My headshots on LinkedIn have also assisted in several job offers!

I couldn't afford to move just yet, and I didn't want to move during the holidays, so my goal was to move in February. I did not say anything to the local manager. October through December was a rollercoaster ride. Things slowed down and the local manager tried to train me more. Eventually she saw that I hated the job and offered me a different position within the company. Unfortunately, before I could completely tran-sition, they needed to find someone else to fill my current position. I ended up doing two jobs instead of one for the same pay.

Meanwhile, everyone at Sprouts loved me. And I loved Sprouts. I loved being a cashier. I could go into work, do my job, be social, and leave. Beyond cashiering and cleaning, there were little other requirements of me. I could have easily been promoted to head cashier or perhaps even manager, but I had no interest in that at all. Since it was a grocery store, I knew they could never pay me enough to be able to cover my bills, even as a manager. If I couldn't make a living off it, why would I take on additional responsibilities? I was happy where I was just being a cashier. Everyone knew that and respected my decision.

Toward the end of November, Sprouts was doing a Grab and Give. We filled large grocery bags full of non-perishable foods and small grocery bags full of deodorants, soaps, lip balms, and other health related stuff. We were selling the bags for $10 apiece and donating them all to the local food bank. All the cashiers were told to promote this and sell as many bags as possible. We were told the cashier who sold the most bags would earn $100. I, being the stellar salesman that I am and wanting an extra $100, started selling five to ten bags every night I worked. The other cashiers were not that interested in doing it, so the manager upped the game by offering other incentives if you sold certain amounts of bags per shift. I started earning all sorts of rewards and was in the lead most of the competition. The manager was both proud of me for selling as many bags as I was and disappointed in the full-time cashiers that they could not match the part time cashier. At that time, I was only working one, maybe two nights a week as another deal I had with the other company during my interview. They did not want me to have two jobs, and I was supposed to be "on call" at night. But since they did not pay me enough to live, they agreed I could keep my part-time job until I got a raise. I wanted to show that I was as committed to them as possible, so I worked as few shifts as I could at Sprouts. The manager at Sprouts asked me to go full time on several occasions and I continuously told him that I couldn't afford it.

In early December the transportation broker had a small company Christmas party for our group that worked in Northern California. I had also agreed to go down south and attend the actual company Christmas party. But things just continued to go downhill with that job. Near the time of the small Christmas party, the company I swore was corrupt made a huge mistake and showed their true colors. Another company and the drivers kept getting into small spats and one day, after the small Christmas party, I just had enough. I was tired of adults acting like children. I was tired of doing two jobs and getting paid for one. Ultimately, I was fed up with having a bunch of responsibilities and no actual authority. I texted a different manager at Sprouts, the one in charge of the schedule, and asked her how many hours she could give me per week if I decided to go full-time. She was absolutely thrilled and immediately talked to the store manager to find out. The two of them told me they could give me 35 hours per week. I mapped out my entire budget from December to February, including the estimated cost to move and decided if I went full time at Sprouts, I could make it work for a couple of months. I emailed the local manager giving her my two weeks' notice and told the manager/scheduler at Sprouts the date she could start me full time.

When I went to work as a QAS the next day, the local manager had my final check for me. She said I would be paid for the hours I had worked, my vacation time, and for the two weeks because I gave notice, but that was my last day working there. I was a little bit disappointed because there were a couple of companies that I really enjoyed working with, and I did have a couple of things scheduled with them in those two weeks. I wanted to be able to say goodbye to them. If you are reading this, you know who you are. I had to turn in my laptop and my phone. I did not copy your phone numbers or emails before I left. I cannot say your companies or your names due to the non-disclosure agreement I signed. I hope you are all doing well. I'm sorry I did not get to say goodbye. On the other hand, I was thrilled to be done.

I told Sprouts they could make me full time right away. They were thrilled, too. The Grab and Give ended in January of

2019. I sold 290 bags, if I remember correctly; I was just shy of 300. My original goal was to sell 100 bags. I had nearly tripled my goal and during most of the contest, I was part-time. Before I went full time, both managers at Sprouts knew my plans to move. Quitting that job was incredibly bittersweet. If cashiering in California paid the bills, I'd still be there. Unfortunately, it doesn't. Everyone understood my situation and I left with a lot of support and love.

HILLARY HITS
THE HIGHWAY

I told my landlord in California that I would be out of the house by February 5, 2019. I am not capable of driving a large truck or towing a trailer across country. I also couldn't afford to hire a moving company to do everything for me. Middle ground was renting U-Haul boxes. U-Haul boxes are U-Haul's version of PODS. They drop them off, you load them, they pick them up, and then they deliver them to your new location. I had packed the majority of my house by myself. The end of January friends came over and helped me pack the rest and then pack the U-Haul boxes. The next week I spent as much time as I could saying goodbye to my friends in California and cleaning the house.

In January, I visited New York for the first time to celebrate my birthday with some good friends. Hammer was the Doc on the *CGC Mellon,* and Derek was a former student turned friend. I stayed with Derek and his husband, and Hammer and I spent a day together. While I was there, Derek suggested I come up with some hashtags for my trip. He knew that I was trying to promote my business and mental health awareness and I wanted more Instagram followers. He suggested I take a lot of pictures and use the hashtag "Hillaryhitsthehighway." I loved his idea: Not only did I use that hashtag but also used "#casey-hitsthehighway," "#sandmetothesouth," and "#timetomove-forward."

I hit the highway, heading south. The first stop was San Diego. Kevin and Mindy had transferred there, and I wanted to see them again. They had also watched Casey a lot for me when I went out of town. I thought he would do all right seeing them and not be so anxious with all the changes. I was wrong. Casey was a mess our entire time in San Diego. He whined incessantly every time I left and wouldn't leave my side when I came back. Despite that, we went all over San Diego and La Jolla. I had a good time. I even found more sand dollars in Coronado!

Kevin and I had talked about my turning HJH Designs into a business. He had asked me several questions about the website and business plan in general. God bless Kevin, he has always wanted to ensure that my website is designed for exactly what I need. He specifically designed it allowing for the amount of time I had and the effort I could put into maintenance. Now that I was moving, and I wanted to make it my business, he wanted to change a few things to help.

Mindy had overheard this conversation, so she and I discussed my plans. Mindy likes my clocks and art and was not against my turning HJH Designs into a business, but she believed that I was a stronger writer than artist. She really encouraged me to write a book. I told her that I had tried to write one a couple times before, but I never got very far even though I had lots of idea. Mindy suggested I write short stories instead. I could write about funny things that happened while I was in the Coast Guard and about serious cases. It could be sort of like "Chicken Soup for the Soul" but with a Coast Guard theme. Writing short stories was in line with my "rule": "mini goals gain control," so I agreed to think about it.

After spending a week in San Diego, I went to Arizona. Since Casey was already a mess and behaved badly on the last trip, my cousin did not want us to stay with him. Instead, we got a hotel room and my cousin brought dinner, and we hung out for a while at the hotel. I was kind of disappointed we couldn't do more. The hotel was attached to a casino and was dog friendly, but the rules stated you couldn't leave your dog in the room by itself. I'm sure people break this rule all the time. I'm equally sure that their dogs don't bark up a storm for hours at a time while they are gone. Instead of letting that get to me, though, I decided to just be thankful for the time we were able to spend together.

I had to stop a few more times at random hotels because Arizona to Texas is a long drive, but the last stop was Lee's house. Originally this was not a planned stop. I love Lee and his family. He is my mentor, after all. But Lee has three kids, three dogs, two cats, and two birds. I thought Casey would lose his mind at their house, and I didn't want to be responsible for any damage he might cause. But after Arizona, the road trip started getting to me, too. I was excited about moving to Alabama, but I was also incredibly scared. Time in the car by myself to think about it wasn't helping. I tried to distract myself. Remembering Mindy's advice about short stories, I used the voice recorder on my phone to record a few. I also wrote while in the hotels at night. I came up with the title for the book, incredibly excited by how creative it is. But the longer I drove, the harder it became to distract myself. I could feel myself slipping into depression. I texted Lee and his wife and asked if Casey and I could stop there. They both knew my fears about all the animals and Casey's anxiety and reassured me that it would be fine. Both said they would love to see me.

Casey is something else. He was not OK in San Diego with a family he knew, but in Texas, with a family he didn't know and their "zoo," he was right at home. The entire time we were there, he picked only one fight with one of their dogs. Casey started it, but Lee's dog, Gracie, could have easily ended it. Luckily, Lee's wife broke them up, and Casey learned his lesson. I immediately relaxed because I was with family, and Casey was OK. We stayed for an entire week. Lee was working nights, so I didn't see him as much as I would have liked, but I played board games with the kids and enjoyed several heart-to-heart talks with his wife. Lee's wife knows all about Lee pushing me to move forward with my career when I was in Sabine Pass; also, that I still struggle with anxiety. She re-

assured me that I was making the right decision about moving to Alabama, and that I would not only be OK, but I would
thrive. She added that they were always there if Casey and I
ever wanted to visit.

Confidence restored, I made the final leg to Alabama. I
stayed with one of the Chiefs who had retired when I was stationed in Mobile. Then I purchased one of his houses. He has
been flipping houses ever since he retired in 2011. Originally,
he was scared to do business with a friend, so he was helping
me look at houses without telling me about the most recent
one he was flipping. After finally finding out about it and seeing it, I knew I wanted it. I also knew I wanted to buy from
him. Ordinarily doing business with friends is not something
I would recommend, but I knew how much experience he had
flipping houses. I trusted he'd be honest about all the potential issues with this house, and he was asking a fair price. He
eventually came around and sold the house to me.

My house is three bedrooms, two baths with a game room
and two-car garage. It is 2,030 square feet and in a great neigh-
borhood. The roof, air conditioner, and water heater were all
brand new. The realtor who assisted with my VA loan and
paperwork gave me a bottle of champagne when we closed on
the house. She was my neighbor when I had lived in Mobile
before and knew that Chief and I had been in the Coast Guard.
She suggested I could either drink the champagne or use it to
properly christen the house. I don't drink much and don't like
champagne, so I loved the idea of christening the house. At my
housewarming party, I gave a small speech, named the house,
and smashed the bottle on the sidewalk. I tried to smash it on
the side of the house, but it didn't break. I named the house
Rosmerta after the Celtic goddess of health and prosperity.
I hope Rosmerta watches over Casey, me, and all our future
guests for as long as we reside here.

HARD TIMES AND GOD

When I started this book, I talked about being raised Baptist and God talking to me. I also mentioned going to different churches while serving at different units. When some people go through tragic events, their relationship with God becomes stronger. In my case, a lack of a relationship with God became very apparent to me. I didn't fully realize it until my book was being edited, but I was not taught to love God or have a relationship with God. God is not and has not ever been my friend. I wrote the story in the beginning of the book about my youth pastor giving me a way to make a godly decision. He gave me that answer when I told him that God never talked to me. Going through his process, I made the decision to join the Coast Guard, and I had peace with God. Or so I thought.

Throughout this book I mention good things that happened to me; things I consistently thought "this will have to go in my future book." At one point in my life, I attributed all those things to God. I was in the Coast Guard, where God wanted me to be, and he was rewarding me for it. There were two problems with that line of thought, though. One, my atheist friends had just as many, if not more good stories and rewards in their lives; and two, what did it mean when bad things happened in my life?

Do you know what I remember about church when growing up, besides being bullied and condemned to hell for going to a public school? I remember the pastor banging on the pulpit, face bright red and sweaty, yelling different parts of the sermon. I remember that communion, when it did happen, was strictly forbidden if your heart was not absolutely, 100% right with God. There was time to pray before communion so you could be sure your heart was in that condition. I prayed and prayed and prayed but was never quite sure if I remembered all my sins, and if I was truly forgiven for all of them. I had no idea if my heart was right with God, so I was terrified to take communion. I was equally terrified if I did not partake my mom would wonder why. I did not want to tell her my heart wasn't right with God, so, I'd partake, and then I'd spend weeks praying for God to forgive me for taking communion, along with all my other sins!

I remember the original pastor leaving; I think his family decided to be missionaries, and the new pastor wanting to change things a little bit. The new pastor wanted the public-school kids to be welcome. He wanted some modern music. I remember losing half the congregation. Over half the people in our church found different churches to attend.

I remember learning about Jesus dying on the cross for our sins. I was saved twice, believe it or not. The first time my mom very awkwardly sat my sister and me down, told us about God dying on the cross, and asked us if we wanted to pray and accept him into our hearts. I have no idea if we really knew what we were doing, but we prayed that prayer and were hopefully saved. The second time the same sermon was preached during Sunday school and I had a bunch of questions I wanted to ask. During the prayer they asked if anyone wanted to accept God into their hearts. I raised my hand, thinking I could ask my questions. But when the lady came to get me, I was guided to say the same prayer all over again, no questions being asked or answered.

I think I was eight when I was baptized. It was explained, and I was given a choice, I suppose. I didn't put up a fight, but now that I'm older, I'm curious what would have happened had I said no. Back then I didn't tell my mom no. That really wasn't an option most of the time, so I didn't even really think to say it.

Even though, at that point, I was saved and going to heaven, I still remember being told that sinners were not under God's umbrella of protection. So, every time I chose to sin, God would not be able to help me until I asked for forgiveness.

Fast forward to when I started having mental health issues. I think I had a pass while I was on the *Mellon* although I am not sure why, except Christians always conveniently know when to make exceptions to the rules. For one thing, I don't think anyone at that time knew I had an actual plan to kill myself. They knew how poorly I was being treated, so they understood why I hated the unit. Some of my depression was also blamed on all the rain and grey skies in Seattle, which was probably part of it.

I also very specifically remember being depressed and talking to certain Christians about it. The standard responses were, "Have you been reading your Bible?" or "Have you prayed about it?"

If my answers were no, then those were my magical solutions. If my answers were yes, it usually turned into some sort of argument, ending with the Christian saying, "God made you in his image. Are you saying God made a mistake?"

So, there I was already depressed and then I felt extremely guilty on top of that. Of course, God didn't make a mistake. God is perfect. Obviously, I made a mistake. I was not being protected because of my mistake. That is why I was sick. It was entirely my fault. I brought it on myself.

Let me say this loud and clear, for everybody in the audience, depression is a medical diagnosis due to chemicals in your brain not functioning right. You cannot just pray it away. No one tells a cancer patient to read their Bible and pray. Well, they may tell them that, but they are telling them that on the drive to the chemo appointment. Unfortunately, the mentally ill are not usually driven to therapy by a concerned friend. They are certainly not encouraged to take any medication. They are just told to read and pray. Reading and praying doesn't fix chemical imbalances. Get real help.

For a very long time, I not only took responsibility for what I did wrong, but I took responsibility for everyone's actions. If any bad thing happened, it was my fault. I was not reading my Bible enough. I was not praying enough. I was not hearing God answer me. I was not under his umbrella of protection. I felt guilty all the time. I actually joked, "I should have been born Catholic instead of Baptist because of the guilt I always feel."

Manipulative assholes can smell guilt and depression. I don't have time to write about all the people who took advantage of me because I always took responsibility for everything.

Now, combine that amount of guilt with also walking the line or being on the weight program for twelve years. I swear I've tried every diet or "lifestyle change" I've ever been told to try. I've worked out with personal trainers. I've completely starved and dehydrated myself, which according to science, meant I should have died. But the weight, if it came off, never stayed off. I was where God wanted me to be, right? So why was I struggling so much? That had to be my fault, too.

In earlier chapters maybe you were wondering why I wasn't, on the whole, more assertive. Maybe you were wondering why I waited so long to become assertive. The doctors telling me to work out more or saying that my blood work was normal (when it wasn't healthy) fit into the narrative that I just was not enough. It also costs a lot of money to pay for your own endocrinologist and blood work.

I wrote about different churches I attended. I attended more than I wrote about, as well. Here is the problem with church. If the church is just like the church I grew up in, I don't like it. If the church is different, I cannot convince myself that they are a "true church." Obviously, a church that preaches love and tolerance or a church that allows everyone to participate in communion every week, is a church that is manipulating or interpreting the Bible in such a way as to allow their congregation to continue comfortably living in sin. I cannot be a part of that, either.

I remember going through therapy and learning how to think differently. I tell different stories in this book of lessons I learned or things that happened. There is no real way to capture it all. As I began learning that I was taking responsibility for everyone's actions and that not all bad things were really my fault, I felt my life falling apart even more. Imagine how I felt when I found out I had not one, but two, medical diseases that make it extremely hard to lose weight. Was I really that bad a person to deserve not just one but two lifelong diseases? As I began to love myself more, I began to truly hate God.

In my mind, I will never be able to please God. In my mind, I will never be enough for him. I do not believe he talks to me. The methods to make a godly decision only works for certain decisions, as not all paths are clearly 100% right or 100% wrong. What do I do in the case where it is just a list of pros and cons? Where is God for those decisions? Did God make a mistake when he made me? My body doesn't function the way it is supposed to. Some of that is probably my fault but I made the best decisions I knew how to make at the time. So maybe he didn't make a mistake when he made me. Was I not under his umbrella of protection? Maybe I wasn't but I didn't know how to get under it, either, and I wasn't getting answers from the Bible or from praying. If God made me, then God knows I'm not getting whatever message he is trying to send me. If God made me, he knows how to actually send me that message. I'm tired of taking responsibility for God's actions. I'm not the one to blame in this situation; he is.

I sold my clocks and worked in a consignment store in Cotati, California. I wrote a little about that earlier. I said that I really got into crystals while working there. The store primarily consisted of crystals because it was associated with a healing center. The owner of the store had started the healing center first. When "patients" started asking where to find the things recommended to them and the healers began writing books, the store became the solution.

After the fires in 2017, the owner invited healers in from all over California and held free fifteen-minute sessions for anyone in the community who was interested. The owner was aware of some of my health problems so invited me to attend. She had a specific healer she wanted me to meet who she thought could really help me out.

I'm not sure there has ever been a day in my life that caused me so much confusion. On the one hand, I was so flattered that the owner thought of me and wanted to help me out, and I wanted to attend. On the other hand, I had never heard of many of the healing methods, so I was scared to death I'd be practicing some sort of witchcraft and thus invite demons into my life. After all, I was raised to believe that tarot cards and palm readings were the exact same thing as playing with a Ouija board. All of those things invited the devil right into your life.

I met with four different healers that day. One lady scared the absolute hell out of me. If she had been the first healer I met, I would have run out crying and never returned. Luckily, she was the third. I did not get anything out of bar healing. If you enjoy that, I'm very happy for you. I don't think there is anything wrong with it, but it was a complete waste of time for me. The nutritionist/kinesiologist/iridologist/reiki master/tarot card reader (the healer the owner recommended) was amazing!! I loved her. She gave me some of the same advice my other nutritionist gave me, reinforcing that I was at least making some sound decisions, and she gave me some other advice. I loved it all. No demons have haunted me since the tarot readings.

The healer that changed my life was the fourth healer: The Angel Healer. At first, I thought she was going to be the same as the bar healer. She had me lay down on a massage table and she said she would focus on my chakra points while calling the angels. Ok. I could take another nap. I didn't mind.

Once I lay down, she told me to shut my eyes and imagine tree branches and roots growing out of my feet. The roots extended all the way down to the center of the Earth. I was to imagine the center of the earth as bright orange and being connected to it through my feet. As I began imagining these things I thought, "Ok, this is basically meditating. I'm down with meditating."

But then I felt a warmth surge through my body like I've never felt before and suddenly I was under some weight. I wasn't scared, though. I wasn't suffocating. Instead, it felt like a weighted blanket. I was very comforted. I liked it except that I was afraid to like it. My entire body was saying relax and my mind was saying, "Now you have a demon in your body."

As the session continued, the healer very gently touched my chakra points. Then she moved down to my feet and placed one of her hands on each of my feet. She told me beforehand that she would be "grounding" me. While her hands were still on my feet, a third hand gently touched my chest. I know, I'm 150% sure that that hand was an angel's. While my body was still fighting my mind, and I was still unsure of what all this meant, I also did not want to move. I did not want the session to end. I did not want that hand to go anywhere. If I had not had my church in my head, I would have been more at peace than I have ever been in my entire life.

But I'm not that easily convinced. I'm a true skeptic by nature. The angel healer had to have tricked me in some way. Maybe one of the other healers sneaked in the room while I was "meditating." Maybe she set something else on my chest that I thought was a hand. Maybe I was crazier than I thought I was. Add delusional to my mental health issues, please. Maybe I wasn't delusional. Maybe it was some sort of placebo effect.

I told The Roommate about it, after making him promise not to laugh at me or call me crazy for like an hour. The Roommate didn't think I had done anything wrong (like invite a demon in) nor did he think I was crazier than I already was. The Roommate basically had the same thoughts about the Angel Healing as I had about the bar healing. If I felt better that was great. Good for me. The Roommate was in no hurry to make an appointment for himself, though.

I talked to Elad about it. He believed every word I said and believed an angel was with me. Elad said that angels presented themselves to humans all the time in the Bible. He asked why I would doubt that they would present themselves to me.

I saw the Angel Healer one more time before I left California. I felt the same warmth and weight. Instead of placing a hand on my chest, though, my hands felt like they were levitating the entire hour. Angels were holding my hands.

Some Christians may say that God and the angels are on the same team. They may say that God sent the angels on his behalf; the angels were God's way of talking to me. I'm not buying into that. If I wanted to tell a good friend something incredibly important, I would not tell five other friends and hope that they relay my message correctly. I would tell my friend myself. Sorry, God, you do not get a pass on this one, nor do you get a pass if you were trying to relay your message through other humans. If you want to talk to me, do it yourself.

In the next chapter, I compare fighting health issues to fighting an addiction. A lot of the twelve-step program involves believing in a higher power. I believe in the angels. I ask Michael to protect me, especially when I drive. I ask Rafael to heal me. I thank them at the end of the day that I was not badly hurt. I do not thank them for keeping me alive. I'm not sure that is something I'm thankful for just yet. I also thank the rest of my angels for being by my side and ask them to be with my loved ones, too.

I do not want to hate God. I do not know how to mentally wrap my head around him, though, and I do not trust humans to tell me. I will not continue to feel like I'm "less than." I will not continue to try to have a relationship with someone who clearly does not want one with me. I'm completely done with that life—most days—after you've hurt me enough times.

I've tried a couple of churches in Mobile, including the "gay church." I was hoping to find compassionate, open-minded humans that I could be friends with. I figured the God thing might also sort itself out eventually, if he decided to stop being so stubborn. I will not bash the churches as there is really no need for that. I will say that I did not find what I was looking for. My "hunger" to continue searching is not really that strong. Maybe someday I will find this so-called loving God that some Christians claim to know. Maybe I never will. If there is a heaven, I hope that I still have a ticket in. I was saved twice, after all! If I don't have a ticket, there's comfort in knowing that I will not be (suffering) alone somewhere else.

HEALTH, HAPPINESS, AND PROSPERITY

It didn't take long for this book to transform from short stories to an actual story that flowed. The beginnings of the book were choppy and, thank God for editors, but as soon as I started writing about my time on the *Mellon*, I was on a roll and had a good flow. Once I started to see that it was going to be an actual book, I was told by several people that I needed to think about what the theme of the book would be, so I could make sure to stick to the theme and not be disorganized. My original idea was to really focus on my mental health issues and push people to get help if they needed it. Two things prevented me from choosing this theme. One, I am more than just my mental health issues. My story is more than just my mental health. And two, a good friend pointed out to me that if getting help was easy, both of us would have gotten help a lot sooner than we did. In fact, she pointed out that if things were as simple as I was making them seem when I was telling her about the book, she and I would both still be in the Coast Guard. She was right. Getting help is not easy and even after I got help, I still lost my career.

I did not want to write a book that ripped the Coast Guard to shreds. I'm pretty sure I could get in big trouble for that, but I also do not regret joining, and I do not think the organization, as a whole, is a terrible organization. I still have a lot of friends in, and I'm still proud of all their accomplishments. I'm proud of all my accomplishments, too.

So, how could I write a book showing my accomplishments

and my pride while also telling my entire story, highlighting my mental health issues, and encouraging people to get help? Elad suggested I write the book from my perspective now versus my perspective as I was going through everything and show that transformation is possible. I loved that idea and I sincerely hope I hit that mark.

While I "graduated" from therapy in July 2018, and then again in October 2018, after my emergency sessions, I still call Elad from time to time when I need him. I hate making this analogy as I have never been an addict, but I kind of think mental health is like an addiction. First off, in order to change, you have to admit you have a problem. Once you admit you have a problem, you have to want to get help and want to change. No one can make that decision for you. Depending on your age and your specific situation, people can force you into therapy or into a psych ward, but ultimately you have to choose if you are going to go through the program or not, just like rehab. Therapy is not easy. Therapy requires a level of honesty and vulnerability that cannot be described in a book. And good therapists or psychologists are not easy to find, as I have learned through my experience with the Pastor and the VA. I've also had friends share their horror stories with me. I thank God every day for Elad. I don't know if I could have shared my story with anyone else.

An addict must avoid certain people or situations where they might be encouraged to use again. I, too, had to reevaluate certain friendships and situations that I was in that made my health worse, including my career in the Coast Guard. I also had to evaluate me and my behavior. I do not know all twelve steps in the twelve-step program or the order of them. I do not know if you must complete the steps in their exact order. I do know one of the steps is making amends with people you have hurt in the past. Along with cutting certain people out of my life who I considered toxic, I have also tried to make amends with people who I hurt. Some people chose to forgive me, and others chose not to. I know I only have control over my actions, and I have to leave the rest to my higher power. I'm trying my best to do that.

My original diagnosis was a borderline anxiety disorder and I was on the spectrum for depression but was not clinically depressed. After time with Elad, he determined that along with the anxiety disorder I also had post-traumatic stress disorder (PTSD.) PTSD can stem from one traumatic event or from a series of traumatic events. My PTSD stems from my time on the *Mellon* and my series of medical issues that I still struggle with, especially when I have a medical appointment. I have spun out before, during, and after several medical appointments. Just like an addict attends AA (or other) meetings, I still talk to Elad for occasional tune ups. Just like an addict struggles every single day to stay clean, I struggle every single day with my health issues, hormone imbalances, anxiety, and depression. There are nights when I cry myself to sleep. There are days when I hate everyone and everything. There are times when I am so paralyzed with fear that I am not capable of making simple decisions. My anxiety, fear, and shame tell me that I do not deserve anything good in my life. If something good is in my life, I inevitably think that it is a mistake, and it will not last for long. I am not fully healed yet, but I am making progress.

At every opportunity, the old Hillary settled for comfortable hatred over the unknown even with more pleasant possibilities. The old Hillary would still be in California, working two to four jobs, seven days a week, trying to make ends meet. If the old Hillary had moved to Alabama, and that is a big if, she would have gotten another part-time cashier job at a local store. The old Hillary judged everyone and did not have any compassion for herself. The new Hillary has her own business. The new Hillary meditates before she goes to bed. The new Hillary calls Elad when she is spinning out. The new Hillary, full of anxiety, goes to craft fairs and flea markets, turns on the master salesman in her, and promotes her business. The new Hillary just wrote her first book. And as the new Hillary stumbles, grows, and overcomes her obstacles, she will let go of her anxiety, shame, and fear. And all of this is progress.

Some people think my decision to get out of the Coast Guard was my decision or my choice. Some still strongly believe that I should have just eaten healthier or worked out more. A smaller group thinks I literally should have starved myself for eight more years just to have saved my career. Those people strongly believe that I was a complete moron for giving up a pension. I made a lot of mistakes while I was in the Coast Guard. I ate healthy following the rules and guidelines I was given during the weight loss camp and worked out on a regular basis. When I was on the line for weigh-ins, I starved myself to meet the standards. After I met the standards, I binged in celebration. This quickly became a habit or an eating disorder without my even realizing it and lasted for years. There are people who watched me do everything "correctly," who know that I gave my best effort and did all I could to meet the standards and stay in. There are other people who met me during binges or after I had given up and probably swear my problems are all self-created. At different times I have believed both of those statements. Somewhere in the middle of all of that is the truth. I was 26 pounds over the weight requirement when I was discharged. I don't know if I could have lost that, so I don't know if getting out was fully my choice or not. I do know that it was the right thing for me. I do know that my health, physical and mental, was fading quickly, and I would not have gotten better had I stayed in and tried to lose those twenty-six pounds.

Perhaps if I were an addict and my tune ups with Elad could be considered AA meetings, perhaps this book could be my way of becoming a sponsor. Getting help is not always a possibility and certainly is not easy. Sometimes improving your life requires a major life change. All of this is scary as hell. All of it is worth it. If you are in a bad situation, if you are suicidal, if you have anxiety, if you are an addict, if you struggle in any way, please look for a way out, even if the way out is unconventional and against "logical" advice—such as giving up a "stable" career. You have your fear, anxiety, depression or whatever else, but you also have a gut. And in your gut, you know what is best for you. You are stronger than you think. Take a leap of faith. Your health and your life literally depend on it.

If you have never been in a bad situation, never been addicted to anything, never battled suicide or other mental health issues, then I hope this book has opened your eyes a little bit to what it is like to live with these things. I hope that you will look for more opportunities to help the people in your life and show more compassion toward them. If someone reaches out to you for help, please listen to them. Actually listen to them. Listen to understand them, not to respond to them. They should talk more than you do. Understand that you will never actually understand what they are going through. Let them know that you love them or support them or both. Encourage them to get help or make a change in their life, but do not try to force them to do either. Be patient as they begin and go through their journey, especially as they stumble on their journey. You are not perfect; don't expect them to be.

I cannot stress enough how hard it is to find a good therapist. I talked about the Pastor in this book. I've spoken to two VA psychologists so far. I'm pretty sure you are not supposed to leave an appointment with a psychologist feeling homicidal. Both of the so-called psychologists asked me questions only to interrupt me part way through my answers. Both of them were extremely arrogant. One of them interrogated me, literally, in order to make sure I was not suicidal. He forced me to tell him my reason for living and forced me to take a plastic bracelet with the Veteran's Suicide Hotline Number on it. I understand that suicide rates, especially among Veterans, are extremely high. I promise you that interrogating patients is not the way to lower those statistics. There are only four people on this Earth that know my true reason for living, including the above-mentioned VA psychologist. I regret telling him. That was my first meeting with him, and I did not and do not trust him. He should not have that information about me. I have never felt more uncomfortable in my life.

Unfortunately, several of my friends have told me similar horror stories about military, civilian, and VA therapists, clergy, and psychologists. I am not writing this to scare anyone. I'm writing this because it is the truth. If you are trying to help someone you love, you need to know that they may not like or feel comfortable with the first person they go to see. This does not mean they do not want to get help. This does not indicate they are worse off than you thought they were or that you should give up on them. And for those of you who are experiencing mental health issues or who have been interrogated, shamed, judged, betrayed, or hurt by so-called therapists, clergy, and psychologists, please do not give up your search for help. There are more resources out there. It's an exhausting journey, believe me I know, but it is worth it when you find the right person or right thing that works.

Life and recovery are a journey. I am still on mine. I'm not perfect. I have been hurt, and I have hurt a lot of people, as well. I constantly try to meld worlds and find balance. I bounce between depression and extreme anger. I cry myself to sleep. I advocate for compassion. I post a lot of my story and truth on social media. Sometimes I'm too aggressive about it because these wounds are not healed. Sometimes I connect with a complete stranger in the middle of the night and assure them that they are not alone. I know that I am stronger than I have ever given myself credit for. I am broken. But I am also beautiful. I will never again forget that I am beautiful.